HUMAN AUTOEROTIC PRACTICES

HUMAN AUTOEROTIC PRACTICES

Manfred F. DeMartino, M.A.

HUMAN SCIENCES PRESS
72 Fifth Avenue   3 Henrietta Street
NEW YORK, NY 10011 ● LONDON, WC2E 8LU

Library of Congress Catalog Number 78-8766

ISBN: 0-87705-373-1
      0-87705-403-7

Printed in the United States of America

9 987654321

Library of Congress Cataloging in Publication Data

Main entry under title:

Human autoerotic practices.

   Bibliography: p. 361
   Includes index.
   1. Masturbation—Addresses, essays, lectures.
2. Masturbation—Psychological aspects—Addresses,
essays, lectures.   I. DeMartino, Manfred F.
[DNLM: 1. Masturbation. WM612 D372h]
HQ447.H85   613.9'5   78-8766
ISBN 0-87705-373-1

Dedicated to two truly inspirational pioneer sexologists—
psychotherapists, Dr. Albert Ellis and Dr. A. H. Maslow

"He that will not apply new
remedies must expect new
evils; for time is the greatest
innovator."
Francis Bacon

CONTENTS

FOREWORD

Although scores of books and hundreds of articles have been written on the subject of autoeroticism or masturbation, none of them has been definitive. Manfred DeMartino has now provided us with a definitive work on the subject. As author and compiler, DeMartino has gone through the existing significant information in this area extracting almost all the really important papers and chapters that have so far been published on autoeroticism and has beautifully woven them into a comprehensive volume. He has omitted virtually no notable aspect of this topic and has managed to include a marvelously representative selection of papers by an imposing array of authorities. If an informed reader or professional perused only a single volume on masturbation and acquired all the information needed for a thorough understanding of this area of human sexuality, s/he would do very well with DeMartino's *Human Autoerotic Practices: Adjustment Through Autoeroticism.*

I am tempted to stop this Foreword right here and

merely urge you on to the rest of the interesting material in this volume. However, after reading this book and thinking about some of the other writings I have done in addition to those included in DeMartino's book, I feel sorely tempted to make still another summary of the advantages of masturbation for human living. For I now see that my previous listings in this respect are somewhat fragmentary, and I could easily, and more comprehensively, add to them. Moreover, largely because of space limitations, Manfred DeMartino has been forced to omit some material on auto-eroticism that he had originally planned to include in this volume. I shall therefore conclude this Foreword by summarizing some of the major advantages of masturbation that can be culled from my own writings and those of many of the authorities whose chapters appear in *Human Auto-erotic Practices.*

I have already listed, in Chapter 18, "The Art and Science of Masturbation," some of the leading objections to masturbation that have been made by various authors; and I have answered them in some detail. Here, under various major headings, are some of the main benefits that humans can derive from masturbating (and this list itself is hardly exhaustive!):

SEXUAL ADVANTAGES OF MASTURBATION.   People can often achieve better sex through resorting to autoerotic practices than they would achieve if they only resorted to interpersonal sexual contacts. For example:

1.   They can help establish the philosophy that sex is good in, by, and for itself; and that there is nothing whatever wrong about experiencing it as a fine thing in its own right.

2.   They can explore various kinds of self-stimulation and discover which ones are maximally satisfying for themselves.

3.   They can frequently learn, through masturbating, enjoyable forms of sexuality that they can subsequently use to achieve satisfactory modes of sex participation with others.

4.   They can often judge just how sexually responsive they personally are, and determine how big or little a part they wish sex pleasure to play in their lives.

5.   They can manage to repeat enjoyable arousal and orgasm almost at will, without any restrictions from a sex partner. They can thereby participate in sex more frequently than they are likely to do with other individuals.

6.   They can best schedule their sex activities, as well as their resting periods, between activities, since they do not have to depend on the participation of their partners.

7.   They can avoid making undue demands on the time, energy, and sexuality of their partners, thereby often helping these partners have maximum sex satisfaction and minimum pain or frustration.

8.   They can in many cases (especially if they are females) have more intense and more satisfying forms of arousal and orgasm than is likely with their regular or special partners.

9.   They can best train themselves in suitable sexual fantasies, since they have no interferences or distractions from their partners, and may focus on what is most pleasing and useful to themselves in this connection. Once they learn how to fantasize best during masturbation, they can often transfer this learning to their sex affairs with others.

10.   If they have unusual sexual desires or have some kinds of handicaps or deficiencies (such as inability to come to orgasm in a reasonably short period of time), they can often cater to these desires or overcome these handicaps more effectively through masturbating than they can with sex partners.

11.   They can often focus better on their own sexual sensations and pleasures than when they are distracted or

interfered with by the presence of partners. As in the case of fantasy, their learning to focus may then be transferable to their sex acts with others.

12.   They may be less limited in their use of mechanical objects (such as dildos), special apparatuses (such as vibrators), fetishes (such as certain objects of clothing), or other sex aids than they would with a partner present.

13.   They may be able, in many instances, to engage in much longer periods of arousal and near-orgasm than they would with partners; they may also be able to prolong the duration of their orgasms.

14.   They may naturally have, with no intent or special technique on their part, more intense orgasms through masturbation than they are likely to have with others; and they may usually come to orgasm, if they wish to do, much faster through autoerotic practices than through any other mode of sexuality.

15.   During masturbation, they can be observed by a partner, and may thus bring themselves and the partner special arousal and satisfaction. They may also be able to learn about their own sexuality and gratification by their partner's observations.

16.   They may naturally build up considerable sexual tension when they do not have sex play and orgasm; this kind of tension may be satisfactorily (or more satisfactorily) released through masturbation.

17.   Because they find masturbation easily available and ideal for experimental purposes and because they have minimal restrictions in participating in it, they therefore can practice it at whim and may increase their sex desire and proclivities.

18.   They may have inhibitions about having sex with partners, particularly because they are too shy or ashamed to engage in interpersonal sexuality, and may therefore be afforded a very active sex life despite these kinds of inhibitions.

19. They may have specific sexual handicaps that prevent them from easily acquiring partners—such as a low sex drive, inability to come to orgasm quickly, or unusually small sex organs; and they may be able, in spite of these handicaps, to lead an active sex life through masturbation.

20. They may have specific nonsexual handicaps that prevent them from easily acquiring partners—such as small stature, physical deformity, diseases, or homely features; and they may be able, in spite of these nonsexual handicaps, to lead an active sex life through masturbation.

EMOTIONAL ADVANTAGES OF MASTURBATION.
People can often achieve greater emotional health and satisfaction through resorting to autoerotic practices than they would achieve if they only resorted to interpersonal contacts. For example:

1. They can adopt a philosophy of enjoyment that not only aids them in their sexual but in their general life. They can seek more emotional satisfaction and less pain.

2. They can especially see the value of giving to themselves, and not merely to others; and while not becoming entirely autistic or self-centered, they can add a hedonistic philosophy to that of social interest—or choose, if that is their wish, to become more devoted to themselves than to others.

3. When they are forced by conditions or circumstances to be alone, and this is against their wish and they feel lonely, they can divert themselves into the pleasurable pursuit of masturbation and thus feel much better.

4. They can use autoerotic pursuits to distract themselves from anxiety, self-downing, depression, and other disturbing feelings. Masturbation will not solve these basic emotional problems; but as a distraction technique it is one of the best and will at least serve as temporary palliation for emotional distress in innumerable instances.

5.   Masturbation can be used as a shame-attacking and guilt-attacking homework assignment. In rational-emotive therapy (RET) and other forms of cognitive-behavior therapy, a good many "shameful" acts are given as homework assignments for individuals to practice, to show them that nothing is intrinsically "shameful"—that people only attribute "shame" or "guilt" to certain acts. As such an assignment, masturbation can prove very helpful emotionally.

6.   People can use masturbation to gain confidence in their own ability to arouse themselves and bring themselves to orgasm; and when they gain such confidence, they tend to feel much better and stop downgrading themselves, sexually and in other areas of their lives.

7.   When people's lives are filled with few enjoyments and many frustrations, masturbation can easily remain as one of their frequent pleasures and distractions. It may enhance their lives and make them feel much happier and less depressed.

8.   People can use masturbation as a goal-directing and prothinking activity. Given the problem of satisfying themselves sexually, and not having interpersonal outlets easily available, they may think up various forms of masturbatory activities that will help them live more happily; and they may also develop useful goal-directed attitudes and pursuits in the process.

9.   People can use masturbation as a form of self-exploration, to discover exactly what they like and do not like sexually. Thus, they can explore their own likes and dislikes as well in other important areas of their lives. They can also become more risk taking and adventurous through these avenues of enjoyment.

10.   People can not only distract themselves from disturbed feelings by masturbating, as mentioned above, but they can also directly release bodily and emotional tensions thereby. The release of tension through masturbation fre-

quently helps men and women relax, get ready for other pursuits, and restfully sleep when they want to do so.

HEALTHFUL ADVANTAGES OF MASTURBATION.
People often achieve greater physical and general health through resorting to autoerotic practices than they would probably achieve if they only resorted to interpersonal sexual contacts. For example:

1.   Undesirable pregnancy and abortion are avoided.
2.   The possibility of acquiring venereal diseases from others and acquiring various other diseases, such as colds, coughs, respiratory ailments, skin infections, and the like is minimized.
3.   People often aid their physical health by managing to obtain regular sexual release and satisfaction; and sometimes by going through involved physical exercises as they masturbate.
4.   Women, in particular, may help overcome premenstrual tension or other physical conditions associated with their menstrual cycles when they masturbate.
5.   Masturbation often leads to relaxed sleeping conditions and to concomitant conditions that aid some people's physical health.
6.   When physically ill or disabled, people can often masturbate when it would not be practical for them to have interpersonal sex experiences, and they may thereby help themselves back to a healthier condition.

RELATIONSHIP ADVANTAGES OF MASTURBATION.
Although masturbation, when resorted to by oneself, is obviously a solitary pursuit, some people actually achieve better relationships with their partners or mates than they would probably achieve if they only engaged in sexual contacts with these partners. For example:

1.   When one partner or mate wants much more sex than the other, masturbation enables one partner to be steadily satisfied and, at the same time, not impose on the other. This kind of consideration for the other partner frequently enhances the love relationship between the two.

2.   When one partner or mate temporarily wants less sex than the other partner—as when one is in the last stages of pregnancy, is ill, or is disabled—masturbation may again enable one partner to be steadily satisfied sexually without imposing on the other. An ill or disabled partner may especially appreciate the other's masturbating; and their relationship may be considerably bettered thereby.

3.   When one partner wants sex only occasionally or intermittently, the other partner may keep up his or her level of arousal and interest in sex by masturbating, and may therefore be ready for sex when the first partner wants to be available again. Otherwise, both partners might sink into a kind of sexual apathy and inertia and their sex and love lives might be impaired.

4.   People often make themselves hostile toward each other because one partner wants the kind of sex that the other does not, or for various kinds of nonsexual reasons. When they resort to masturbation, they are able to get some of the kind of sex that they cannot obtain from their partner, and thereby hostility abates: since one partner is no longer sexually deprived and the other is not imposed on.

5.   Masturbation allows both partners a large measure of freedom and self-satisfaction; when they know that they have this freedom they tend to tolerate some of the restrictions of an enduring relationship much better and consequently have a more loving relationship.

6.   Masturbation frequently helps bring about better attitudes on the part of both partners toward themselves and toward others.

7.   People who resort to masturbation when they are

mated and who find unusual or extra satisfactions in this kind of autoerotic activity tend to feel less overconstrained by the mating relationship and to adjust better to their partners.

8.   As noted in a previous section of this Foreword, people who learn self-satisfying sex acts in the process of masturbating can often bring these acts to their participations with others and thereby enhance their interpersonal sex relations.

OTHER ADVANTAGES OF MASTURBATION.
Millions of people throughout the world have always found and still find a great many other advantages when they resort to masturbation that they would not find if they only participated in interpersonal contacts. For example:

1.   They save a great deal of time and energy arranging for masturbatory pursuits rather than always having to arrange for interpersonal sex.

2.   They can easily intersperse their masturbatory activities with nonsexual acts, while they often do not do the same with their interpersonal sex contacts.

3.   They can masturbate with just about no paraphernalia, room requirements, space requirements, etc.; while they often have trouble in these respects when having sex with a partner.

4.   They can engage in masturbation most inexpensively, while other forms of sex often require some kind of monetary outlay.

5.   They can easily and quickly keep themselves out of potential sex, love, or general trouble by resorting to masturbation. If they could not masturbate, they might sometimes be tempted to resort to various kinds of unethical or criminal behavior.

6.   They can use masturbation in symbolic, religious, value laden, and other ways and, if they wish, derive unifica-

tion experiences and other profound nonsexual experiences from engaging in it.

You will note, in the foregoing list, some fifty advantages of masturbation. The list is hardly exhaustive and could undoubtedly be increased to more than a hundred.

All of which proves—what? Merely that autoeroticism is a major and important part of human behavior. That is the main message of the authoritative statements on this subject that Manfred DeMartino has amassed in this book. And the book itself, because it is so definitive, informative, and unequivocal, is a telling and trenchant message in its own right. I am sure that it will be widely—and helpfully—read.

REFERENCES

Ellis, A. *The folklore of sex.* New York: Boni, 1951. (Rev. ed.) New York: Grove Press, 1961.

Ellis, A. *The American sexual tragedy.* New York: Twayne, 1954. (Rev. ed.) New York: Lyle Stuart and Grove Press, 1962.

Ellis, A. *Sex without guilt.* New York: Lyle Stuart, 1958. (Rev. ed.) New York: Lyle Stuart and Hollywood: Wilshire Books, 1965.

Ellis, A. *The art and science of love.* New York: Lyle Stuart, 1960. (Rev. ed.) New York: Lyle Stuart and Bantam Books, 1965.

Ellis, A. *The sensuous person.* New York: Lyle Stuart and New American Library, 1972.

Ellis, A. *Sex and the liberated man.* New York: Lyle Stuart, 1976.

Ellis, A. *The intelligent woman's guide to dating and mating.* Secaucus, New Jersey: Lyle Stuart, 1978.

Albert Ellis, Ph.D.

Institute for Rational-Emotive Therapy
New York

PREFACE

Perhaps the most dramatic and striking change that has occurred during the past few decades in the area of human sexuality has been in regard to the attitudes by eminent sexologists toward the practice of autoeroticism. While in bygone years most of the noted authorities (even those in the 1940s) stated, much to the dismay of persons of all ages and particularly adolescents, that the use of masturbation led to one form of psychopathology or another, now leading sex therapists (e.g., Ellis, 1960, 1976; LoPiccolo, 1972, 1976; Kaplan, 1974; Barbach, 1974, 1975) and others (Dodson, 1974) openly recommend its use in counteracting sexual dysfunction, especially in women. (Long before it was "fashionable" to do so, occasionally this writer encouraged women who had sexual problems to indulge in autoerotic activity. Not surprisingly, those who were able to accept such a revolutionary suggestion found it beneficial.) For the first time also, sex therapists and the like are making reference to their own current autoerotic activity (see chapters by Dodson, 1974; Ellis, 1976; and LoPiccolo & Lobitz, 1972).

Actually, the use of masturbatory behavior for therapeutic purposes was first recommended by some practitioners many years ago. Dr. G. V. Hamilton, a pioneer sexologist-psychiatrist stated in his well-known book, *A Research in Marriage:* "Not so long ago our predecessors were so sure that masturbation can destroy the body as well as the mind that they even listed locomotor ataxia . . . as one of its possible consequences. In recent years a new guess in the matter has led some physicians to prescribe masturbation for persons who find it inexpedient or impossible to have ordinary sex intercourse" (1929, p. 422).

Significantly, too, movies now can be purchased from reputable and scientific sources that are specifically designed to teach women and men how to derive the best results from masturbation. And, more and more women's groups are springing up in which the practice of autoeroticism is openly discussed in great detail, (Dodson, 1974; Hill, 1976). National television programs (talk shows) are also beginning to devote increasingly more time to the topic of masturbation. (The first time the word masturbation appeared in national reputable publications was in 1948.)

Furthermore, a number of current prominent sex therapists, unlike practically all proclaimed sexologists of the past generation, have pointed out that not only is the practice of autoeroticism perfectly acceptable and psychologically helpful, but its *lack* of use may be associated with the presence of emotional problems. For instance, Dr. Harold Greenwald, the well-known clinical psychologist-sexologist, has remarked: "I have observed that many people who have severe sexual problems have never masturbated" (1971, p. 54). And Dr. James Leslie McCary, the highly regarded psychologist-sex therapist, has stated, "Indeed, those who do not practice masturbation, or have never done so, are far more likely to be suffering from an emotional or sexual problem than those who have masturbatory experience" (1973, p. 156). Moreover, the renowned psychiatrist-sex therapist Dr. Helen Singer Kaplan has commented: "In contrast to men, where the absence of adolescent masturbation raises a suspicion of psychiatric disturbance, women who never have masturbated are not necessarily pathological. Even so, absence of masturbation is a frequent finding in the histories of women who later complain of orgastic difficulties" (1974, p. 110). Especially interesting and significant is the observation by the noted psychoanalyst Dr. René A. Spitz that, in his clinical practice, those persons who first learned of the practice of masturbation during late adolescence (the twenties) tended to be emotionally disturbed (1962).

While no one should ever feel *compelled* to engage in autoerotic behavior, nevertheless, in light of the overall research it is unmistakeable that the use of masturbation by persons of all ages is both "normal" and often quite beneficial and helpful, providing no guilt feelings are experienced. Unfortunately, however, many people of both sexes including those of very high intelligence (DeMartino, 1974), still experience some feelings of guilt and apprehension in regard to masturbatory activity. Kinsey and his associates with respect to males stated: "While college men more often admit their experience, there are males in some other groups who would admit almost any other kind of sexual activity before they would give a record of masturbatory experience" (1948, p. 499). And in reference to females they remarked: "There is no other type of sexual activity which has worried so many women" (1953, p. 170). More than 20 years later Morton Hunt observed: "Yet, aside from pubescent boys (who are often proud of their new accomplishment), most persons who masturbate remain more or less guilt-ridden about it, and nearly all of them are extremely secretive about their masturbating and would be horribly embarrassed to have anyone know the truth" (1974, p. 66).

Consequently, the need for mass education relating to the normalcy of the practice of autoeroticism continues to exist. Because of this need, and in view of the increasing number of females (especially) and males (to some degree) engaging in masturbation, as well as what appears to be the dawn of a new era concerning the psychotherapeutic value of autoeroticism, this writer decided it would be useful at this time to publish a scientific and practical book on the practice of autoeroticism by females and males and its benefits. The readings presented in this book, therefore, were chosen on the basis of their being scientifically sound and applicable to the sexual lives of females and males.

This book consists of six main sections: Part 1 contains studies that deal mainly with autoeroticism from a psychological viewpoint; Part 2 is concerned with masturbatory activity during the period of adolescence; Part 3 considers the autoerotic practices, fantasies, etc. experienced by women; Part 4 pertains to the autoerotic practices, fantasies, etc. of both women and men; Part 5 deals with the use of autoeroticism in the treatment of sexual dysfunction; and Part 6, which was written by this author, summarizes some of the reported research on autoeroticism and brings together some of the more important research and clinical findings related to masturbatory activity by women and men not covered in the studies included in this book.

The classic writings on the subject of autoeroticism are incorporated in this volume and the contributors read like a Who's Who in the field of human sexuality. Included are such highly regarded authorities as Dr. Lonnie G. Barbach, Dr. Diane B. Brashear, Dr. Alex Comfort, Lester W. Dearborn, Betty Dodson, Dr. Albert Ellis, Havelock Ellis, Dr. Seymour Fisher, Dr. Clelland S. Ford and Dr. Frank A. Beach, David Cole Gordon, Morton Hunt, Dr. Helen Singer Kaplan, Dr. Joseph LoPiccolo, Dr. William H. Masters and Virginia Johnson, Dr. James L. McCary, and Dr. Robert C. Sorensen.

While I hope that this book will be of value to sex educators, sex therapists, marriage counselors, psychiatrists, psychotherapists, psychiatric social workers, medical students, physicians, nurses, and men and women in general, one thing seems certain: all who read this book will never again wonder about the normalcy or usefulness of the practice of autoeroticism.

Syracuse, New York   Manfred F. DeMartino, M.A.
1978

ACKNOWLEDGMENTS

Sincere thanks is made to the following for permission to reprint portions of their previously published material.

Freud, S. *The Basic Writings of Sigmund Freud,* Trans. and Ed. by Dr. A. A. Brill, New York. Copyright 1938 by Random House, Inc. Copyright © renewed 1965 by Gioia Bernheim and Edmund R. Brill. Reprinted by permission.

Hunt, M. *Sexual Behavior in the 1970s.* Chicago: Playboy Press, 1974. Reprinted by permission of the publisher.

Kaplan, H. S. *The New Sex Therapy.* New York: Brunner-Mazel, 1974. Reprinted by permission of the publisher.

Kinsey, A. C., Pomeroy, W. B., and Martin, C. E. *Sexual Behavior in the Human Male.* Philadelphia: Saunders, 1948. Reprinted by permission of Dr. Paul H. Gebhard.

Kinsey, A. C., Pomeroy, W. B., Martin, C. E., and Gebhard, P. H. *Sexual Behavior in the Human Female.* Philadelphia:

Saunders, 1953. Reprinted by permission of Dr. Paul H. Gebhard.

Levin, R. J. The Redbook Report on Premarital and Extramarital Sex: The End of the Double Standard? *Redbook,* October 1975. Reprinted from Redbook Magazine, October 1975. Copyright © 1975 by The Redbook Publishing Company. Reprinted by permission of Redbook Magazine.

Levin, R. J., and Levin, A. Sexual Pleasure: The Surprising Preferences of 100,000 Women. *Redbook,* September 1975. Reprinted from Redbook Magazine, September 1975. Copyright © 1975 by The Redbook Publishing Company. Reprinted by permission of Redbook Magazine.

Masters, W. M., and Johnson, V. E. *Human Sexual Inadequacy.* Boston: Little, Brown, 1970. Reprinted by permission of Dr. W. H. Masters and the publisher.

McCary, J. L. *Human Sexuality,* Second Edition. New York: D. Van Nostrand Company, 1973. Reprinted by permission of the publisher.

From *Adolescent Sexuality in Contemporary America* by Robert C. Sorensen, Copyright © 1972, 1973 by Robert C. Sorensen, by permission of Harry N. Abrams, Inc.

Wagner, N. Sexual Activity and the Cardiac Patient. In Green, R. (Ed.), *Human Sexuality.* Baltimore: Williams and Wilkins Co., 1975. Reprinted by permission of Dr. Richard Green and the publisher.

AUTOEROTICISM VIEWED PSYCHOLOGICALLY

INTRODUCTION

The chapters that comprise Part I deal with autoerotic activity mainly from a psychological standpoint and all of the authors agree that the practice is perfectly "normal" in human beings of all ages and at all levels of development. In Chapter I, by Lester W. Dearborn (former Chairman, American Association of Marriage Counselors), which is regarded as a classic, some of the archaic attitudes toward masturbation are discussed as well as their origins, and a review of the early research concerning the incidence of autoeroticism is presented. Dearborn also comments on some of the misconceptions relating to masturbation as well as the use of masturbatory behavior during infancy, childhood, and adolescence. The experiencing of fantasy during masturbatory activity is also discussed as are the different autoerotic methods employed by males and females. Dearborn concludes his pioneering treatise on masturbation by reaffirming his fervent belief in the normalcy of the practice: *"Masturbation, according to the best medi-*

cal authorities, causes no harm physically or mentally. Any harm resulting from masturbation is caused entirely by worry or by a sense of guilt due to misinformation. "

Dr. Albert Ellis, the internationally famous and highly prolific, pioneering sexologist-psychotherapist, stresses the normalcy of masturbation by both sexes during the entire life span, including marriage, in Chapter 2. However, he points out that autoerotic activity may be viewed as unhealthy "if an individual *exclusively* and *compulsively* uses it as a sex outlet *when other sex outlets are easily available.* " He further states that erroneously believing masturbation to be abnormal can cause a person to suffer psychologically and vehemently attacks the notion that masturbation is harmful if practiced to "excess." Very important, as Ellis emphasizes, "it is invariably social seclusiveness that leads to the use of masturbation as a sole sex outlet rather than the latter leading to the former."

Chapter 3, by Patricia Brooks (a psychiatric nurse), is of historic significance inasmuch as it is one of the very few readings on masturbation to have been published in nursing journals until 1967. After criticizing nursing journals for having ignored discussing the practice of masturbation, even though many nurses (i.e., pediatric, public health, psychiatric) "may be confronted with masturbatory behavior in their patients," Brooks emphasizes the importance of recognizing the naturalness of the activity in understanding the growth process during infancy, childhood, and adolescence. She also points out that masturbatory behavior by hospitalized adult patients may serve different functions or needs, and attendant nurses, therefore, should assume an accepting and professional attitude toward the practice and try to understand the underlying motives for its use. As Brooks observes: "It is behavior that is useful for patients and should be understood by nurses."

Chapter 4, by David Cole Gordon (clinical psychologist), comes from his small but unique and important book,

Self-Love. In the first part of this work Gordon enumerates the many benefits derived from the use of autoeroticism, especially in regard to "psychopaths," "highly sexed individuals," "aging widows," "bachelors," unmarried women, the disabled, and those who are homosexuals or have homosexual tendencies. The reasons for engaging in masturbation are also discussed. In the second half of Gordon's excerpt attention is devoted primarily to the unification process that occurs within an individual during orgasm attainment, and especially as a result of masturbation. Some comments are also made concerning the intensity of sexual pleasure obtained from coitus as compared to masturbation. The fact that many males (particularly college males) continue to engage in autoerotic activity after marriage is also noted. Gordon believes that masturbation "is not only an intense unification experience" but has an added advantage over other forms of sexual expression since it is an experience a person "can have at will and which permits him to indulge without the psychological distraction of a coital partner of the opposite sex." The reasons why autoeroticism should be, but is not, the most satisfying (unifying) of all sexual experiences are also analyzed.

Chapter 5, by the noted English sexologist, Dr. Alex Comfort, was taken from his very successful book, *More Joy.* In this chapter Comfort states that learning to masturbate is more important in the lives of females than males because while most males spontaneously start doing so in early adolescence, this does not occur in the case of females. Even so, males do have to learn how to use masturbatory activity as a means of delaying their orgasmic response during intercourse. And as Comfort observes, women who are not able to attain an orgasm during coitus almost always have to first be taught how to accomplish this by themselves before they can experience orgasms in intercourse. Consequently, boys only have to be taught not to feel guilty about masturbating while girls have to be "actively encouraged to explore their own bodies." For, according to Comfort, unless a woman knows what is stimulating to her, she cannot help her male partner produce such a reaction in her. After attacking the belief that masturbation will prevent heterosexual encounters, as Comfort states, the mother who discovers her daughter masturbating should be happy because "she's learning a skill." Furthermore, the mother should encourage her daughter to continue the practice because of the enjoyment derived and because the activity serves as a sexual learning experience. Comfort, however, does not feel that a young girl should use a vibrator because "it's inclined to damp down sensitivity with prolonged use." And as he points out, a daughter who doesn't masturbate should be taught to do so, but preferably by means of books or sex education rather than parents. Lovers, moreover, should engage in both hand-genital contacts with one another as well as view each other masturbating "both for excitement and instruction." Sexually experienced adults, suggests Comfort, should reevaluate their masturbatory practices and try to discover new autoerotic techniques. Finally, the stated object of masturbation "is both to enjoy and learn more about the responses of which you are capable."

In Chapter 6, Dr. Diane B. Brashear* [a SIECUS (Sex Information and Education Council of the U.S.) Board member and marriage and sex counselor], presents the positive statement of SIECUS relating to the use of masturbation. And, as would be expected, the stand taken by this highly respected organization is that not only is autoeroticism a normal or "natural" aspect of sexual expression for persons of all ages, but it is also beneficial in a number of ways. Masturbation, for instance, can provide a good way of learning about the pleasures associated with one's own

*Dr. Brashear was a SIECUS Board Member in 1974.

body as well as enlighten one concerning what is personally sexually pleasurable, and it can also enhance a person's responsiveness in sexual relations with others. Moreover, the use of autoerotic activity as stated by Brashear can help increase one's feelings of self-confidence, counteract feelings of boredom and despair, and make life more enjoyable and exciting. Furthermore, masturbatory activity can release general feelings of tension in a perfectly desirable manner as well as reduce premenstrual tension. SIECUS's attitude toward masturbation is well illustrated by Brashear's observation: "To know and enjoy oneself is a prerequisite for a positive self-concept, self-realization, and self-esteem, qualities essential for positive human growth."

Chapter 1

MASTURBATION

Lester W. Dearborn, B.S.

Director, Boston Marriage Counseling Service, and Former Chairman, American Association of Marriage Counselors.

Since we began to study the sex life of man no other subject has been more frequently discussed, no other practice more roundly condemned and more universally practiced than masturbation. Masturbation is any stimulation of the sexual organs for the pleasure involved and for the release of tension.

What was the probable origin of the old ideas and taboos regarding masturbation? The knowledge may help to set at rest the feeling that "where there is smoke there must be fire." The fact is that many people feel there must have been a reason for the belief that masturbation resulted in harm, or otherwise the impression would not have prevailed.

Excerpted from *SUCCESSFUL MARRIAGE* by Morris Fishbein & Ernest W. Burgess. Copyright © 1947, 1955, 1963, 1970, 1971 by Morris Fishbein. Reprinted by permission of Doubleday & Company, Inc.

When people lived in tribes that fought with other tribes, group survival was of paramount importance. The elders of the tribe considered it a social sin to waste sperm by any practice that did not procreate children. The spill of spermatozoa by Onan (which in the past has been erroneously referred to as masturbation) came under tribal interdict. The condemnation did not occur because of the loss of an easily renewable supply of spermatozoa, but rather because of Onan's anti-social attitude in refusing to father offspring.

The attitudes expressed during the twenty-two centuries marking the period from Hippocrates to Brady's[1] writings in the 1890's bear definite similarities in their obvious ignorance of body structure, causation of disease, lack of objectivity, and almost complete absence of a scientific approach to this subject. From the 1890's to the beginning of World War I there was a period of transition. During this period came a growing interest in psychiatry, the beginnings of the movement for preventive medicine, and an emphasis on the need for a scientific approach to the study of cause and result. While the notion still persisted that masturbation might cause insanity and that it was without doubt a harmful practice, we do get glimpses of a more enlightened attitude. Many insisted that the practice might be more widespread and less harmful than had been believed. For the most part, however, these pleadings for an enlightened attitude were greatly overshadowed by the persisting influence of Tissot[2] in France, who blasted the eighteenth-century world by his *Onana, A Treatise on the Diseases Produced by Onanism.* This book is steeped in ignorance and personal bias. Tissot could not be expected to have known the nature of semen or the nature of the male sex hormones. He could, however, have exercised intelligence in the deductions he made from the available facts. Tissot's book went through numerous editions and was translated into several languages. It became the main source book of those who felt impelled to write about the viciousness of "self-abuse." About this time, or in 1763, an English contemporary[3] published an unsigned booklet about *tabes dorsalis*, or *locomotor ataxia*, one cause of which he said was "the immoderate loss of so pure a fluid as the semen." Tissot agreed with him and spoke of the preciousness of the seminal fluid, the loss of one ounce of which enfeebled one more than the loss of forty ounces of blood. For these beliefs, there was not, of course, the slightest scientific evidence.

Tissot attributed most of the known disorders of his day to the loss of semen; he added a few new ones born of his own observation. He accepted a statement that he had known "simple gonorrhea, dropsy, and consumption to depend on the same cause." The appalling liberties which Tissot took with scientific fact are emphasized best by his contention that sexual relations were apt to cause epileptic fits, the belief being that "coitus is a kind of epilepsy," considering the "orgasm as a convulsive symptom." Such statements, born of the man's imagination, caused immeasurable suffering for generations to follow. One effect credited to masturbation, which has been more persistently believed in than any of the others, is that masturbation supposedly caused insanity. As if Tissot had not done enough to cripple man's mind with fear, Rozier,[4] writing fifty years after the seventh edition of Tissot's work, added insanity to Tissot's list. By 1839 the belief that masturbation caused insanity was well rooted.

In 1839, a Dr. M. S. Gove[5] published her work *Solitary Vice*, in which she quoted the sixth report of the State Lunatic Hospital at Worcester, Massachusetts, to the effect that masturbation was "third in point of power to deprive its victim of reason." Beginning with Gove appear admissions by various authors of the universality of the practice; at the same time attempts had not been made to explain why the dire consequences which they ascribed to masturbation did not manifest themselves in every case. Gove unconsciously hinted at the naturalness of masturbation in the statement that the greater part of those who communicated with her on the subject had not been taught to masturbate and did not know that anyone else did. At another point she unwittingly intimated that worry was responsible for the symptoms supposedly caused by masturbation itself.

In 1840 an anonymous writer[6] took issue with the authorities prior to him, contending that the disorders attributed to masturbation were not caused directly by it. He declared that they had *no proof* that they were so caused. Here was the first demand for a scientific approach to the whole subject. In the next sentence the writer slipped back into the old groove and described what he considered the one and only disorder due to masturbation, namely dementia praecox or schizophrenia.

Dr. E. T. Brady in 1891 was one of the first to question the part that masturbation was supposed to play in the causation of insanity. While he seemed to have no doubt about the perniciousness of the practice, he did state, "But it is very probable that its importance as an influence has been greatly exaggerated, particularly in connection with the causation of insanity." Modern marriage counselors are still having to deal with the heritage of belief and a carry-over of the old taboos.

In a paper published in 1888, in *Medical News,* Lawson Tait,[7] one of the leading gynecologists of his time, adopted what we would consider today a rather wholesome attitude toward masturbation and sex education. He said, "It is a sad misfortune that all sexual questions are so completely hidden from children at puberty." Apparently he had no doubt that there were evil effects from masturbation, but he raised a serious question as to what those evil effects might be. He was among the first to try to divorce religious morality from a condition that he considered merely physical. He seemed to feel there might be some harm in masturbation so far as the male was concerned, although he said, "The evil effects of masturbation have been greatly overrated." In women, he questioned whether or not it was carried on to such an extent as to do any harm. He admitted that there were few boys who failed to masturbate at some time, but he felt the practice was comparatively rare among girls. In this he reflected the attitude of that period, when many considered that females were lacking in passion, since they felt they had no need for it. This concept of female sexuality was not exploded until sexologists gathered convincing statistics to the contrary at a relatively recent date.

In 1907 Dr. Frederick Sturgis[8] attempted to make a study of the frequency of masturbation without any consideration of its supposed evils or disabling sequelae. His admittedly conservative estimate was that 60 per cent of both sexes masturbate at some time in their lives, but he held that were the whole truth known the figure would be nearer 90 per cent.

The writings of three men have probably had more direct influence upon the thinking and behavior in this country in the last half century than have those of any other writers, largely because their books when published bore the stamp of authority and were generally approved by religious leaders, educators, and social workers. The books of G. Stanley Hall,[9] Winfield Scott Hall,[10] and Sylvanus Stall[11] have probably, in the past, been on the bookshelves in more homes and schools and public libraries than is presently true of the modern treatises on the subject. The influence of this last writer has been particularly bad because of the absence of any scientific approach to the subject and the wholly emotional manner in which it was handled. Stall said:

> *No boy can toy with the exposed portions of his reproductive system without finally suffering very serious consequences.*

He favored sex education, but in this matter it was with the thought of saving boys from these terrible consequences. He says:

> Nothing so much favors the continuance and spread of this awful vice as ignorance, and only by being early and purely taught on this important subject can the coming boys and men be saved from the awful consequences which are ruining morally, mentally, and physically thousands of boys every year.

After lecturing on the moral aspects of the subject he tells us that the next to suffer is the nervous system:

> In the act of masturbation the nerves are wrought upon in such a manner as to produce most serious results.

Then, in addition to the mental and moral changes which are supposed to have taken place, he details the dreadful physical results.

I have quoted from Stall's chapter on "Self-Abuse" because he does not produce one iota of scientific evidence to substantiate any of his statements, yet his influence and that of others like him are still affecting the emotional lives of thousands of people at the present time.

The influence of Freud, the whole psychoanalytic school, and Havelock Ellis, more than anyone else, have made sexology a godchild of medicine. More specifically, for contributions on this subject credit is given to Bernard, Bigelow, Davis, Hamilton, Kinsey, Kirkpatrick, Popenoe, and others.

Now two trends are manifest in the literature on masturbation. First is a tendency to consider masturbation in any form, under any circumstances, and with any frequency completely harmless. The writers holding this view knew that the sequelae attributed to it by preceding generations were groundless. Their newly acquired objectivity taught them to view the matter in a different light, to observe that much of animal life masturbates when deprived of any other outlet for its sexual drive. Hence they assumed it to be completely harmless.

At this same time, students interested in psychiatry and psychoanalysis began to see new dangers in the practice, such as fixations, repressions, psychoneuroses, maladjustment to the sexual phase of marriage, and other mental effects. Many of these dangers have since been proven false; many are in the process of being so proved. Many of our present writings are still being influenced by the thought that we mustn't go too far in releasing restrictions for fear we may be encouraging complete abandonment which may lead to possible if not definable untoward results. However, there is a growing accumulation of modern literature which frankly reveals the truth (see bibliography).

PREVALENCE

What of the prevalence of masturbation? Tissot stated one reason for his writing the book was that the practice was so general. Almost without exception, particularly so far as boys were concerned, authors of treatises on this subject have expressed the belief that if it was not universal it was a habit indulged in by the majority of males. (The study of masturbation in females did not come until much later.) Sylvanus Stall said:

> I wish I might say to you that but very few have ever known of this vice, but I do not believe that such an assertion would be true.

In other words, he, too, accepted that it was pretty generally practiced. It is the one thing about which these early authors were right as proven by the following studies:

W. L. Hughes,[12] Peck and Wells,[13] W. S. Taylor,[14] Kinsey,[15] Exner,[16] Lilburn Merrill,[17] and Dickinson and Beam.[18]

As to the prevalence of masturbation, all of the studies that have been carried on by competent investigators under well-credentialed auspices indicate that well over 90 per cent of all males have had a history of masturbation. While these studies vary somewhat in exactness, running anywhere from 90 per cent to 98 per cent, a study by Dr. A. C. Kinsey of Indiana University published in 1948 sets the figure at 94+ per cent. There will be little disagreement with this figure on the part of modern students of the subject. In 1929, Dr. Katherine Davis[19] published her study of college women wherein she reported admitted masturbation by 65 per cent of them. Since for most of them to admit masturbation was a matter of confession, we might easily add 10 per cent as a factor of error, as other studies, notably Hamilton's[20] and my own unpublished but recorded research, indicate that the figure among females runs somewhere between 75 per cent and 80 per cent if we are talking about a group of single women who have reached the age of twenty-five. In both sexes the frequency of the experience varies greatly, but the average single woman will report masturbation from two to three times a month, particularly just before or after her menstrual period, whereas the average single male reports two or three times a week. Checking this against the Hamilton report, we find that 49 per cent reported masturbation three or more times a week, and the Kinsey study, as reported by Glenn Ramsey,[21] shows 46 per cent of males who report a frequency of from one to six times weekly or more.

It may be safely assumed, therefore, from all the studies to date that were we to take the histories of men and women who had reached the age of twenty-five we would find that masturbation has played a part in the lives of more than 90 per cent of all males and about 70 per cent of all females, with the frequency running from once or twice a month up to several times a week, and that no evidence has been presented to prove that the greater frequency was any more productive of harm than the lesser.

Since all of this is pretty generally accepted by professional students of the sex life, it is a dereliction of responsibility not to bring these facts to the attention of millions of people who could profit by the knowledge. In regard to this subject it might be said that today we are living in two worlds, one in which the normality of occasional masturbation for release of tension and for the physical and emotional satisfactions involved is accepted as normal, and the other, a larger world (though admittedly it is growing smaller), in which there is a persistence of the old ideas based on the dogma of the past. If you believe that I have been overemphasizing the influence of the past in present-day thinking on this subject I refer you to a statement made by Dr. Maurice Levine, who in listing misconceptions says that one misconception is "that masturbation causes psychoses."

> *This is a misconception which has been exceedingly harmful and one which is extraordinarily persistent. In spite of the mental-hygiene teaching of the past fifteen or twenty years, many parents and doctors still believe such incorrect ideas, and still punish and threaten children who masturbate. One child-guidance clinic found recently that about 75 per cent of the parents of its child-patients remembered having threatened the children with the dangers of masturbation. It is important that physicians know that this is a mistake; many still do not.[22]*

It would seem that in overcoming this problem in the larger sense we have simply to tell the truth. In doing so we must avoid the use of expressions which indicate the bias and prejudice begotten of our own early training. It is of little avail to try to release a person's fears by admitting the normality of the practice and denying that it has any unhealthy consequences, while at the same time showing your own distaste by using such words as, "It isn't nice," "Well-adjusted young people find better things to do," "You should give your attention to more constructive things," and similar condemnations. All such statements are vague, without meaning, and just as productive of emotional conflict as were the consequences attributed to masturbation in the past.

I have run across many instances where the feelings of improperness concerning the practice was having an untoward effect on personality adjustment which, if not as drastic as were the fears of the past, was definitely unwholesome in its result. Every marriage counselor has met innumerable instances in which the conflict over masturbation and its possible consequences has had a profound result in the lack of sex adjustment in marriage. In personal guidance, counselors run across many cases in which worry over masturbation has been a major factor in maladjustment because of feelings of inadequacy and attitudes of self-condemnation. Whenever a person has not been particularly concerned about physical or mental consequences, the very thought that the practice indicated a lack of character development still led to self-castigation and to unwholesome sex attitudes.[23]

Masturbation in Infancy

Infancy is the period in which most of the harm is done by the unwholesome attitude of adults. In their over-concern regarding this practice they engender fears and worries in the mind of the child. What is a wholesome attitude? First, we must understand that the child masturbates because he finds pleasure in it. The practice may begin very early, often when the child is still in the crib. Whether the practice begins at this time or later, it is spontaneous in the vast majority of cases. Despite the dire warnings of early writers

concerning servant girls and playmates as sources of instruction in this practice, the majority of people who have
talked with me cannot remember ever having received instruction from another; rather the practice began either as
an urge or through some natural handling of the sexual
organs. This is particularly true of the female. There are
boys who report that they first became interested after
hearing other boys talk about it or observing such behavior
on the part of another. Even when they clearly remember
sex play with other children they seem to feel that their
interest in their own sexual organs preceded the group
experiences. Most people claim that they do not know how
or when they began but only that they have been doing it
from a very early age. Many girls report that the interest
came coincidentally with the onset of menstruation; an
even larger number say that they had no particular interest
in it until some time in their later teens.

Some recent literature* dealing with this habit in infancy has been rather forthright and free from fear-inspir-
ing admonitions. A few writers are aesthetically critical, but
the tendency is to deal with it more and more as a fact and
as an accepted part of the child's development.

It is only fair to consider one factor which might give
a parent some slight concern. Concerning the very young,
we have no evidence that there is any tension release but
rather that the organs are being manipulated because of
sensory satisfactions. Because each episode does not come
to a definite end, masturbation can be a prolonged activity
to the exclusion of other interests, thus overemphasizing
the child's pleasure interest in himself, which may later
handicap social development.

*Dr. Benjamin Spock, *Baby and Child Care*, Pocket Book edition,
1946; Hannah Lees, "The Word You Can't Say," reprint from *Hygeia*,
May 1944.

A child should be trained in good habits of hygiene, proper diet, proper elimination, and proper sleep. He should be encouraged to be active and interested in his play. If he appears to be unduly and overfrequently interested in his sex organs, this problem should be discussed with the family physician, who will inquire into the possibility of adherent tissue or conditions which cause itching, thus drawing the child's attention to that area. If, however, the physician declares everything to be normal and you know that the habits of hygiene are well regulated, when you observe the child masturbating, do nothing about it; do not scold or punish him or make the incident seem important. If you wish to distract his attention, do so by presenting another interest. Do it on the basis of "Let's do this" rather than "Stop doing that." If it becomes a matter of public display, then social values are involved. Correction should be a matter not of what he is doing but where he is doing it. We need have little worry, because the happy, well-adjusted child finds life so interesting and is busy at so many things that masturbation will play a very minor part in his activities.

In the unhappy child where there is an obvious preoccupation with masturbation this should be regarded as a symptom of a deeper problem. Any attempt to correct the symptom without getting at the cause will undoubtedly cause greater tension and make matters worse. In a case such as this a parent is well advised to seek the counsel of a child specialist.

Masturbation is common as an adolescent practice in both sexes, with all evidence pointing to the fact that there is a higher percentage among males than among females. However, at the age of fifteen there is every indication that at least 50 per cent of the girls have masturbated and that the percentage increases as the group gets older; there are many more girls masturbating at the age of nineteen or twenty than were doing so in their middle teens. All that can be said about the harmlessness of masturbation in the earlier period can be repeated here. It is true, however, that masturbation itself is likely to take on a somewhat different meaning to the adolescent, as each experience becomes an episode in itself, leading to orgasm, unless this climax is definitely suppressed or inhibited. It is also a psychological as well as a physiological act, as fantasy is a component part of the experience. Dr. Hamilton pointed out that the desirability of fantasy construction as part of the act and suggested that this made a more complete autoerotic experience, encouraging easier and more successful transition to heterosexual relations than does the masturbation which is purely sensory and without imagery.

There is great variety in the reported content of fantasies. Whatever it is, it consists of use of the imagination concerning sexual experience, intensifying the erotism to the point of orgasm. This can be a satisfying experience; it can help to relieve emotional tensions, and it effectively concentrates the sexual sensations in the genital area where they should be located, this being an effect especially to be desired in the female. If fear has not been engendered in the young person's mind he will quickly pass from such an episode to other life activities without particular concern, making the experience helpful and relatively unimportant. Unfortunately, because of the teachings of the past, thousands of young people still find themselves unable to pass from such an experience without deep feelings of anxiety. Consciousness of guilt, feelings of sin, and fear of consequences are the crippling sequelae of those who live in this second world. Thus, the feelings of inferiority and self-condemnation, plus the anticipation of eventual harmful consequences, carry over into adult life and often adversely affect the chance for good sex adjustment. Happily, however, the type of sexual incompatibility in marriage which springs from this cause can be eliminated by proper education; this would also be true where it has been a factor in personality maladjustment.

Much credit for the successful application of modern psychology to the problem of masturbation should go to Dr. Walter F. Robie of Baldwinsville, Massachusetts, whose books, *Rational Sex Ethics, The Art of Love,* and *Sex and Life,* first emphasized the modern point of view in this field.

The physical structure of the male does not admit of a great deal of variety in masturbatory practice, and it is usually accomplished manually. However, some variations are reported, such as making coital movements against the bedclothes, or using a pillow for the purpose, or pressing against objects.

In the girl, however, because her construction permits it, there is considerable variation. While it appears that the use of the finger on the clitoris is the most usual form, running a close second is what has been referred to as thigh-rubbing, in which the girl presses her thighs together or crosses her legs and squeezes the inner muscles of her thighs, thus bringing pressure on the labia and incidentally on the clitoris. At this she may become quite skillful and can prolong the experience or bring herself to orgasm at will. Many girls who use this method, however, report that they stop short of orgasm. This may be due to the fact that thigh-rubbing is often used as a substitute after admonition by the parent who has observed some digital exploration. A frequent statement of older girls and women is that they remember having been told, "Don't you ever let me catch you touching yourself again." A household term for masturbation is "playing with oneself"; this often develops a concept in the mind of the child that the harm lies in hand contact. The girl, therefore, can indulge in thigh-rubbing with less consciousness of guilt because she is not "playing with herself."

Other methods are also reported, such as pulling panties, nightgown, pajamas, the bed sheet, or other materials tightly between the thighs, then making motions that excite the clitoris. Instrumental masturbation, that of putting something in the vagina, is not as often reported as some of these other methods.

Some forms of masturbation may act as a drawback to marriage adjustment, not because of any harm in the behavior itself, but because the transition from a particular form of masturbation to acquiring satisfactions in intercourse may later become difficult. It has been my experience that in the female those who report that they pass from clitoral stimulation to manipulation of the whole vulva, with emphasis upon stimulation of the vaginal orifice, very quickly made an adjustment to coitus; they will often report they have orgasm at the first experience or shortly thereafter. Those who for a number of years have used only the clitoris find it more difficult to make such a transition, but where they have been relieved of guilt feelings and have a cooperative and skillful husband, such an adjustment will likely be made sometime within the first six months. Those girls who have denied themselves the direct form of masturbation and have used substitutive measures, such as various forms of pressure, or breast rubbing, often force themselves to stop just prior to orgasm because they have developed a fear of the orgasm, having conceived the idea that the wrong or harm lies in the release itself. In such cases, or in any case where orgasm has been suppressed, they may have developed a habit of non-response and carry this over into their marital relations, later to report that they have little or no satisfaction in coitus and an inability to come to a climax. In discouraging a form of direct masturbation in children one may be unwittingly encouraging a substitutive form which acts as a deterrent to achieving orgasm in intercourse. Also, the guilt feeling which caused a girl to withdraw from direct fondling of her own organs is apt also to cause her to resist manual stimulation on the part of the husband in his attempts at precoital excitation.

It has been my experience that the male who has mas-turbated with a sense of guilt which has driven him to get it over with as soon as possible and to suppress any accom-panying fantasy is likely in consequence to find himself bothered in early marriage by premature ejaculation. The one who has engaged in masturbation reservatus, delaying the orgasm at will, has thus prepared himself to be a more adequate partner by having developed a technique that makes it possible for him to stay with his wife as long as it is necessary for her satisfaction.

In conclusion I wish to emphasize that every sex educa-tion program should include information concerning the normality of masturbation; this should be given to adults as well as to youth because it is through misinformed adults that the old superstitions are perpetuated. I think the kind of statement we ought to make and stand by should be something as follows:

> *Masturbation, according to the best medical authorities, causes no harm physically or mentally. Any harm resulting from masturbation is caused entirely by worry or by a sense of guilt due to misinformation.*

I would make this kind of statement and challenge anyone to prove otherwise. Let us have respect for the normalities of life and for the good sense of our young people who have little time to be overconcerned with sex. Let's stop equivocating. Tell the truth and shame the devil!

NOTES

1. E. T. Brady, "Masturbation," *Va. M. Month.,* 18:256–60, 1891–2.

2. S. A. D. Tissot, *A Treatise on the Disease Produced by Onanism,* New York, translated and published by Collins and Hannay, 1832. (First French issue prior to 1767.)

3. Anonymous, *A Practical Essay Upon the Tabes Dorsalis,* 1763.

4. Rozier, *Des Habitudes secretes ou Des Maladies Produites par onanisme chez les femmes,* 3 ed. Paris, 1830.

5. M. S. Gove, *Solitary Vice,* Portland, 1839.

6. Anonymous, *An Hour's Conference with Fathers and Sons, in Relation to a Common Fatal Indulgence of Youth,* Boston, 1840.

7. Lawson Tait, "Masturbation-Clinical Lectures," *Medical News,* 53:1–3, 1888.

8. F. R. Sturgis, "The Comparative Prevalence of Masturbation in Males and Females," *Am. J. Dermat. and Genito-Urin. Dis.,* II:396–400, 1907.

9. G. Stanley Hall, *Adolescence,* 1907.

10. Winfield S. Hall, *From Youth into Manhood.*

11. Sylvanus Stall, *What a Young Boy Ought to Know,* 1905.

12. W. L. Hughes, "Sex Experiences of Boyhood," *J. Social. Hyg.,* 12, 1926.

13. M. W. Peck and F. L. Wells, "On the Psycho-sexuality of College Graduate Men," *Ment. Hyg.,* 7, 1923.

14. W. S. Taylor, "A Critique of Sublimation in Males: A Study of Forty Superior Single Men," *Genet. Psychol. Monog.,* 13, 1933.

15. Dr. A. C. Kinsey, Dr. Wardell B. Pomeroy, Dr. Clyde E. Martin, *Sexual Behavior in the Human Male,* 497–516, 1948.

16. M. J. Exner, *Problems and Principles of Sex Education,* copyright by International Committee of Y.M.C.A., 1915.

17. Lilburn Merrill, A summary of findings in a study of sexualism among a group of one hundred delinquent boys, *J. Juven. Res.,* 3, 1918.

18. R. L. Dickinson and Lura Beam, *A Thousand Marriages; a Medical Study of Sex Adjustment,* 1931.

19. K. B. Davis, *Factors in the Sex Life of Twenty-Two Hundred Women,* 1929.

20. G. V. Hamilton, *A Research in Marriage.*

21. Glenn V. Ramsey, "The Sexual Development of Boys," *Am. Journal of Psy.,* Vol. 56, April 1943.

22. Dr. Maurice Levine, *Psychotherapy in Medicine,* 1942.

23. Albert Ellis, Ph.D., *The American Sexual Tragedy,* 210, 1954.

BIBLIOGRAPHY

Adams, Dr. C. R., *Preparing for marriage.* New York, E. P. Dutton, 1951, p. 55.

Baruch, D. W., *Parents can be people.* New York: D. Appleton-Century Co., 1944, Chap. 9.

Ellis, A., *The American sexual tragedy.* New York: Twayne Publishers, 1954, pp. 154, 201.

Frank, L. K., & Frank, Mary, *How to be a woman.* Maco Magazine Corp. 1954, p. 35.

Kinsey, A. C., Pomeroy, Wardell, B., Martin, C. E., *Sexual behavior in the human male.* Philadelphia, W. B. Saunders Co., 1948, pp. 497–516.

Levy, J., M. D., & Munroe, R., *The happy family.* New York: Alfred A. Knopf, 1938, p. 134.

Chapter 2

MYTHS CONCERNING AUTOEROTICISM

Albert Ellis, Ph.D.

All recent studies, including Kinsey's, have shown that up-
ward of 90 per cent of young males masturbate even when
they frequently have available heterosexual outlets.

It is certainly true that masturbation can be a psychologically unhealthy practice—if an individual *exclusively and
compulsively* uses it as a sex outlet *when other sex outlets are
easily available.* Severely neurotic or psychotic individuals,
for example, may become fixated on masturbational modes
of sex activity and be entirely incapable of obtaining sex
satisfaction in any other way. Or they may masturbate to
the accompaniment of bizarre, intensely sado-masochistic
or otherwise weird fantasies. Or they may masturbate continually when they have no sexual desire and are incapable
of orgasm. But these are relatively rare cases, and the indi-

From *The Journal of Social Therapy,* 1955, I, 141–143. Reprinted by
permission of the author and the publisher. Copyright is owned by
Corrective and Social Psychiatry. Originally this article was entitled *Masturbation.*

viduals falling within these categories invariably are generally disturbed persons whose sexual peculiarities are
merely one aspect of their more inclusive personality disorders.

More frequently, young males will resort exclusively to
masturbation as a sex outlet, not because they do not desire
heterosexual relations, but because they feel social-sexu-
ally inadequate, and retreat to sex solitude rather than run
the risks of heterosexual courtship. Here again, however,
their exclusive masturbation is a symptom of their general
personality disturbance, and is not necessarily a sex problem in itself. It is not their masturbating which is abnormal,
but their fear of social-sexual contacts with members of the
other sex.

Assuming that masturbation may be a symptom of disturbance when it is exclusively and compulsively practiced
though other sex outlets are freely available, it is certainly
not abnormal or perverted when it is practiced as a substitute for, say, heterosexual outlets that are *not* easily available. Not only during childhood and adolescence, but
during the entire span of an adult male's (or, for that matter, female's) life, autoerotism leading to orgasm is a harmless form of sex activity—provided (1) that the masturbator
does not erroneously *believe* masturbation to be harmful or
abnormal, (2) that when socially approved non-masturba-
tional outlets are available he also resorts to them, and (3)
that when other sex outlets are not available he remains
interested in them and makes some effort to try to find
them.

Several bugaboos against masturbation are still raised
in many sexual and psychological texts. It is frequently
noted, for example, that autoerotism is an "immature"
mode of sex activity which is appropriate for youngsters but
not for adults. This is nonsense, since the Kinsey and other
data conclusively show that adult males (and, especially,
females) of all ages frequently masturbate, and often do so

even after marriage. Masturbation becomes "immature" only when it is *exclusively* and *compulsively* practiced even though other outlets are easily available.

It is sometimes alleged that masturbation mitigates against sex adjustment in marriage, leading to impotence in males and frigidity in females. The available facts do not support this conclusion and some of them directly contradict it. Masturbators (especially females) often tend to be more potent and less frigid than non-masturbators—possibly because the higher-sexed individuals tend to masturbate more frequently than do lower-sexed ones.

Sex texts frequently state that masturbation is not essentially harmful but that it may easily be practiced to "excess." This is sheer drivel. Both male and female sex physiology is such that as soon as an individual has gone beyond normal sex limits, he or she automatically becomes sexually fatigued and quite incapable of further orgasms. Only seriously psychotic individuals, who will go so far as to masturbate when they have no sexual desire, will normally masturbate to "excess."

Writers with underlying prejudices against masturbation often allege that it is harmful because it leads to social or sexual seclusiveness. But, on the contrary, it is invariably social seclusiveness that leads to the use of masturbation as a sole sex outlet rather than the latter leading to the former. It is, moreover, an individual's rigid, puritanical sex notions which frequently make him (or her) so ashamed of heterosexual participations that he cannot face nonmasturbational forms of activity and hence exclusively resorts to masturbation. If the sex apologists would show more concern about these puritanical attitudes, which they themselves help to inculcate, than with the so-called evils of masturbation, they would be rendering a far greater human service and be contributing to the decline of masturbation by logically encouraging approved heterosexual alternatives.

Chapter 3

MASTURBATION

Patricia A. Brooks, M.S.

This author, a psychiatric nursing specialist, has accused nursing publications of avoiding a subject which many nurses must deal with in the course of taking care of sick adults and well children. Masturbation, she reminds us, has certain roles in the normal process of development. In adulthood, too, it serves certain functions—some pathologic, some normal. But in every case, it has some purpose. When a patient uses this behavior, it is the nurse's therapeutic responsibility to try to find out why.

Masturbation, known also as auto-eroticism and "self-abuse," is behavior that may be encountered by many

Miss Brooks, who is a graduate of De Pauw University School of Nursing, Greencastle, Ind., earned a master of science degree at Rutgers, The State University, Newark, N.J. She is a clinical nurse specialist in the Mental Health Clinic at Denver General Hospital in Colorado.

nurses. Pediatric and public health nurses, in particular, are frequently faced with this behavior; having to cope with it, however, means that they also are in a position to educate parents and help correct misconceptions. Psychiatric nurses also may be confronted with masturbatory behavior in their patients. Yet, despite the general relevance of the subject, only one article on masturbation has been published in nursing journals in the past 10 years.[1] Perhaps general societal taboos have had a greater effect on nursing attitudes than we would care to believe!

Many persons are so conditioned that even the word "masturbation" arouses disgust and anxiety. Such a reaction in nurses will influence their response to a patient and prevent them from examining the behavior for the clues it may give in understanding the patient and in uncovering more significant problem areas, areas in which nursing intervention can be therapeutic.

DEVELOPMENTAL ASPECTS

Understanding the role of masturbation in the growth process is essential for understanding normal development. The infant, as a first step toward mastery of himself and his environment, begins to explore the world about him. Naturally, his own body—fingers, arms, legs, and eventually, the genitals—provides a ready source of manipulable objects. Early selection of the genitals for exploration is random, but the pleasurable sensation is for the infant a new way of experiencing his body. His interest, however, is transient as other apsects of the world claim his attention.

In time, however, the infant learns that his genitalia will consistently provide him with pleasurable sensations. Since the genitalia are always available, masturbatory activity may then become a substitute for other delayed satisfactions, or it may be used to soothe. Some primitive cultures have recognized this soothing effect and have utilized masturbation in getting an infant to sleep. Others recognize masturbation as the first behavioral link in the process of reproduction, and Hofling and Leininger note that ". . . such activity is not only physically harmless in itself, but it is of definite survival value for the human species."[2]

Yet, Western society works to restrict masturbation from its onset. Invariably, the mother or other significant persons react with anxiety, alarm, or anger when they discover a baby touching his genitals. The baby's hands are removed from his genitalia, or slapped; disapproval is expressed verbally or nonverbally. Even when there is no overt attempt to stop the masturbation, the mother's anxiety is communicated to the infant by means of empathy, producing in him a corresponding feeling of discomfort.[3] If the anxiety level of the mother is high, the behavior which elicited the anxiety may be dissociated, or pushed from awareness, by the infant.[4] Repetition of such patterns over a period of time may cause the infant to remove genital sensations from his awareness, leaving an important aspect of himself denied to him.

Discovery of masturbation in an older child may result in direct disapproval expressed in the common folklore of the society; for example, threats that it will lead to mental illness, permanent physical damage, or to transient conditions such as "eye trouble" or acne. Threats of castration or isolation and other types of punishment are also used. These methods of dealing with masturbatory activity give rise to needless anxiety and fear in many children; when the disapproved behavior is continued in secret, guilt also occurs.

In adolescence, masturbation again becomes a normal behavior pattern. Pearce and Newton consider it ". . . a helpful preliminary in learning the individual patterning and timing of stimulus and response of the lust dynamism."[5] Masturbation allows the person to experience sexual pleasure without the complication of a relationship with another person. If a teen-ager is able to discover his sexual sensations without excessive anxiety or guilt, he should then be more successful in proceeding to normal heterosexual adjustment. Masturbatory activity may, of course, take place within the context of a relationship as, for example, in the mutual masturbatory play often found among peers of the same sex in the preadolescent period.

The adolescent who was severely reprimanded for masturbating in childhood, or burdened with misinformation, will be in conflict, experiencing on the one hand the pleasurable release masturbation provides (including its gratification of the normal sex need) and the guilt engendered by his concept of the behavior as evil or harmful. Trying to solve his dilemma, the adolescent may attempt to avoid all sexual stimuli and to use extreme willpower, but then he experiences guilt and disgust when he fails in this avoidance. His conflict may express itself in physical symptoms such as weakness, aches, pains, severe fatigue, and neurasthenia.[6] If the conflict over masturbation is severe, the adolescent might find that gratification of his sexual needs through indiscriminate heterosexual relationships would be less threatening to his self-image. However, not all adolescents masturbate or engage in promiscuous sexual activity; many sublimate their sexual needs through fantasy or with preliminary sexual activity—"necking" or "petting" with the opposite sex.

The harmful aspect of masturbation—even excessive masturbation—is not physical damage; rather, it is the emotional trauma that occurs because of guilt and anxiety. And, constantly trying to avoid masturbation (and the need to keep sexual feelings dissociated which lies behind this preoccupation) may prevent the formation of any type of relationship with the opposite sex.

Excessive masturbation at any age is a symptom, or clue, that some needs of the individual are not being met through interpersonal relationships; moreover, these needs may be entirely unrelated to sexuality.[7] Nursing intervention, based on identification of the unmet needs—as well as of the immediate purpose the masturbation is serving—is directed toward helping the individual develop more effective methods of attaining gratification. Once the patient is able to attain the gratification by other means, the masturbatory behavior should decrease.

GUIDANCE FOR PARENTS

Society does place restrictions on sexual behavior, including masturbation. Parents, therefore, need to find ways to help children meet society's expectations without threats, misinformation, and severe disapproval.

How do parents accomplish this? There is no easy outline to follow, but if they recognize the normalcy of the behavior in the growth process they may tend to not overemphasize the masturbation or, at least, to not respond with threats or misinformation. Parents also can attempt to pay special attention to the child when he is not masturbating. Engaging him in other activities is useful, but if they are introduced following each episode of masturbation, they serve only to focus attention on the masturbatory activity.

Parents also must be aware of their own reactions and feelings about masturbation. Otherwise, rationalizations for parental action may be formed, and disapproval of the child's behavior may be carried out on a more covert level. If the relationship between child and parent is such that the child needs to rebel, masturbatory behavior might fulfill this function and become the basis for a power struggle between child and parents. In general, though, parents can help their children toward normal sexual adjustment by not becoming alarmed about masturbation. What they need to add is love, attention, and creative stimulation, as well as reasonable and consistent limit setting.

FUNCTIONS IN ADULTHOOD

Masturbation in hospitalized patients may serve a variety of functions—some pathologic and some merely transient substitutes until the patient goes home. The function would be considered pathologic to the extent that it enables the individual to avoid recognition of an unmet need and inhibits initiation of more appropriate or more acceptable methods by which he can meet the need.

For the patient who has integrated some regular means of achieving sexual satisfaction prior to hospitalization, masturbation may merely be a means of gaining temporary relief of sexual tension. In another patient, masturbation may serve him as it did in childhood, reducing anxiety and producing pleasurable sensations. It may also be used to drive others away and thus help a patient avoid relationships with persons of the same or of the opposite sex. Even the *discussion* of masturbatory behavior may serve this purpose.

Most psychiatric nurses have observed situations such as the one in which a patient begins to masturbate openly after one week on an acute treatment ward. His behavior is upsetting to both the staff and other patients. The staff may be in conflict between the desire to respond therapeutically (which usually means with acceptance) and their own personal reactions to the behavior (which often includes the wish to punish). Other patients often respond with increased anxiety to a patient who so flagrantly violates a rigid taboo or who so openly demonstrates their own "private" problem. Patients' reactions may then lead the staff to justify their own disapproval, seclusion, or discipline of the masturbating patient even though there is no subsequent decrease in the behavior or any observable help to the patient.

It is important to consider masturbation as a *clue* to the purpose it serves the patient. Caudill states that a patient in a mental hospital has five sources for satisfaction of his immediate needs: 1) his doctor; 2) the nursing staff; 3) the use of the physical space on the ward; 4) the other patients; and 5) himself—as related to his psychological resources and the manipulation of his body.[8] When the patient is unable to obtain adequate satisfaction from the first four sources, he is forced to turn to himself as a last resort, a last resort because self-satisfaction is not as satisfying as satisfaction gained through relationships with others. Caudill further says that a patient's inability to communicate adequately with the doctor and staff, coupled with repetitive pathologic experiences in the hospital and the deprivation of usual living habits, may lead him to depend on the fifth resource.[9] This may be especially true on "back" wards where there are many patients and few staff, where environmental and interpersonal stimulation and gratification are of low intensity and low caliber.

To understand masturbation, the staff should look at the pattern in which it occurs. Does the patient masturbate after being brushed off by the doctor, the nurse, or another patient? Does he start to masturbate after a fight has begun, or whenever he is left alone for a long time? Does the pattern seem to be one of relieving anxiety or of maintaining self-control? What does the patient seem to gain from masturbation? In each instance, the nurse needs to observe the situation and then promptly help the patient clarify his thoughts and feelings at the stressful moment and review the events which precipitated his anxiety. Such intervention should decrease the level of his anxiety and allow more attention to be focused on alternate methods of behavior. With this type of nursing intervention, masturbation should become less necessary and, therefore, be used less frequently to attain satisfaction.

A young married patient in the course of an individual interview described the use of masturbation for relief of anxiety. Although this patient had previously expressed very tolerant ideas regarding masturbation during a group therapy session, the strength of the societal taboo easily can be seen in her projection of blame for initiating the activity during her childhood. "I was hit on the head with a baseball. After that I started to masturbate. I'd get nervous and then I'd masturbate. It would make me more nervous because I felt guilty about it. I never would have started to masturbate if it weren't for that baseball. My whole personality changed. This was when I was ten."

Masturbation, in itself, was not the problem for this patient; rather, it was aspects of her life that aroused her anxiety and her pattern of turning to herself for satisfaction rather than to other people. There also was indication that she may have had difficulty in accepting herself as a sexual person. Areas such as these would be the focus of nurse intervention.

Masturbation also may be a belated attempt at integrating the sexual aspect of the self. During psychotherapy, a patient may begin to experience previously dissociated feelings and thoughts and may need to pass through the adolescent masturbatory phase on his way to normal sexual adjustment.

An attempt at exploration and integration can be illustrated in a nurse-patient interview with a 13-year-old boy with childhood schizophrenia.

PATIENT: Did you ever jerk a boy off?

NURSE: No.

PATIENT: Do you know what that means?

NURSE: Yes, what does it mean to you?

PATIENT: Pull on it.

NURSE: And what happens?

PATIENT: It gets hard.

NURSE: Have you done that before?

PATIENT: Yes.

NURSE: What do you think about?

PATIENT: I guess what the boy's pulling on.

NURSE: Do you mean his penis?

PATIENT: Yes. Sometimes I do it in bed at night and it tickles.

NURSE: That's called masturbating. What do you think about when you masturbate?

PATIENT: About a girl pulling on it. What's the name of the part the girl has down between her legs in the front?

NURSE: Vagina.

In this interview the nurse focused on clarifying information given by the patient and providing appropriate titles or correcting misinformation when necessary. A non-verbal message that such behavior was acceptable also appears to have been conveyed.

Masturbation, as an activity or as a focus of discussion, may provide an effective means of avoiding a relationship with the nurse. An attractive young male patient discussed his masturbation problem at length in the second interview with a young female nurse; he also discussed sexual fantasies with her. The use of erotic material so early in the relationship was considered to be an avoidance maneuver. In other words, obsessive preoccupation with masturbation as a topic prevented a more meaningful focus and was an attempt to drive the nurse away. However, nursing intervention at this time was focused on remaining with the patient and listening to him but not on promoting further exploration of the masturbation. In these situations, it is particularly important for the nurse to be aware of her own reactions to the patient so that she will not unwittingly increase the patient's pathology by becoming caught in the patient's avoidance maneuver. The following excerpt was taken from the second interview with this patient:

PATIENT: I masturbate quite a bit.

NURSE: What feelings do you have about masturbating?

PATIENT: Well, I enjoy it but I'd rather do it in reality than by myself.

NURSE: I'm not clear what you mean by "in reality."

PATIENT: In other words, I think I would prefer to make my dreams come true. I'm all alone and I'd rather be with a woman. I do it more frequently at home.

NURSE: What does being at home have to do with your masturbation?

PATIENT: It's a frustrating situation. I live with my two sisters who are young women. I don't think I would ever approach them in a sexual manner.

Later interviews with this patient showed that he was quite unable to relate to women; through masturbation he was able to avoid, in part, a physiologic need for relating. Masturbation served also as a tension-release mechanism for the seductive relationship the patient had formed with his sisters. The masturbation, however, was only a clue to problem relationships, relationships which the patient did not understand and could neither cope with nor change. The topic of masturbation did not come up in later interviews, but the initial discussion of it had provided some clues to early transference reactions.

Discussion of masturbation may also serve the opposite function; it may increase closeness. In the twenty-first group therapy session of a group of schizophrenic patients, sexual topics—ranging from masturbation to homosexual experiences—were introduced for the first time. Even though this was highly charged material, a growing support and trust for each other in the group made the discussion possible and tended to deepen the group's relatedness.

However, even within one session, the purpose the discussion serves may vary. When the focus on homosexuality increased the anxiety level within the group, the conversation again reverted to masturbation. Toward the end of this session, two of the young men engaged in obsessional competition for the status of having the worst problem.

> MR. J.:   I masturbated twice a day for six years; as a nurse, what do you think of that?
>
> NURSE: I don't think anything about it. (shrugging)
>
> MR. D.:   Well, I masturbated three times a day for a year!
>
> NURSE: Do you want a prize or something?
>
> MR. D.:   No! It's a terrible problem. You should know about this—what it does to your physical condition.
>
> NURSE: I wonder why you want me to "know it all" right now. You're kind of putting me down.
>
> MR. J.:   Because we need help with it.
>
> NURSE: And I don't care about you?
>
> MR. J.:   You don't realize how important this is.

As the anxiety in relation to both topics increased, the patients continued to focus on masturbation to avoid more useful areas of discussion as well as to express their demands for care and their anger at the leader for not protecting them from this anxiety.

Masturbation also may be used to gain attention or to avoid being aware of loneliness. These aspects have not been discussed in this paper. Rather, the emphasis here has been on understanding masturbatory behavior as a clue to unmet needs and on basing nursing intervention upon this recognition in order to help the patient develop alternate methods of achieving satisfaction. The intervention might not be specific to the masturbation at all, but may, instead, focus on general problems in the patient's inter-personal relationships. If problems are reduced, the need for masturbatory behavior might also decrease.

Masturbation serves different patients in different settings, and the purpose it serves can vary for an individual from one time to another. It is behavior that is useful for patients and should be understood by nurses.

NOTES

1. Juzwiak, Marijo. Masturbation; the hush-hush subject. R.N. 26:59–65, Mar. 1963.

2. Hofling, C. K., and Leininger, Madeleine M. *Basic Psychiatric Concepts in Nursing.* Philadelphia: J. B. Lippincott Co., 1960, p. 170.

3. Sullivan, H. S. *The Interpersonal Theory Psychiatry,* ed. by Helen S. Perry and Mary L. Gawel. New York: W. W. Norton and Co., 1953, p. 41.

4. *Ibid.,* p. 145.

5. Pearce, Jane E., and Newton, Saul. *The Conditions of Human Growth.* New York: Citadel Press, 1963, p. 112.

6. Sullivan, *op. cit.,* p. 391.

7. Hofling and Leininger, *op. cit.,* p. 395.

8. Caudill, William. *The Psychiatric Hospital as a Small Society.* Cambridge, Mass.: Published for the Commonwealth Fund by Harvard University Press, 1958, p. 33.

9. *Ibid.*

Chapter 4

THE BENEFITS OF AUTOEROTISM—
UNIFICATION AND SEXUALITY

David Cole Gordon

THE BENEFITS OF AUTOEROTISM

When no guilt, fear, or anxieties are involved, the sexual or physical satisfaction that flows from any type of sexual activity which proceeds to orgasm should theoretically leave a person sexually satisfied and well adjusted psychologically. Sexual arousal creates many physiological as well as psychological tensions which are resolved and relaxed by the climactic orgasm, following which the individual returns to a normal state. Sexual tension or frustration, particularly when prolonged, sets up a disturbance in the individual which can impair not only his work efficiency but his personal serenity. It is quite obvious that people are happier and more well adjusted when sexual excitation can be resolved by orgasm.

One of the common misconceptions and unsubstantiated notions, that are so rife in the literature of masturbation, is that the practice of autoerotism particularly by women leads to an aversion to normal heterosexual relationships and injures their capacity to achieve orgasm in marital or normal intercourse. This is testified to by many physicians and writers including, surprisingly, Havelock Ellis.

The opposing and prevailing view is that onanists tend to be more potent and less frigid than non-masturbators, suggesting that indulgence in masturbation frequently indicates that the person is more highly sexed then the abstainers.

We have already seen how the practice of masturbation can prevent suicides which certainly must be regarded as a valuable social benefit. Masturbation furnishes an invaluable outlet which permits sociopaths and psychopaths to act out their overheated sexual fantasies which they might otherwise stage as sexual crimes violating not only innocent victims but the social mores and morals. It acts as a defense for society protecting it against highly sexed individuals with strong instinctive cravings and inadequate ethical and sexual inhibitions. Many of our sexual crimes are committed by precisely this type of individual who refuses to resort to masturbation because he regards it as unmanly, a viewpoint that is particularly prevalent among the lower socio-economic classes. The outlet where it is resorted to not only protects society, but also the individuals involved against becoming criminals and risking imprisonment.

What about the sex lives of aging widows, confirmed bachelors, old maids, and those unfortunates who suffer from a deformity or disabling illness that makes them unattractive to the opposite sex or unable to obtain a sexual companion? Are these to be denied any sexual gratification? As naive as most of us still are about sexual practices, the statistics indicate that potency, as well as desire, contin-

ues into advanced as well as old age. Autoerotism represents the sole outlet for these individuals who are
bombarded, as all of us are, with the sexual stimuli that
pervade our culture and appear in all of our advertising and
communication media.

The practice is also a great outlet for those who are
troubled by homosexual cravings. There are overt and actively practicing homosexuals, latent homosexuals, and
overt homosexuals who for any of a variety of reasons, but
mostly because of fear of society, abstain from active homosexual acts. Masturbation furnishes them with an outlet
that permits them to indulge in vicarious expression and
satisfaction of their desires without breaking the law, risking disease or getting involved in the violence and physical
risks that are an integral part of the random sexual life of
homosexuals. . . .

Among the minor though important benefits assigned
to onanism is a frequent aid to the sleeplessness caused by
the physical restlessness and psychical irritation resulting
from insufficient sexual gratification. The release of tension through orgasm frequently relaxes a person sufficiently so that he can sleep, providing it does not cause him
to lie awake worrying about the practice.

Why We Masturbate

With all that has been written about sex in all its forms, of
which masturbation is just one, nothing has been said or
written which explains why man engages in it and why it is
so potent a drive. All of the Freudian discussion about
pleasure and instinct and all of the psychoanalytic and eru-
dite words tell us nothing basic. Why is the sex drive so
strong? If the answer is pleasure, then why is it so pleasant?
It is over in a split second. Why then will men and women
risk life, liberty, marriage, reputation, money and limb for

a single sexual encounter? It is not necessary to sustain life as are food and water. Why then will men and women leave careers, jobs, hearth, home and family for a satisfactory sexual relationship? Why has sex become so all important in our society and a satisfactory sex life a key desideratum to happiness? Masturbation is important only as one aspect of sexuality and because of the tremendous amount of needless suffering that it causes. For that matter all sexual activity, even of the so-called normal heterosexual variety, probably produces more psychic conflict, pain and suffering than all of man's other activities put together. Certainly more psychoanalytic hours are logged discussing sexual problems, in and out of marriage, than any other single area of confusion. Sex becomes a problem almost from the time we are born until we die. It is not uncommonly the last thing in a person's mind before he dies. Why? Before we attempt to answer this question let us examine some of the reasons others have suggested to explain the phenomenon of sexuality, particularly as it relates to masturbation.

The key concepts for the understanding of Freud's theory of masturbation are his theories of the instincts and the pleasure principle. Freud defined instincts as the forces which we assume to exist behind the tensions caused by the needs of the id which represent the somatic demands upon mental life.

The two basic instincts Freud assumed were Eros, the life instinct, and Thanatos, the destructive instinct. Of Eros, Freud indicated that the instincts of self-preservation as well as the preservation of the species fell within its bounds and that its aim was to establish ever greater unities and to bind together. About pleasure and unpleasure Freud believed that the raising of the tensions governing the ego's activities is in general felt as unpleasure and their lowering as pleasure.

As we can see by the foregoing definitions, Freud believed that Eros was one of the two basic instincts and combined with the pleasure principle explained the practice of masturbation in infancy. If, however, Freud's theories are correct, why don't they explain equally well and consistently why men and women continue to masturbate? Why should something that was normal and natural suddenly become abnormal and pathological? When does it slip into the realm of pathology? The day after marriage? The day after turning twenty-one? Or the day after the commencement of an affair? All Freud really tells us is that man has a sexual instinct and finds masturbation pleasant. He does not come to grips with the question as to why it is so pleasant and why, in the wake of the problems it brings, men and women find it so hard to discontinue, and, when they do, why the consequences are frequently so disastrous.

Another theory as to why man masturbates is that the activity represents man's aboriginal sexuality as well as expressing all of his suppressed and asocial components. Man even today can obtain gratification from his own body much in the same manner as primordial man did who could indulge in sexual pleasures much as he felt like it and as the opportunity presented itself.

Still another view might be called the "forbidden fruit" theory. This position believes that the very forbidden nature of the practice and its surrounding taboos not only contributes to and enhances its pleasure value but acts as stimulant. The theory is that if it were commonly permitted it would lose most of its charm.

Another theory is that masturbation and the accompanying feelings of guilt and anxiety derive much of their potency from the fact that they represent a breaking away from one's parents and constitute a child's first act of independence. A child depends upon his parents for all of his basic bodily needs, but onanism is a pleasure he can obtain by himself and from his own body and frees the subject from the social obligation of gratitude. The onanist only has himself to thank for the pleasure he receives. Since the tendency is to make us thankful to some higher powers for all our gratifications, autoerotism becomes a symbol of opposition to the parents. It is found that children whose masturbatory activity is disregarded by the parents generally tend to give up the habit most easily. The habit is most rigidly fixed whenever the child feels that he is contravening the parental will and he continues the indulgence through neurotic stubbornness. Many children masturbate when they are threatened with punishment. . . .

UNIFICATION AND SEXUALITY

Man is never more unified than during orgasm. His mind is totally quiescent at climax whether it is obtained as a result of normal heterosexual intercourse, homosexual activity, or masturbation. And, as with all of his other unification experiences, he seeks to repeat them as often as possible. It should be reemphasized here that the unification experience is so profoundly satisfying not just because man becomes one with himself, but because he also becomes one with the world and others, and for that brief moment in eternity all of his earthly problems are resolved.

Physiologists can explain the unique biological dynamics of the sexual orgasm and measure the various bodily responses such as respiration, blood pressure and tachycardia. Their studies provide valuable and long overdue scientific information as to what happens to the body during sexual activity. There is a more basic but non-measurable reason why the sexual orgasmic experience is so profoundly satisfying that man pursues it to the extent that he does, and frequently sacrifices in its pursuit such things as family, friendship, money, and position. It is possible the reason is that procreation is the creation of life itself and, therefore, is the unification experience par excellence. . . .

Let us turn now to masturbation and self-love, the subject of this book. We quoted earlier the famous dictum that coition is a poor substitute for masturbation. The first human clinical evidence to support this is in the findings of Masters and Johnson. They concluded that while the number of experiments was not sufficient to allow a truly empirical position, the corpus contraction patterns initiated in response to automanipulative techniques were of greater intensity and duration than those resulting from coitally induced orgasmic experience. Their study subjects also reported that the autoerotic experience was more intense than, although not necessarily as satisfying as that resulting from heterosexual intercourse.

They also found an interesting correlation between tachycardia and autoerotic activity and that the heart rate was usually elevated significantly during the late plateau and orgasmic phases of the sexual cycle. They reported rates from 110 to 180 + beats per minute. More variation in orgasmic intensity was reflected in the heart rates of the female rather than the male, and the highest cardiac rates of all were produced during female masturbatory sessions rather than intercourse.

Scientific support for the superior satisfaction obtained from onanistic activity at times also seems to be adduced by Carpenter's[1] study of free-living male rhesus monkeys. He theorized that some autoerotic behavior could be anticipated, but probably would only be observed in the case of isolated or immature males. Nevertheless, he observed three instances of self-stimulation to the point of ejaculation in adult, mature males while they were in association with females.

[1]C. R. Carpenter, "Sexual behavior of free ranging rhesus monkeys (Macaca mulatta). I. Specimens, procedures and behavioral characteristics of estrus. II. Periodicity of estrus, homosexual, autoerotic and nonconformist behavior." *J. Comparative and Physiological Psychol.*, Vol. XXX, III (1942), 113–142 and 143–162.

Even though these studies are not conclusive they at least point to the fact that the orgasm in masturbation is frequently more intense than the one experienced in coition. Then, why would it not be more satisfying? To many men it undoubtedly is. Masturbation is still quite common after marriage and occurs only with reduced frequencies. It is most frequent according to Kinsey among college educated males where 69 percent had continued to indulge in autoerotism after marriage. The figure drops to 42 percent among men of high school level and 29 percent of those of grade school level. The drop in incidence may be attributed to the bias against the practice not being manly. Another reason perhaps may be that in the lower social classes the husband's demands take precedence over the wife's indisposition or lack of inclination.

In many cases, the autoerotic activity is confined to the periods when the husband is separated from his wife. Some married males will go for long periods without indulgence, but go back to it as an outlet for their sexual desires when they are apart from their wives as in wartime. This is most common among college men. Sometimes autoerotic activity results from the wife's disinclination to have as frequent sexual relations as her husband would like. Onanism is frequently practiced during the periods of pregnancy, menstruation, and illness when regular intercourse is not feasible.

It is suspected that masturbation among married men is more common than the statistical data indicates. It is self-evident that men, when queried, hesitate to admit that they have masturbated after marriage without qualifying their admission. There are in addition some men who engage in self-stimulation as a means of adding sexual variety to their lives and who continue to masturbate regardless of the amount of sexual intercourse they may have.

In the light of the foregoing which shows the superior intensity of the onanistic experience, and our analysis of the unification experience as man's most important raison d'etre, we see why the masturbation habit is so hard to break. It is not only an intense unification experience, but it is one he can have at will and which permits him to indulge without the psychosocial distraction of a coital partner of the opposite sex.

Theoretically, it would seem that onanism should be the most satisfying of all sexual activities. The reason that it is not, is not just because of the religious and social opprobrium attached, although they are contributing factors to the anxiety and guilt which we have seen always attached to the practice. Perhaps the basic reason why it does not offer as much satisfaction as heterosexual intercourse is that, while it is a key unification experience in that it unifies man with himself, it does not unify him with others.

It now should be clear where homosexuality fits in. It combines the unification with oneself, with unification with another, but not another with whom one can procreate. Nevertheless it is still preferred by many in spite of all the risks and condemnations attached, to the solitary practice of onanism. Ultimate satisfaction would seem to be simultaneous unification with oneself with others and with the universe. This may only be possible in heterosexual coitus among our sexual activities. We may enquire then, if that is so, then why does the evidence seem to point to the fact that the autoerotic experience is not only more intense but of longer duration than the heterosexual variety? As suggested above, the reason probably lies in the psychic and psychosocial distraction of the coital partner who must be accommodated and satisfied. It is one of the great tragedies of mankind that sexual relationships should have so many overtones and complicating factors involved, and that what should be the simplest and most natural of human acts has become all too frequently, so difficult. . . .

Chapter 5

MASTURBATION AND LEARNING

Alex Comfort, M.B., Ph.D.

This is now a more important learning experience for the woman than for the man, because quite a few girls don't embark on it spontaneously. Men almost universally masturbate for enjoyment from early adolescence on—they may also use it to desensitize themselves and avoid over-rapid response in intercourse: the second of these has to be learned, but not the first. Women who do not climax or who are frigid in intercourse almost always have to be taught in the first instance how to produce an orgasm themselves, before learning to transfer that ability to the sexual situation. This strongly suggests that while boys need only be told to enjoy masturbation without guilt, adolescent girls should be actively encouraged to explore their own bodies. The idea that this is a beautiful love-secret to be taught them only by an idealized betrothed falls down on the inexperience and anxiety of a lot of the unidealized men they'll meet. If they don't know their own responses they can't help a man to stimulate them. The idea that learning in this way will cause them to get stuck with noncoital responses is a piece of theoretical folklore. Shy and anxious people of either sex can get stuck with masturbation because it's nonrelational, but that is as a consequence of their original withdrawnness.

To the mother who finds her daughter masturbating and wants to know what to tell her, the answer is, rejoice and be exceedingly glad that she's learning a skill, and hope that if you were worried by old superstitions you didn't show it and put her off. As to "telling" her, say it's something she'll be able to enjoy all her life, a practice for adult lovemaking, and the only way to learn her own responses; warn her against disturbed people who say it's sinful or harmful. Don't give her a vibrator—some adults find that effective, but it's inclined to damp down sensitivity with prolonged use, and is better kept for people already sexually active. If your daughter doesn't masturbate, there would be a case for teaching her if parental teaching wasn't apt to be mistimed and intrusive: books, or instruction in a group as a part of normal sex education, would be a better idea.

Lovers should not only masturbate each other, but watch each other masturbate—both for excitement and instruction. Few women respond best to finger insertion which men tend to use with the idea of simulating intercourse. If your man watches how you do it, he can vary that for new sensations.

One of the most useful things any sexually experienced adult can do is to re-evaluate masturbation. When we start it as kids we don't have the experience to do this, and most of us stay with the technique we learned then and use it as an occasional occurance. As an adult you can go back over this—it's something you enjoy and accept and you now have the privacy to do it properly. If you never saw yourself masturbate, use a mirror, settling down to it naked and in the most comfortable posture. A male should consciously look for new techniques: try with your left hand if you normally use the right (you'll be surprised at the difference), use the foreskin if you normally retract it—if you're circumcised, try wetting or oiling the glans and rubbing only that. A woman should similarly try things she hasn't normally tried—the clitoris alone, if you use the whole-hand method, and vice versa. The object is both to enjoy and to learn more about the responses of which you are capable. If any other part of you seems to need attention, notice. If you have a fantasy, notice that. Then try the same things with your partner watching. He or she will learn new things too.

Chapter 6

"HONK! IF YOU MASTURBATE!"*

Diane B. Brashear, Ph.D.

The May 1974 issue of the SIECUS Report included ten important position statements adopted by the SIECUS Board of Directors. This article by SIECUS Board member, Diane B. Brashear, expands on the statement concerning masturbation, which reads as follows:

It is the position of SIECUS that:

Sexual self-pleasuring, or masturbation, is a natural part of sexual behavior for individuals of all ages.

It can help to develop a sense of the body as belonging to the self, and an affirmative attitude toward the body as a legitimate source of enjoyment.

Dr. Brashear, a SIECUS Board member in 1974, is now in private practice as a marriage and sexual counselor and is Director of the Brashear Center in Indianapolis, Indiana.

*From SIECUS REPORT Vol. III, No. 2, November 1974. Reprinted by permission of the author and the publisher. Copyright © Sex Information and Education Council of the United States, New York, 1974.

It can also help in the release of tension in a way harmless to the self and to others, and provide an intense experience of the self as preparation for experiencing another.

Masturbation, and the fantasies that frequently accompany it, can be important aids in maintaining or restoring the image of one's self as a fully functioning human being.

As infants discover the joy of their bodies, they learn the pleasure and positive experience in touching their fingers, toes, and genitals. Parents delight in their child's skill in labeling body parts correctly. "Where's your eye? Your nose?" is a favorite parent-child game which aids the child's cognitive development as well as communicating positive value about the named body parts. The pleasure in discovering ourselves is as natural to our development as eating and sleeping. But, how many parents say, "Where's your penis? Your vagina? Vulva? Clitoris? Testes?" Parents do not take pride in their child's discovery of his or her genitals. Instead they indicate through games and non-verbal cues that these unnamed parts should remain un-named and unused, forgetting that inevitably they will be covertly discovered.

The word masturbation, as well as definition about this behavior, is confusing. Some prefer that the term be re-stricted to self-stimulation purposefully directed to sexual arousal and orgasm. Others suggest that masturbation in-volves a variety of sexual behaviors, and argue that auto-eroticism which includes dreams, fantasies and physical self-stimulation may more accurately reflect human experi-ence. Nevertheless, masturbation and whatever it connotes has historically been and currently is a topic of great con-cern. Most professional literature appears to be preoc-cupied with symptoms and problems related to masturbation. Havelock Ellis was known to have written,

"There is no end to the list of real and supposed symptoms as a result of masturbation," an ambivalence still shared by many. Today studies and written material about masturbation support the theme "masturbation is normal." It does seem, however, that few sources, with the exception of some popular "how to do it" books ever say that masturbation is good. Is it too farfetched to suggest that mothers be helped to feel free to say to their children, "Masturbation is a good way of enjoying your body" in a way similar to getting a good night's sleep makes you feel fine the next day?

Masturbation can be important, helpful, comforting, and good training to prepare an individual for later, more involved sexual, other-directed response. And yet, sex therapists note that negative attitudes formed in childhood about masturbation can be related to turned off adults who have generalized negative feelings about all sexual expression. The absence of masturbation is a frequent finding in histories of women with orgastic difficulties. "Giving permission"—a common theme in today's sex counseling—often is gained by recommending and teaching masturbation to sexually dysfunctional adults. What better way to learn what pleasures us than ourselves, to bring about and experience our sexual feelings and responses without risking feelings of having to perform to outer imposed norms or to the projected needs of a partner, and free of the fear of reprisal or defeat.

Masturbation is often viewed defensively as substitute behavior for something "better." However, no studies have shown that people who are free of handicaps are likely to stay with exclusive masturbation, especially when a partner is available. "I have to masturbate" can also sometimes be an angry accusation to an unsatisfactory partner. The concept that self-pleasure can of itself be acceptable and positive seems wanting. Giving to oneself is difficult for many individuals. We work so *others* can be proud, so *others* can appreciate, enjoy. Self-denial, self-discipline is a virtue. To enjoy oneself, "to give to me" and to play on behalf of oneself does not come easily to adults well socialized to our work ethic—acceptable for children, yes, but not for responsible grown-ups! This may be why it is easier to excuse masturbation as acceptable sexual behavior on many other grounds than inherent self-pleasuring. Why the need to excuse it at all? The essence of this pleasurable act lies in the dimension to self-awareness and self-confidence that it may provide and that otherwise may not be found. A dramatic result can be the development of self-confidence in one's own competence. This occurred with a twenty-five-year-old man afflicted with cerebral palsy who proudly told me that in his world filled with constant reminders of his dependency on others, masturbation was one thing he could do for himself and he did a "damn good job!"

Masturbation can and does alleviate premenstrual tension for many women. It can confirm to individuals that they are sexual beings who are sexually responsive, to the enhancement of their self-image. Self-pleasuring and its accompanying fantasies can be a rich experience in an otherwise tedious existence. It was so for one man who confided that the sexual fantasies and self-pleasuring he anticipated and experienced helped him get through the long day as he sat in his chair at the nursing home. Or, it can be a comfort as it was to my widowed friend who reported that masturbation was a preferred behavior at the peak of her grief for the lost lover who had been her husband. Our sexuality has no parameters but is a part of our total being—thus it is natural to experience our bodies joyfully rather than in fear or guilt, in such a way that the experience is a positive one.

To know and enjoy oneself is a prerequisite for a positive self-concept, self-realization and self-esteem, qualities essential for positive human growth. Isn't it time that professional sex therapists and counselors, those of us who see masturbation as positive, pleasurable, comforting behavior, take an affirmative stand for it? The SIECUS Position Statement does just that.

People should not have to apologize for their sexuality and those sexual expressions of it that are private and nonexploitive. I believe that one's sexuality can become a positive force and as self-affirming as any other dimension of our being. In too many instances individual human potential is thwarted and denied because of sexual fears, threats and self-doubts. Assent to our sexuality must begin within ourselves. Can we permit us and others to be sexual? This may be what is best about the SIECUS Position Statement. It gives us that permission. I applaud SIECUS for taking a stand to insure to individuals their right to be sexual. I am concerned that those of us who agree with this Statement take heart from SIECUS and communicate this message widely. I will venture that the more the SIECUS Statement is promoted, the more helpful the positive connotation of masturbation will be.

My greatest concern is not so much with the acceptance of this Position Statement among sex educated persons, as it is with the communication of the essence of this message to all individuals. That concern accounts for the title of this article. How do we reach individuals and share such a positive attitude? Merely saying such formerly taboo words as masturbation usually elicits shock or puzzlement accompanied by a putting off polite response. Yet most people are interested and eager for information, permission and comfort about their sexuality and sexual behaviors. The fact that we know that the majority of individuals do masturbate, in contrast to the strong taboo in talking about it, presents a puzzling dichotomy to communicators, educators and counselors. In this society, new ways of communicating some personal messages have become playful, creative and fun. Therefore, suggested a friend, why not spread the message as others do? How about a bumper sticker "Honk! If You Masturbate!"? Would this cause silence and shock? Or, perhaps, the noise of responding horns might be a fitting, contemporary and affirmative orchestration for our own sexuality. Sex need not, nor should it, be always solemn. All affirmations of life build bulwarks against the life- and joy-destroying forces we daily live with.

Part II

AUTOEROTICISM DURING ADOLESCENCE

INTRODUCTION

The chapters presented in Part 2 deal with the autoerotic practices of female and male adolescents, and, as will be observed, some new and interesting changes appear to be taking place in the sexual lives of present-day young people (ages 12 to the mid-twenties).

In Chapter 7, Dr. Robert C. Sorensen (a social psychologist) reports a study that involved 411 adolescents (females and males) ranging in age from 13 to 19 years that was "based upon a national probability sample that conforms quite closely in its composition to the entire adolescent population of the country as reflected by the 1970 census data." This study represents the most comprehensive investigation of adolescent masturbatory activity since the ones undertaken by Kinsey et al. (1948, 1953). Data pertaining to the practice of masturbation (as well as other sexual behavior) were obtained through the use of an anonymous questionnaire. The findings reported by Sorensen include the following: (1) The respondents were more defensive in regard to autoerotic activity than any of the other sexual practices investigated. (2) Some 39% of the females and 58% of the males signified having masturbated at one time or another. (3) The majority of females who masturbated started before or at the age of 12 years, while most of those males who had done so began before or at the age of 13. (4) The younger females and males in the sample indicated that they had first masturbated at a much earlier age than did the older adolescents. (5) Autoeroticism was more prevalent among nonvirgins (62%) than virgins (34%). (6) Males not only engaged in masturbation more frequently than did females but they also enjoyed it more. (7) Some 93% of the females and 89% of the males who were "currently masturbating" stated that they had experienced a fantasy or daydream at one time or another while masturbating. (8) A much greater number of those who used marijuana enjoyed the practice of masturbation than did nonusers, and more "pot" users fantasied during the act than did nonusers. The aim of the study described by Ibtihaj Arafat and Wayne L. Cotton in Chapter 8 was to "determine if an individual's gender is related to differences in patterns of and attitudes toward masturbation, in regard to frequency, cause, effect, regularity, feelings, and awareness of the practice." The participants in this investigation comprised 205 female and 230 male college students in the New York City area between the ages of 17 and 30 (most were in the age range 20 to 22). A self-administering questionnaire was used to collect the data, and, in reference to masturbatory practices, the subjects were asked about their *"present"* activity. Some of the findings revealed by Arafat and Cotton were the following: (1) Significantly more males (89%) than females (almost 61%) reported that they were "presently" masturbating. (2) While most of the respondents began masturbating during the ages of 9 to 16 years, somewhat more of the females started doing so before 9 years of age and after 16 than did males. (3) A significantly higher percentage of the females than males stated that orgasms achieved from masturbation were of greater intensity than those reached during intercourse. (4) No significant difference was disclosed with respect to the sex of the participant and the frequency with which masturbation was practiced. (5) Self-discovery was the primary way in which both sexes learned about masturbation (the second most prevalent source was friends). (6) The main reason given by both sexes for having masturbated was because of being "horny"; "pleasure seeking" was the second major motive described. Other reasons noted were feelings of being lonely, frustration, mental strain, and absence of mate. (7) Although a much higher percentage of the females than males indicated feeling depressed after having masturbated, a somewhat higher percentage of males than females reported feeling guilty as a result of the practice. For some subjects masturbatory behavior resulted in feelings of a "fear of becoming insane" and of being "perverse." (8) While slightly less than half of both sexes revealed that when involved in "regular sexual activity with a partner" they did not have a desire to masturbate, approximately 20% of the subjects stated that experiencing coitus had no effect on their masturbation frequency. More males than females, however, signified masturbating occasionally even when experiencing "frequent sexual activity." (9) Quite significantly, more females (5.50%) than males (1.46%) indicated that they masturbate more *often* when involved in frequent sexuality. (10) About 40% of both sexes expressed a fear of being discovered while engaged in autoeroticism.

Chapter 7

VARIOUS ASPECTS OF MASTURBATION BY TEENAGE BOYS AND GIRLS

Robert C. Sorensen, Ph.D.

DEFINITION AND NATURE OF MASTURBATION

We define masturbation as the act of manipulating one's sex organs in order to induce sexual pleasure without the participation of another person. Although young people sometimes masturbate in the company of others and can therefore be said to be sexually stimulated by the presence and example of others, physical stimulus during masturbation is applied to the sex organ only by the person himself. We did not include in our definition those forms of masturbation involving physical contact with another person.

In our questionnaire we defined masturbation as follows. For girls: "Most girls sometimes play with their sex organ while they are growing up. If a girl does this in order

to experience a pleasant sensation, it is called masturbation"; for boys: "Most boys sometimes play with themselves sexually while growing up. If a boy does this and has
an erection, it is called masturbation."

Forty-nine percent of all adolescents say they have
masturbated; 58% of all boys and 39% of all girls have
masturbated at least once. . . . The incidence and frequency
of masturbation vary among the diverse sexual behavior
groups studied here.

There are no respondents with whom we spoke who
are not aware of masturbation as a form of sexual behavior.
However, only 18% of the boys and 16% of the girls acknowledge that their parents have talked to them about
masturbation. . . .

INCIDENCE OF MASTURBATION

Age at First Experience

Although in some cases masturbation first occurs after the
individual has begun having sexual intercourse, most masturbation begins before the first sexual intercourse, sometimes years before. More girls masturbate at an earlier age
than do boys. Most girls who masturbate have masturbated
before the age of thirteen; the majority of boys who masturbate have had their first masturbation experience before
the age of fourteen. . . .

Younger boys and girls in our sample report a much
earlier age of first masturbation than do their older counterparts. We do not know why this is true, but we must
assume that the explanation lies within one or more of
these assumptions:

1. Children are masturbating at an earlier age than
    in the past.

2. Younger adolescents recall with greater accuracy the date of prepubescent first masturbation.
3. Younger adolescents are more candid about masturbation even though they have guilt feelings, particularly if masturbation is habitual. Their candor may result from the fact that they are not expected to engage in intercourse rather than masturbation. . . .

Age at Which Boys and Girls With Masturbation Experience First Masturbated

	All	*Boys*	*Girls*
10 or under	20%	12%	33%
11	11	12	8
12	14	15	13
13	29	36	18
14	18	17	19
15–19	8	8	9
Total	100%	100%	100%

Masturbation Among Virgins

Masturbation is less common among virgins (34%) than among nonvirgins (62%); and among virgins 49% of the beginners,[1] compared with 32% of the inexperienced,[2] have masturbated. . . .

When we view the incidence of masturbation by male and female virgins, we have a different perspective of the sexually inexperienced and the sexual beginners. Proportionally twice as many boy beginners masturbate as do in-

[1]Sexual beginners had only beginning sexual experience but no forms of sexual intercourse.
[2]Sexually inexperienced adolescents had no sexual experience.

experienced boys; but about the same proportion of girl beginners masturbate as do inexperienced girls. . . .

Masturbation Among Nonvirgins

Sexual intercourse stimulates some young people to masturbate for the first time. We can conjecture that some boys and girls want to experience through masturbation the same pleasure they receive in sexual intercourse. Unfortunately, our survey did not tell us whether or not adolescents whose masturbation begins after the first sexual intercourse had previously engaged in sexual petting. In any case, we see a substantial rise in the incidence of masturbation among those who have had sexual intercourse.

Sixty-two percent of all nonvirgins masturbate, as compared to 34% of all virgins. . . .

Masturbation jumps nearly 50% from male virgins to male nonvirgins . . . and, again, virtually 50% from female virgins to female nonvirgins. . . .

Incidence of Masturbation Among Virgins and Nonvirgins

All boys		All girls	
Virgins	*Nonvirgins*	*Virgins*	*Nonvirgins*
41%	69%	28%	53%

PLEASURES AND PAINS OF MASTURBATION

. . . Young people consider masturbation pleasurable and useful not only for sexual release but also for psychic and sexual stimulation. Things they would not ordinarily think about or would not feel comfortable thinking about are somehow licensed in the masturbation experience.

Enjoyment and Fantasy Thinking

Fifty-nine percent of all adolescents who have current masturbatory experience agree that they usually enjoy masturbating a great deal or somewhat. Six percent say they do not enjoy their masturbation at all.

Proportionally more boys claim to enjoy masturbating than do girls. Sixty-five percent of the boys enjoy masturbating a great deal or somewhat, compared to 49% of the girls. . . .

Masturbation and fantasy thinking go well together for many young people: each is a solitary activity that meets an otherwise unmeetable need. From what adolescent respondents tell us about their experiences in masturbation, it seems clear that fantasy thinking substantially enhances the psychic pleasure of the experience. Moreover, for the sexually inexperienced fantasy thinking is clearly a substitute for real experience. Only 11% of the boys and 7% of the girls who are currently masturbating say they never daydream or fantasize during masturbation. . . .

Age makes a difference in the amount of daydreaming and fantasy during masturbation. Not as many older as younger girls daydream most of the time during masturbation; older girls report more often than younger girls that they daydream some of the time. Older boys are virtually the same as younger boys in the frequency and intensity of their daydreaming during masturbation. . . .

While differences are not large, the inexperienced are more likely to daydream most of the time or never than any of the other sexual behavior groups. . . . Although a majority of the inexperienced (80%) daydream most or some of the time during masturbation, only 71% of the virgins, compared to 89% of the nonvirgins, daydream most or some of the time when they masturbate. . . .

Fewer girls than boys say they daydream most of the

time during masturbation, but girls are almost twice as likely as boys to say they daydream some of the time. . . .

The basic categories of fantasy thinking differ between boys and girls among the sexually inexperienced. Our depth interviews reveal that they include the following:

For boys:

      *Sex with someone who is forced to submit

      *Sex with more than one female

      *Group sex

      *Sex when one is forced to submit

      *Varying degrees of violence to the other person

      *Oral and anal sex

For girls:

      *Sex with a male who is much admired

      *Sex with one or more males when one is forced to submit

      *Inflicting mild violence on the other person

      *Oral sex (passive)

No significant frequency of homosexual fantasy thinking was discovered among boys or girls.

Many needs are satisfied through these varieties of fantasy thinking. The orgasm, or climax, comes faster and, with girls, is better assured by fantasies. Hostilities toward others can be satisfied sexually through masturbation, as can desires for experiences people do not want to have in reality. Some young people feel that masturbation is good training for sexual intercourse: some girls learn not only what an orgasm is like but also the best manual techniques to produce one.

Some young people relieve their doubts and insecurities through the medium of masturbation. . . .

Role of Marijuana

Marijuana users enjoy masturbation in substantially greater proportions than nonusers. Twenty-seven percent of the marijuana users, compared with 8% of the nonusers, get a great deal of enjoyment from masturbation: 48% of the users, compared with 38% of the nonusers, enjoy masturbation somewhat. . . .

The association between marijuana usage and enjoyment of masturbation is reasonably uniform among boys and girls who are currently masturbating. Although boys as a whole enjoy masturbation more than all girls, the girl marijuana users enjoy masturbation at the same levels as do all boys. Thus, for example, 20% of the girl marijuana users enjoy masturbation a great deal, compared with 19% of all boys and 4% of the girl nonusers; 44% of the girl users enjoy masturbation somewhat, compared to 51% of the boy users. . . .

Marijuana users, more often than nonusers, tend to fantasize during masturbation. Fifty-eight percent of the users, compared to 48% of the nonusers, fantasize most of the time during masturbation. Thirty-seven percent of the users, compared to 26% of the nonusers, fantasize some of the time during masturbation. However, 15% of the nonusers, compared to 3% of the users, never fantasize while masturbating. . . .

Guilt Feelings

. . . The strong enjoyment of masturbation by many is one indication that young people may not feel guilty about it. But because one can feel guilty about what one enjoys, we asked all those who masturbated during the preceding month: "How about feelings of guilt, anxiety, or concern about masturbation? Do you have such feelings often, sometimes, rarely, or never?" Fifty-one percent of all adolescents responded that they rarely or never have such feelings. . . .

A smaller proportion of girls than boys feel guilty about masturbation either often or never, but substantially more girls feel guilty about masturbation sometimes. Older girls and boys report proportionally twice as often as their younger contemporaries that they never feel guilty about their masturbation. The older girls (29%) most frequently express no guilt feelings about their masturbation; 19% of all boys assert that they often have guilt feelings about their masturbation. . . .

Personal Privacy and Disgust: Implications of Findings

. . . Among the sex practices we discussed, there seems to be none about which young people feel more defensive or private than their masturbation. A few young people felt that questions dealing with masturbation in the personal interviews were an intrusion.

We uncovered no superstitions about masturbation dealing with impotency, the spoiling of later sexual experiences, or mental illness. What we did uncover were some suggestions of adolescent personal distaste for the fact that they handled their own bodies in order to achieve sexual relief. Handling one's own body and the various ways of manipulating one's sex organs seem to be offensive to some people. Unlike sexual intercourse or even more deviant forms of sexual behavior, the word *masturbate* grates for many when mentioned out loud. Masturbation, though a private matter, is considered socially unacceptable by many, and some may feel that their self-esteem or even sexuality is compromised by admission of masturbation.

Masturbation is even the one form of sexual activity that some young people classify as abnormal for themselves—solitary, contrived, and devoid of all affection except for one's self, which is being treated as an object. "To play with oneself" is a derogatory term often used in other contexts as an unrewarding or useless form of activity.

Because of the problems anticipated in obtaining a candid response from some adolescents about their masturbation, we deliberately worded our initial question on the subject to foster openness. Although we gave respondents the printed instruction at the top of the page, "If you have *never* masturbated, please skip to the next yellow page," we asked this leading question: "How old were you the very first time that you masturbated?" We did this, knowing that the problem was not one of encouraging adolescents to say they masturbated when they did not, but that the problem was to be sure they would deal honestly and candidly with the question if in fact they have ever masturbated. We are confident that the results on masturbation do not suffer from overreporting. If anything, masturbation is underreported, despite our efforts.

SALIENT FINDINGS

1.   There seems to be no sex practice discussed in this study about which young people feel more defensive or private than masturbation. Superstition is seldom a factor. Self-esteem, embarrassment, and personal disgust seem to be the major inhibiting factors.

2.   Fifty-eight percent of the boys and 39% of the girls of all ages say they have masturbated one or more times.

3.   Most girls who masturbate have done so before or while they were twelve years old; 33% of all girls with masturbation experience had done so before they were eleven years old. Most boys who masturbate have had their first masturbation experience before or while they were thirteen.

4.   Younger boys and girls masturbated at a much earlier average age than did older adolescents.

5.   Masturbation at least once is less common among virgins (34%) than among nonvirgins (62%).

6.   Thirty-seven percent of all nonvirgin adolescents who have current intercourse experience also masturbated within the past month.

7.   Fourteen percent of all adolescents currently masturbating *never* masturbated to orgasm during the past month.

8.   Boys masturbate more frequently than girls. Of those currently masturbating, 43% of the girls and 21% of the boys masturbated once or twice during the past month; 12% of the girls and 22% of the boys masturbated eleven or more times during the past month.

9.   Of those currently masturbating, 65% of the boys, compared to 49% of the girls, enjoy their masturbation a great deal or somewhat. The sexually inexperienced more frequently report a great deal of enjoyment from masturbation than members of any other sexual behavior group.

10.   Only 11% of the boys and 7% of the girls who are currently masturbating say they never daydream or fantasize while they are masturbating.

11.   Some adolescents masturbate in order to test their ability to have an orgasm and to gain pleasure from it.

12.   Marijuana users enjoy masturbation in substantially greater proportions than nonusers. Of those currently masturbating, 27% of the marijuana users, compared to 8% of the nonusers, report a great deal of enjoyment. More marijuana users fantasize during masturbation than nonusers.

13.   Fifty-one percent of all masturbating adolescents rarely or never express feelings of anxiety or guilt about their masturbation. Sexual adventurers most frequently report often having guilt or anxiety feelings about masturbation.

14.   Of those adolescents currently masturbating, 80% believe they masturbate about as much as other boys or girls their own age.

Chapter 8

MASTURBATION PRACTICES OF COLLEGE MALES AND FEMALES

Ibtihaj S. Arafat, Ph.D. and Wayne L. Cotton, Ph.D.

Abstract

In this study, the authors have examined the masturbation practices of both male and female college students, attempting to test some of the premises long held that men and women differ significantly in such practices. The findings indicate that while there are differences in many of the variables examined, there are others which show striking similarities. Thus, they open to question a number of assumptions held regarding differences in sexual needs and responses of males and females.

. . . Increased openness in discussion of sexual practices generally, together with more sophisticated knowledge of human sexuality (Shearer, 1972), changes in mores, and a reevaluation of sex socialization have given new dimensions to ideas regarding masturbation.

Abridged from the *Journal of Sex Research,* 1974, *10,* 293–307. Reprinted by permission of the *Journal of Sex Research.* Originally this article was entitled "Masturbation Practices of Males and Females."

It is, however, with regard to women that these changes show the most impact. Today sex practices of women are being discussed at all levels, although it appears from material in the field that male patterns of masturbation are stressed much more in the available data. It is the purpose of this study to provide more information on the subject so as to produce a more current evaluation by conducting a comparative analysis of men and women in regard to their habits of masturbation. The information, therefore, has been gathered from both males and females. . . .

The objective of the present study is to attempt to determine if an individual's gender is related to differences in patterns of and attitudes toward masturbation in regard to frequency, cause, effect, regularity, feelings, and awareness of the practice.

REVIEW OF THE LITERATURE

Masturbation is defined by the researchers as any sort of bodily self-stimulation that results in excitation of the genitals. It commonly involves handling or rubbing of the sexual organs, or bringing them into contact with some foreign object. Most writers use the term masturbation to mean the sexual stimulation that leads to climax or orgasm (Shearer, 1972:17). . . . For purposes of this study, however, we are primarily interested in masturbation as a *solitary* activity, and include that in our definition. . . .

In addition to the discharge of sexual tension, masturbation serves such purposes as the reduction of anxiety, expression of hostility, fantasizing of sexual experimentation, and an assertion of sexual identity in anticipation or recall.

Attitudes that are held concerning masturbation are of a mixed nature. In America, attitudes reflect the influence of two major sources: the Judeo-Christian tradition, and presently discarded medical opinion developed more or less in line with this tradition.

However, many religionists today, while not ready to accept masturbation as moral, are more willing to excuse and tolerate it. Medical opinion for many years, and occasionally today, has been influenced by religious and moral traditions. . . .

The total effect of Western traditions was to make masturbation a highly censored and punishable behavior, one that could have such terrible results as insanity, death, and possible damnation. Thus parents felt justified in going to extremes to save their children. Masturbation clinics were conducted under medical supervision, and aluminum mitts were sold to parents for incarcerating the children's hands at bedtime (Malfetti and Eidlitz, 1972). . . .

It is important to keep in mind that some social pressure is leveled toward masturbation among adults in nearly all societies, and for adolescents in many as well, certainly in Western cultures. Therefore, informants are more likely than not to underestimate the frequency or deny the behavior that is socially condemned. For most people, masturbation probably represents an inferior form of sexual activity in which adults should not participate. One of the exceptions are the Tesu of New Ireland, who expect the adult woman to engage in a form of masturbation when sexually excited and lacking a sex partner. . . .

Edwardes and Masters (1962) describe masturbatory practices in the Middle East and the Orient, especially with regard to children and adolescents, but indicate a fairly high prevalence among adults as well in the traditional cultures. Again, it is quite probable that masturbation occurs among adults in more cultures than is generally admitted to or supposed.

It is not possible to state with complete accuracy the prevalence with which solitary masturbation is practiced. Data derived from the questioning of thousands of people by means of surveys in clinical settings such as the studies . . . by Kinsey et al. (1948, 1953) show that it is extremely common among both males and females of all ages. . . .

Although masturbation is usually considered to be a phenomenon of adolescence, many boys and girls discover orgasm long before puberty. Prior to puberty the male like the female is capable of orgasm, though it is not accompanied by ejaculation. Self masturbation is responsible for the first ejaculation experienced by most American boys. This form of stimulation serves as the chief sexual outlet during the early years of adolescence. Studies in which female adults have reported about their adolescent activity have given percentages clustering from about 30 to 60 percent, although some investigators have reported a much higher or lower figure (Kinsey, 1953). Kinsey reports that by late adolescence, about two-fifths of girls have had experience with masturbation, but only about half of these are actively pursuing the practice at any particular time. As for males, according to Kinsey (1948), the frequency of masturbation is progressively reduced in post-adolescent years, although it may continue through adult life. He found that 69 percent of American husbands who have graduated from college masturbate at least occasionally.

However, little is known about the frequency of masturbation among girls. All research findings indicate that it is less often, and is by no means a regular occurrence. . . .

Masturbation has been discussed by a number of researchers (Ford and Beach, 1951; Himelhock and Fana, 1955; Marshall and Suggs, 1971; Bergler, 1954; Bernard, 1969; Brecher, 1969) but none of them has covered the points to the extent to which they are discussed in the present study.

Methods and Procedures

A self-administered questionnaire was used in collecting data for this research. Six hundred students were chosen at random from three university campuses among all the campuses in the New York Metropolitan area; 435 respondents (72.5%) returned the completed questionnaires, while 165 questionnaires were either incomplete or were not returned to the researchers. Of the 435 completed questionnaires, 52.87 percent (230 questionnaires) were completed by male respondents, and 47.13 percent (205 questionnaires) were completed by female respondents. The age of the respondents ranges between seventeen and thirty, with the majority in the age group of 20–22. The questionnaires consisted of twenty-seven questions. The first seven questions cover the demographic characteristics of the respondents such as sex, age, religious affiliation, marital status, ethnicity, and school classification. Questions 8–12 discussed attitude formation of the respondents such as: how did the respondent become aware of masturbation, age at which he became aware of it, age he began masturbating, awareness of parents' attitude on masturbation, and description of the parents' attitude. Questions 13–15 discussed whether during adolescence masturbation was discussed among the respondent's peers, whether peers' attitude affected respondents' attitude on masturbation, and how it affected the respondent's attitude. The following five questions (16–20) discussed the respondents' masturbatory practices, asking if he (she) now masturbates, and if he answered no, why not? If his answer was yes—how often, under what conditions he masturbates, and how he feels after masturbation: afraid, guilty, satisfied, depressed, or perverse. Questions 21, 22, and 23 inquired about the masturbatory practices of the respondent if he (she) has other sexual outlets on a regular basis, and if, whether these affect masturbatory practices, whether he discusses his masturbation with his partner, and whether the partner also masturbates. The last four questions (24–27) measured the degree of the anxiety respondents have in being discovered in the act of masturbation, where they masturbate, own masturbation frequency compared to the frequency of others, and whether the frequency of orgasm due to masturbation is equal, less than, or more than the frequency of orgasm during sexual activity with a partner.

Percentages were used in the tabulation of data to facilitate comparisons, in addition to the Chi-Square test, which is used to show whether a relationship exists between the dependent and independent variables in the study. The independent variable used was the sex of the respondent, and the dependent variables were the age he (she) started masturbating, intensity of orgasm during intercourse with a partner, frequency of masturbation, reasons for refraining from masturbation, how respondent became aware of masturbation, reasons for masturbation, feelings after masturbation, effect of regular sexual activity on masturbation practices, fear of being discovered, and frequency of masturbation as conceived by respondent in comparison to others.

The data were collected over a period of four months —September 1972–February 1973, and the analysis was done during the year of 1973.

ANALYSIS AND DISCUSSION

As previously stated, the main objective of this research is to try to determine if there is any relationship between gender and masturbatory practices, and if so, what the relationship is.

The sample used in this analysis was made up of 52.87 percent (230) males and 47.13 percent (205) females. Of both sexes, 75.86 percent (330) of respondents report that they presently masturbate, and 24.14 percent (105) that they do not. More males (89.13 percent) than females (60.98 percent) masturbate. These figures very nearly coincide with available data from Kinsey, et al., cited above.

Kinsey reported that 90 percent of the males and 60 percent of the females in the United States masturbated at least once in their lives. The difference in the present study lies in the fact that different questions were posed to find out if masturbation is engaged in *at present,* while Kinsey asked if respondents had *ever* masturbated. In addition, the respondents in the present study were limited to college students, while Kinsey's sample included respondents of more diverse backgrounds, although he did break his data down to show variations according to educational background. Also, a large number of the respondents here are still in the stage of late adolescence, and this is the time of sexual experimentation and high frequency of masturbation. Many of those who do masturbate for a limited period of their lives, do it during adolescence. . . .

As for the relationship between sex and the age one begins to masturbate, most people (males and females) begin masturbating between the ages of 9 and 16, but there is a higher percentage of females who begin masturbating between the ages of 17 and 21. The researchers believe that this difference comes from the variation of the primary effect of orgasm on the individual. According to theoretical information, sexual stimulus in males is more closely related to the development of testicle function whereas the similar function for females is related to specific glandular development.

. . . A substantially higher percentage of females (33.33%) than males (9.27%) experience a higher intensity of orgasm during masturbation than during activity with a partner. However, the majority of both sexes (51.22% of the males and 45.84% of the females) stated that the intensity of orgasm during masturbation is less than during intercourse.

. . . No significant difference was found to exist between sex of respondent and frequency of masturbation. The data show that most people who do masturbate, regardless of sex, do it on the average of several times per week or several times per month.

As for the reasons for refraining from masturbation on the part of those who do not masturbate (105 respondents or 24.14%), a higher percentage of the females (76.25%) stated that they refrain from masturbation due to lack of desire, compared to 56.00% of the males who do not masturbate because of the same reason. However, a higher percentage of the males (32.00%) than females (13.75%) who do not masturbate thought of masturbation as a waste of energy, immoral, and producing cheap feelings. The rest of the respondents (12.00% males and 10.00% females) who do not masturbate gave inhibitions, guilt feelings, and religion as reasons for refraining from masturbation.

. . . The highest percentage of both sexes (58.70% males, and 49.76% females) stated that they first became aware of the process by self discovery. The second highest percentage (30.87% males and 29.27% females) became aware of the process through friends. This reflects the strength of the peer group relationship and its affect as a socialization agency. The lowest percentage (1.30% males and 1.46% females) learned by discussion with parents or by overhearing parents talking about it. Parents usually refrain from discussing such topics with their children. A similar percentage learned from siblings (2.61% males and 3.90% females). However, a higher percentage of females (15.61%) than males (6.25%) learned from strangers or by coincidence.

When the respondents were asked about the cause of masturbation, 47.45 percent males and 39.24 percent females stated that they felt horny, 21.17 percent males and 24.30 percent females gave pleasure seeking as a cause, 12.41 percent males and 16.36 percent females masturbated because they felt lonely, 11.31 percent males and 9.35 percent females stated that they were suffering from frustration and mental strain, and only 7.66 percent males and 9.02 percent females gave the absence of a mate as a reason.

... While the majority of both sexes (68.22% males and 57.4% females) stated that they have physical but no emotional satisfaction, 11.02% of the males compared to 24.08% of the females stated that they feel depressed after they masturbate. However, a higher percentage of males (12.71%) than females (9.74%) have feelings of guilt, 3.39% of the males and 7.14% of the females fear becoming insane, and 4.66% of the males and 1.30% of the females feel perverse.

As for the effect of other sexual activities on the frequency of masturbation ... about half of both sexes (45.37 percent males and 48.80 percent females) stated that there is no need for masturbation if they have regular sexual activity with a partner. However, almost 20% of both sexes in the sample stated that sexual intercourse has no effect on the frequency of masturbation and almost 17% of both sexes stated that the frequency decreases but is still regular. A higher percentage of the males (16.59%) than females (9.60%) stated that they masturbate occasionally even though they have frequent sexual activity. On the other hand, a higher percentage of females (5.50%) than males (1.46%) stated that the frequency increases, which may reflect the lack of sexual satisfaction with the sex partner on the part of the female. In this case, masturbation is used as an aid in releasing tension.

... Of both sexes, almost 40% stated that they fear being discovered in the act.

When the respondents were asked to compare their frequency of masturbation, as conceived by them, in comparison to others ... a higher percentage of males (69.27%) than females (55.20%) stated that it is equal to the others, while a higher percentage of females (40.00%) than males (13.66%) stated that it is less than others. On the other hand, a higher percentage of males (8.78%) than females (2.40%) thought that they have a higher frequency of masturbation than others, and the same percentages of both sexes stated that they do not know.

CONCLUSIONS

The percentages of both males and females who masturbate appear to approximate the figures given by Kinsey et al. There is new evidence presented herein, however, which indicates many differences between men and women in masturbatory practices, which to some extent modifies existing conceptions concerning female masturbation. There are also some significant similarities. For example, among both males and females who do masturbate, the frequency with which masturbation is practiced is very similar. The majority of both sexes begin masturbating between the ages of 9 and 16 years, although a somewhat greater number of women began the practice prior to age 9 and after age 16 than men.

However, many more females than males reported a greater intensity of orgasm resulting from masturbation than from intercourse, with nearly one-third so reporting, and many more females than males say that they do not masturbate simply from lack of desire. The immediate reasons for masturbating are similar in the two sexes except that somewhat more males than females attribute it to sexual tension (feeling horny). About twice as many females as males report feeling depressed after masturbation, which may reflect the belief that the practice is less desirable in women than in men, although feelings of guilt were slightly more frequent among the male respondents, and fear of being discovered in the act almost exactly the same. More females than males feel that their frequency of masturbation is less than that of others.

These and other findings suggest that although men

and women show many more similarities in habits of masturbation than earlier data or popular beliefs indicate, there are still more interesting differences between the two sexes. Some of these differences may still reflect the traditional feelings about women's sexuality and the double standard associated with it.

REFERENCES

Bergler, E. *Kinsey's myth of female sexuality.* New York: Grune and Stratton, 1954.

Bernard, J. *The individual and sex and society.* Baltimore: John Hopkins Press, 1969, pp. 319–327.

Brecher, E. *The sex researchers.* Boston: Little Brown, 1969, pp. 140–200.

Edwardes, A., & Masters, R. E. L. *The cradle of erotica.* New York: The Julian Press, 1963.

Ford, C. S., & Beach, F. A. *Patterns of sexual behavior.* New York: Harper & Row, 1951.

Himelhock, J., & Fana, S. (Eds.) *Sexual behavior in American society.* New York: W. W. Norton & Co., 1955.

Kinsey, A. C., Pomeroy, W. B., & Martin, C. E. *Sexual behavior in the human male.* Philadelphia: W. B. Saunders Co., 1948.

Kinsey, A. C., Pomeroy, W. B., Martin, C. E., & Gebhard, P. H. *Sexual behavior in the human female.* Philadelphia: W. B. Saunders Co., 1953.

Malfetti, J., & Eidlitz, E. *Perspectives on sexuality.* New York: Holt, Rinehart and Winston, 1972. p. 33.

Marshall, D. S., & Suggs, R. C. (Eds.) *Human sexual behavior.* New York: Basic Books, Inc., 1971.

Shearer, M. L., & Shearer, M. R. *Rapping about sex.* New York: Barnes and Noble, 1972, pp. 11–20.

Part III

AUTOEROTICISM IN WOMEN

INTRODUCTION

All of the studies in this section are devoted to the masturbatory experiences of women, a subject that for many years was rather neglected and poorly understood and is presently receiving increasingly more attention. The main reasons for the new emphasis by sexologists, sex therapists, and others on the use of autoeroticism by women are discussed in Part 5. In Chapter 9 the world-renowned pioneer sexologists Dr. William H. Masters and Virginia E. Johnson Masters, as a result of their firsthand observations, describe in detail the masturbatory techniques utilized by women. Major consideration is directed to the ways in which the clitoris (clitoral body) is stimulated and manipulated during self-stimulation. These researchers point out that women exhibit important individual differences in their methods of masturbating and rarely do they "employ direct manipulation of the clitoral glans." Instead, "women who manipulate the clitoris directly concentrate on the clitoral shaft." Furthermore, as Masters and Johnson note, because of the desire to avoid a feeling of "overwhelming intensity," generally women concentrate on manipulating the entire mons area instead of just the clitoral body. Mention is also made of the marked erotic sensitivity of the minor labia and of the important fact that unlike males, females desire to be stimulated "during the actual orgasmic expression." Very interesting, say Masters and Johnson, is the fact that women who manipulate the clitoral body during masturbation often do not conclude their activity until they have attained several orgasms.

In Chapter 10, Dr. Seymour Fisher, a well-known prolific author and research psychologist, discusses some of his unique and controversial findings relating to the masturbatory activity of 300 married women he studied and who were between the ages of 21 and 45 (the majority were between 21 and 25). Although Fisher found that, in general, his subjects masturbated infrequently, he did discover certain personality characteristics associated with those women who seldom masturbated and least enjoyed the practice. These women seemed to oppose "greater freedom in sexual matters," to place little importance on sex in their lives, and to prefer a routine, orderly, systematic, and clean (not messy) life-style. Such women also expressed a strong belief in God and "religious ideals" (as opposed to church attendance), and in retrospect viewed their mothers as having been "moralistically strict." These women, however, did *not* recall their mothers as being distant, unloving, or neglecting. Moreover, experiences that are new and novel were not generally enjoyed by these women. On the other hand, as disclosed by Fisher, those married women who were "most inclined to masturbate" viewed their mothers as being rejecting and unloving, believed more sexual freedom should exist in our society, and disliked orderly ("clean") and routinized styles of living. In view of these findings, Fisher proposes the theory that masturbation may (1) be "a way of asserting the independence of one's body from mother," (2) be a form of self-assertion, defiance, and independence, and (3) provide a different method (new experience) than the usual of sexual stimulation. A factor that Fisher believes inhibits masturbation is the feeling that the practice is literally "dirty." Consistent with other research, Fisher did not uncover any evidence suggesting that to married women masturbation represents a "compensation for deficiences in other aspects of sexual behavior" or that it signifies the presence of anxiety feelings or psychopathology. Significant too, he did not discover any relationship between "clitoral–vaginal preference" and the amount of enjoyment derived from masturbation or the frequency with which it was experienced. Fisher also discusses the role of fantasy during masturbation in reference to clitorally oriented and vaginally oriented women as viewed by different researchers. And in referring to the ease with which women are able to achieve an orgasm from autoerotic activity as compared to heterosexual encounters, Fisher reiterates a major conclusion of his overall study: "that the presence of the male sex partner introduces an antiorgasmic influence." The presence of the male partner interferes with orgasm attainment by the woman, according to Fisher, not because of his lack of adequate sexual technique but because his presence arouses within her a "concern about object loss beyond the level that is present when a woman stimulates herself sexually." Stated another way, a woman "finds herself a more dependable object to which to relate than she does a man." Interestingly enough, although this basic concept was strongly attacked when it was first expressed several years ago, it now appears to be gaining wider acceptance by women (see Dr. Lonnie Barbach, Chapter 21).

Chapter 11, by this writer, is based on a study of 327 women with very high I.Q.'s that Dr. Albert Ellis has described as "the most comprehensive to date." (1976, p. 105). In this chapter a detailed account of various aspects of the autoerotic activity of women with I.Q.'s ranging from 131 to 187 is presented as well as many of the verbatim comments made by these respondents concerning their masturbatory practices. Some of the important findings revealed in this study include the following: (1) While 81% of the total sample of participants signified having masturbated, the practice was most prevalent among women in the 30–39 and 40–49 age groups and least prevalent among subjects in the youngest age group 16–19 years. (2) Infancy was the earliest age at which autoeroticism was first experienced and the oldest age was 57 years. The median age of first masturbation for the sample of women was 14 years. (3) The most frequent way in which the subjects learned to masturbate was from self-discovery; reading provided the second most predominant way. (4) Of those who had ever engaged in autoeroticism, 82% had attained an orgasm from the experience at one time or another. While a higher percentage of women in the 50–61 age group than any other noted having reached an orgasm from the practice, a smaller percentage of those females in the 16–19 age group than any other signified having done so. (5) The use of fantasy during masturbation was indicated by 70% of those who had ever indulged in the behavior and the highest percentage of women who reported having done so were in the 40–49 year age group. The main fantasy reported involved sexual thoughts of desirable men. (6) Of the various masturbatory techniques used, the predominant one described was manual clitoral stimulation. (7) Some 80% of the women who were married (or had been) and who had masturbated did so while married. And a higher percentage of women in the 50–61 year age group than any other signified having masturbated during their marital years. The reasons given for the practice during marriage were varied with the two main ones being (a) absence of husband and (b) need to reduce feelings of tension after unsatisfactory coitus. (8) The use of masturbation by women, if anything, tends to have a positive rather than a negative effect on their marital sexual life. (9) Only 68% of the participants viewed masturbation as being acceptable. (10) High feelings of self-esteem as well as high feelings of security were found to be significantly correlated with an acceptance of masturbation. (11) The practice of masturbation and nonvirginity go together *more* than do masturbation and virginity.

Betty Dodson is, without doubt, the best-known current woman painter of *erotic* art as well as one of the most ardent feminist proponents of the use of autoeroticism by women. Her first "one-woman show was in 1968 at the Wickersham Gallery on Madison Avenue" in New York City and in 1971 some of her erotic creations appeared in an issue of the *Evergreen Review* (Vol. 15). In addition to being a pioneer erotic artist, as Dodson observes in her very small but highly interesting book, *Liberating Masturbation,* she has also attempted to help women overcome sexual problems through the use of masturbation and other therapeutic approaches. In Chapter 12 she describes in detail and with imagination the procedures a woman can employ in acquiring a greater sense of self-acceptance, self-love, and well-being. Basic to the suggested approach is an acceptance by a woman of her naked body and especially her genital area and the unbridled use of erotic fantasy and masturbation. Dodson notes various autoerotic techniques and also recommends masturbatory activity with a vibrator in the presence of a male partner. Finally, the psychological virtues and benefits of autoeroticism particularly by women are discussed and Dodson concludes her unique discourse by stating: "Masturbation can help return sex to its proper place—to the individual."

Chapter 9

THE CLITORIS

William H. Masters, M.D. and Virginia E. Johnson

Any clinical consideration of clitoral response to effective sexual stimulation must include a discussion of masturbation. The techniques of and reactions to direct manipulation of the clitoral body (glans and shaft) or the mons area vary in each woman. Observations of higher animal patterns of foreplay first sensitized investigators to the clinical importance of effective autostimulative techniques by emphasizing the obvious response that such effective foreplay can develop in the female of the species (Beach, 1947; Ford & Beach, 1951).

Marriage manuals discuss at length the importance of clitoral manipulation as the basis of adequate coital foreplay. Most discussions of initiation and elevation of female sexual tensions have included the questions of why and

Abridged from *Human Sexual Response* by William H. Masters and Virginia E. Johnson. Boston: Little, Brown and Co., 1966. Reprinted by permission of Dr. W. H. Masters and the publisher.

when to stimulate the clitoris. To date there has been little consideration of the infinitely more important questions of how to manipulate the clitoris and how much stimulation usually is required. Direct observation of hundreds of women using mechanical and manual masturbatory techniques through repetitive orgasmic experiences has emphasized the fundamental importance of the questions, "How?" and "How much?"

No two women have been observed to masturbate in identical fashion. However, there is one facet of general agreement. Women rarely report or have been noted to employ direct manipulation of the clitoral glans. In those isolated instances when the technique is used it is limited to the excitement phase only and frequently a lubricant is applied to this normally quite sensitive tissue. Additionally, the clitoral glans often becomes extremely sensitive to touch or pressure immediately after an orgasmic experience, and particular care is taken to avoid direct glans contact when restimulation is desired.

Those women who manipulate the clitoris directly concentrate on the clitoral shaft. Usually they manipulate the right side of the shaft if right handed, and the left side if left handed. Occasionally, women have been observed to switch sides of the shaft during stimulative episodes. A relative degree of local anesthesia may develop if manipulation is concentrated in just one area for extended periods of time or if too much manipulative pressure is applied to any one area.

Women usually stimulate the entire mons area rather than concentrating on the clitoral body. Regardless of whether the clitoris is stimulated by direct means or indirectly through mons area manipulation, the physiologic responses of the clitoris to elevated sexual tensions are identical. Most women prefer to avoid the overwhelming intensity of sensual focus that may develop from direct clitoral contact. Instead, mons area manipulation produces a sensual experience that although somewhat slower to develop is, at orgasmic maturity, fully as satiating an experience as that resulting from direct clitoral shaft massage. Mons area manipulation also avoids the painful stimuli returned to many women when the clitoris is manipulated directly either with too much pressure or for too lengthy periods of time.

The concept of the mons as an area of severe sensual focus is supported by the clinical observation that after clitoridectomy, masturbation has been reported to be as effective a means of sexual stimulation as before surgery (Bonaparte, 1953). Manipulation usually has been confined to the mons area, although sometimes concentrated on the scarred postsurgical site.

Evidence of the extreme tactile sensitivity of the entire perineum in addition to the clitoral body and the mons area has been presented by the Institute for Sex Research (Kinsey, 1953). During the Institute's gynecologic observation, the minor labia were determined to be almost as perceptive to superficial tactile sensation as the clitoral glans. The Institute also considers the minor labia to be fully as important as the clitoris or mons as a source of erotic arousal. While the tactile sensitivity of the minor labia is without question, stimulation of the labia does not provide the human female with the extremes of sensual stimuli that massage of the clitoral shaft or mons area produces.

Another observation of female automanipulative technique should be considered for its clinical import. Most women continue active manipulation of the clitoral shaft or mons area during their entire orgasmic experience. This female reaction pattern parallels their coital pattern of demand for continued active male pelvic thrusting during the woman's orgasmic experience. This female demand for continued stimulation during the actual orgasmic expression is in opposition to the average male's reaction to his ejaculatory experience. Most males attempt the deepest possible vaginal penetration as the first stage of the ejaculatory response develops. They maintain this spastic, deep vaginal entrenchment during the second phase of the ejaculatory experience rather than continuing the rapid pelvic thrusting characteristic of preorgasmic levels of sexual tension. . . .

The human female frequently is not content with one orgasmic experience during episodes of automanipulation involving the clitoral body. If there is no psychosocial distraction to repress sexual tensions, many well-adjusted women enjoy a minimum of three or four orgasmic experiences before they reach apparent satiation. Masturbating women concentrating only on their own sexual demands, without the psychic distractions of a coital partner, may enjoy many sequential orgasmic experiences without allowing their sexual tensions to resolve below plateau-phase levels. Usually physical exhaustion alone terminates such an active masturbatory session. . . .

REFERENCES[1]

Beach, F. A. A review of physiological and psychological studies of sexual behavior in mammals. *Physiological Review,* 1947, **27,** 204–307.

Bonaparte, M. *Female sexuality.* New York: International Universities Press, 1953.

Ford, C. S., & Beach, F. A. *Patterns of sexual behavior.* New York: Paul B. Hoeber, Inc., 1951.

Kinsey, A. C. et al. *Sexual behavior in the human female.* Philadelphia: W. B. Saunders, 1953.

[1]Included here are only a few of the many references that appear in the Masters and Johnson book.

Chapter 10

A SUMMING UP OF FEMININE SEXUALITY

Seymour Fisher, Ph.D.

One form of sexual gratification found by the writer to be very infrequently utilized by the married women in the various samples was masturbation. The average woman said she masturbates "rarely." Relatedly, Kinsey, et al. (1953) found masturbation (to orgasm) to occur, on the average, about once or twice a month in married women.[1] Nevertheless, it is of interest that married women masturbate at all, in view of the fact that they have regular intercourse available. Although some of such masturbatory behavior might be attributed to factors such as the wish for sexual stimulation when the husband is absent from home (for example, away on a business trip), there are suggestions that other factors also play a role. It will be recalled that the writer's findings indicated that women who were

From *THE FEMALE ORGASM: Psychology, Physiology, Fantasy,* by Seymour Fisher, pp. 420–425 © 1973 by Basic Books, Inc., Publishers, New York. Reprinted by permission of the publisher.

least likely to masturbate and who say they least enjoy it are characterized by certain attributes. There was evidence that the more a woman refrains from masturbation the more she is opposed to greater freedom in sexual matters; the less explicitly she acknowledges the importance of sex in her life; the more she prefers a routine that is orderly, systematic, and not messy (unclean); the more she expresses belief in the existence of God and in religious ideals (but is not more religious as defined by formal religious behavior such as church attendance); the more she recalls her mother as having been moralistically strict; the less she enjoys new and novel experiences; and the less she recalls her mother as having been distant, unloving, and neglecting. When the last finding pertaining to the mother was originally interpreted, emphasis was placed on the fact that this was the first instance in which a measure of sexual behavior was significantly linked with attitudes toward the mother rather than the father. In view of the fact that those women who were most inclined to masturbate perceived their mothers as rejecting and unloving, it was proposed that masturbation might be a way of asserting the independence of one's body from mother, a declaration of freedom from her and an assertion of ability to be separate from her. The underlying note of defiance in masturbation is also implied in the fact that amount of masturbation was found to be positively correlated with declaring that there should be more sexual freedom in our culture and in the rejection of orderly, clean, and regulated ways of doing things. There does seem to be a note of self-assertion in the attitude of the woman who is inclined toward masturbation. At the same time, it must be cautioned that there is no evidence that she is *generally* hostile or aggressive or antagonistic to an unusual degree. Her defiance seems to be confined to limited sectors of attitude and behavior. One might almost say that she finds it sufficiently expressive of her defiance to engage periodically in masturbation. The association of masturbation with that which is bad, messy, and immoral needs to be reiterated. Apparently, one of the factors that inhibits masturbation is that it is perceived both figuratively and literally as a "dirty" thing. As noted earlier, this is the only aspect of sexual behavior that was found by the writer to be related to attitudes about being dirty. It is also the only aspect found to be linked with certain aspects of religiosity. Interestingly, Kinsey, et al. (1953) also found the amount of masturbatory behavior to be clearly lower in the religiously devout than nondevout.[2] But they found few, if any, relationships between religiosity and other aspects of sex behavior (except homosexuality and premarital sex contacts). A similar lack of relationship between religiosity and most aspects of sexual behavior has characterized the writer's data. One must also call attention to the link between desire for new and novel experience and masturbatory behavior; the greater a woman's interest in such novel experience the more likely she is to masturbate. From this view, a married woman who masturbates may partially be doing so simply because she wants a change in her usual mode of experiencing sexual arousal. One is reminded at this point that Kinsey, et al. (1953) found that masturbation was positively related to a woman's educational level, even after her marriage and the availability of regular intercourse. If one thinks of the woman who seeks higher amounts of education as being particularly motivated to broaden her perceptions of the world and to learn about its diversity, one could interpret the positive correlation between educational level and amount of masturbation as a reflection of the general relationship between interest in new experience and masturbatory frequency.

Obviously, multiple factors contribute to a woman's motivation to masturbate. Kinsey, et al. (1953) have shown that she will turn to masturbation when other forms of sexual gratification are not available. The writer's data indicate, in addition, that she may turn to masturbation as a way of expressing independence and defiance, and as a way of introducing novelty into her sex life. At the same time, impulses to masturbate growing out of such motivations must overcome inhibitory feelings that define masturbation as dirty and immoral. Amount of masturbation probably represents, then, in each individual case a unique balance among the factors cited that both positively motivate as well as inhibit masturbatory interest. Another point that needs to be reiterated is that masturbation in married women does not appear to be a compensation for deficiencies in other aspects of sexual behavior. Masturbation frequency turned out not be related to orgasm consistency and was also unrelated to preferred and actual intercourse frequencies, strength of orgasm, amount of satisfaction derived from orgasm, and many other indices concerned with sexual responsiveness. One cannot justifiedly think of the woman who masturbates with relatively high frequency (at least if she is not too extremely beyond the range found in samples of normal married women) as trying to obtain substitute gratification for failure in her sexual intercourse encounters. Masturbatory behavior, as it was reported in the various samples studied, is also unrelated to anxiety level or other measures having to do with one's "mental health." There is no support for considering masturbation, in any general sense, a sign of disturbing psychological tensions. This does not rule out the possibility that some individual women might utilize masturbation as a channel for releasing disturbing affect or acting out conflictual wishes, but, of course, any segment of behavior can be adapted to such ends.

Little is known about how married women define their masturbatory activity within the context of their marriage relationship. We do not have data about whether they keep their masturbation secret from their husbands. Do they ever masturbate in the husband's presence? Do they discuss masturbation with their husbands as freely as they discuss other aspects of sexuality? Such information would provide a more accurate basis for evaluating the role of masturbation in the average woman's life. If one had to guess, it is probably likely that most wives conceal their masturbation and rarely talk openly about it. They are probably reluctant to discuss it with their husbands not only because of its "dirty" connotations but also because it could easily be interpreted as depreciatory of the husband's sexual prowess. One negative result with respect to the masturbation findings deserves special comment. The writer discovered that neither masturbation frequency nor amount of satisfaction from masturbation was significantly related to clitoral-vaginal preference. There was not even a hint of a relationship. One might have expected that the clitorally oriented woman who particularly enjoys manual manipulation (which is usually focused in the clitoral area) would also have a special liking for masturbation, which is also manual in character, and in most instances directed to the vicinity of the clitoris (Kinsey, et al., 1953). The fact that this expectation was not fulfilled suggests that the two modes of excitation, although involving analogous anatomical areas, are quite different psychologically. But is this true? It was proposed earlier that what is typical of the clitorally oriented woman is that she prefers a sexual context in which she can feel that she has full possession of her own body, that it is not fused with the body of another. If so, would not the masturbatory situation, which does not involve a sex partner at all, be an even clearer instance of what the clitorally oriented woman prefers? Does this not imply a considerable similarity between the two forms of sexual stimulation? Perhaps so, but the similarity may be only superficial. First of all, there is evidence that although the clitorally oriented woman wants to maintain a sense of being in full possession of her own body, one of the motivations for masturbation is to express a defiant independence (of her mother). That is, masturbation goes a step beyond the simple assertion of self-ownership to a more defiant rejection of any outside hold on one's body. Masturbation may represent psychologically a more radical position with respect to how one wants one's body to be related to others (at a sexual level) than the clitorally oriented woman seeks.

Laing (1959) and others have pointed out another aspect of masturbation that may differentiate it psychologically from the needs of the clitorally oriented woman. In analyzing the act of masturbation they have been impressed with how often it takes on an unreal quality and involves relating to a fantasied or imaginary partner. That is, in the process of masturbating there is an isolation from others and a deviation from accepted norms that imparts to it an unusual aura of unreality. Laing states (p. 40): "The awareness the masturbator has of his body is complicated by the fact that his body has been seduced from real action into participation in an imaginary situation." He adds, "The body as used in the act of masturbation is employed with the express intention of gaining satisfaction by eliminating the problems of coping with other real bodies.... The 'real' other person who is the object of desire becomes merely the shadow of the imagined other. This is one of the problems the masturbator runs into: his imagination casts its shadow over him...." One of the implications of this view is that during masturbation a woman would find that her body takes on somewhat strange, unreal qualities, and in that sense might seem to belong less to herself than it usually does. Relatedly, Laing and others (Masters, 1967) have also remarked that during masturbation the individual is forced to take several divided perspectives toward his own body. He is simultaneously the recipient of stimulation, the giver of stimulation, and perhaps in fantasy still another figure who has been brought into the act. This could mean that masturbation encourages a division of identity as well as multiple modes of regarding or experiencing one's own body. The clitorally oriented woman, who has been speculatively portrayed as motivated to maintain a clear sense of "My body belongs to me," might find the unreality of the masturbatory situation and its encouragement of multiple modes of experiencing one's body to be unacceptable. What about the vaginally oriented woman? One would presume that although the sharing of her body with others, which she could achieve through fantasy during masturbation, might please her, she would find the literal isolation of her body (and the obvious fact that its experiences would be her sole responsibility) to be unpleasant.

A final matter of interest with regard to masturbation derives from the Kinsey, et al. (1953) observation that of the 62 percent of their total sample of women who reported ever having masturbated, only 4 to 6 percent did not attain orgasm. That is, about 96 percent of these women could reach orgasm through their self-stimulation. The 4 to 6 percent who could not reach orgasm may be contrasted with the considerably higher percentages who fail to achieve orgasm while stimulated by a male sex partner. Even after five years of marriage 17 percent of married women have not had an orgasm during their sexual contacts with their husbands. One possible explanation of this difference might be that the 62 percent of women who do report masturbating represent a special selective sample with unusual orgastic potential and that their superiority in this respect would also be evidenced in their sexual response to a male partner. That is, only 4 to 6 percent of them would be completely nonorgastic with a sex partner. However, this is unlikely for two reasons.[3] First, the writer found in his samples that frequency of masturbation had only a chance relationship to orgasm consistency. Furthermore, in the Kinsey, et al. data one finds that even of those women with considerable masturbatory experience prior to marriage, 16 percent still achieved no orgasms at all during the first year of marriage. This 16 percent clearly exceeds the 4 to 6 percent who cannot achieve orgasm through masturbation. There is no obvious simple way to dismiss the apparently greater ability of women to attain orgasm during masturbation than in interaction with a male sex partner.[4] One must conclude that the presence of the male sex partner introduces an antiorgasm influence. Is this antiorgasm influence merely caused by the poorer stimulation techniques of the male as compared to those that a woman can bring to bear on her own body? That is, are women simply more skillful in how they apply stimulation to their own genital areas? Although this may be true in some cases, it is doubtful that it is generally true. One notes, for example, that even among extremely well-educated women, who would presumably have husbands who are well educated (and highly intelligent), 15 percent fail (Kinsey, et al., 1953) to attain orgasm at all after five years of marriage. One would be skeptical that the majority of husbands of such educational (and intellectual) attainment would have neglected during a five-year time span to learn a good deal about stimulating their wives. It is unlikely (although admittedly debatable) that failure to reach orgasm in such a sample would, in any major way, be caused by lack of technique on the husband's part.

There is probably more logic in attributing the male sex partner's antiorgasm effect to his psychological impact. In view of the writer's findings that inhibition of orgasm in women is correlated with fear of loss of objects, one can even specifically suggest that the male partner's negative effect is caused by the concern he arouses about such loss. In many cases the presence of the male sex partner appears to increase the woman's concern about object loss beyond the level that is present when a woman stimulates herself sexually. Although certain difficulties related to role and feelings of unreality were mentioned as possibly arising during a woman's sexual self-stimulation, they seem to have less orgasm inhibiting power than does the presence of the male sex partner. One could say that she finds herself a more dependable object to which to relate than she does a man. It is pertinent to this matter that Kinsey, et al. (1953) found that women with extensive homosexual experience produce higher orgasm rates in their female sex partners than do men in their female sex partners after five years of marriage. Since in this homosexual instance and in that of self-stimulation the person delivering the stimulation is female, the question arises whether the orgasm-inhibiting effect of the male is somehow caused by his being of a different sex. Kinsey, et al. specifically propose that a female may be more capable than a male of stimulating a female adequately because she has a better understanding of the feelings, sensations, and anatomy involved—and therefore has better stimulation techniques.

NOTES

1. The rate in unmarried women tends to be between 50 and 100 percent higher.

2. Kinsey, et al. (1953) found no convincing evidence that masturbation frequency was related to whether a woman was Protestant, Catholic or Jewish. This was also true in this writer's data.

3. It is true that Kinsey, et al. (1953) found amount of *premarital* masturbation to be positively correlated with orgasm consistency during marriage.

4. Kinsey, et al. (1953) point out that women reach orgasm more quickly during masturbation than during intercourse. Further, Masters and Johnson (1966) state (p. 133): "Understandably, the maximum physiologic intensity of orgasmic response subjectively reported or objectively recorded has been achieved by self-regulated mechanical or automanipulative techniques. The next highest level of erotic intensity has resulted from partner manipulation, again with established or self-regulated methods, and the lowest intensity of target-organ response was achieved during coition."

REFERENCES*

Kinsey A. C., Pomeroy, W., Martin, C., & Gebhard, P. *Sexual behavior in the human female*. Philadelphia: W. B. Saunders Co., 1953.

Laing, R. D. *The self and others*. London: Tavistock Publications, 1959.

Masters, R. E. L. *Sexual self-stimulation*. Los Angeles, Cal.: Sherbourne Press, 1967.

*These are only a few of the many references listed by Fisher in his book.

Chapter 11

AUTOEROTICISM: PRACTICES, ATTITUDES, EFFECTS

Manfred F. DeMartino, M.A.

Many intelligent people are still unaware of the fact that masturbation, at all ages and in a variety of situations, is now viewed by researchers in the field of human sexuality as a perfectly normal and healthy form of sexual behavior. Despite the abundance of studies and the findings of researchers, many individuals, particularly those in lower socioeconomic levels, continue to view masturbation as essentially abnormal. A young, single woman of low socioeconomic status, who may, for example, have no hesitation in admitting frequent coitus with different men, may be extremely reticent on the subject of masturbation, either refusing to discuss it or denying point-blank that she has ever experienced it. It is also not unusual to hear married women of various social classes speak freely about extramarital affairs in order to satisfy their sexual needs, while

Abridged from *Sex and the Intelligent Woman* by Manfred F. DeMartino. New York: Springer Publishing Co., 1974.

at the same time rejecting the alternative of masturbation as being abnormal. Public disapproval of masturbatory behavior appears to be a remnant from another era, a belief —hopefully dwindling—promulgated by religious leaders and physicians that masturbation led to neurotic and psychotic disturbances. Certainly, voluminous and conclusive research data are now available to dispel this erroneous notion. . . .

With the aim of obtaining information about the autoerotic behavior of women, we asked our sample of highly intelligent women the following questions: "Has masturbation ever been part of your life experience? If so, at about what age or ages did it occur? How did you learn about it? What methods were used? Was it to the point of orgasm? Was fantasy ever used? If so, describe same. Have you engaged in masturbation since marriage? If so, describe circumstances. How do you feel about the practice of masturbation; is it acceptable to you, good, bad, etc.? Do you feel it has had an effect on your marital sex life in any way? For example, has it helped, hindered, etc.?"

Given the length of the question on masturbation, the responses of the women and our findings have been divided into four parts: occurrence and discovery; methods and orgasm attainment; practice since marriage; and acceptability of masturbation and its effect on marriage.

. . . Although a somewhat higher percentage of the women in the 30–39 and the 40–49 age groups than in any other said they had masturbated, the affirmative and negative percentages in all age groups from 20–29 to 50–61 were rather similar. The youngest age group, 16–19, however, differed sharply: only 51 percent were affirmative about the occurrence of autoerotic behavior as compared to the minimum 80 percent affirmative response in the other four age groups. The negative responses were also dramatically opposed: 48 percent of the youngest group (16–19) denied ever having practiced masturbation, while the percentages in the other four groups were all markedly lower; the highest was the 20–29 age group, which gave a collective negative response of 18 percent. . . .

It is noteworthy, too, . . . that the "No response" replies to the question of occurrence were extremely low. Actually only one woman in the entire sample of 327 failed to be explicit about her status on this issue.

The following sample responses regarding the occurrence of masturbation and manner of discovery are classified according to the woman's age when first experienced.

Infancy to Age Seven

"Infancy to present [3__]." (The numbers in brackets refer to the subject's age at the time of the study.) *Learned?* "Accidentally."

"Two or three, five or six, seventeen to present." *Learned?* "Don't remember."

"Early, cannot remember [and at present]." *Learned?* "Experimentation with friends. Group experiments."

"From about three to present." *Learned?* "I discovered it."

"Seven to present [3__]." *Learned?* "Accidentally, sitting on a railing and while washing in the bathtub."

Age Eight to Fifteen

"Starting about seven or eight." *Learned?* "Little girl friend and I mutually 'discovered' it."

"Perhaps about eight [and at present]." *Learned?* "From my father."

"About seven, more or less, continuing continuously till now." *Learned?* "About eight I discovered it by playing 'horses'—riding on the arm of a couch."

"Very occasionally." *Learned?* "In the sixth grade I sat in the auditorium and, in order to keep from having to go to the bathroom, I discovered how to rub my clitoris."

"Intermittently from puberty to the present." *Learned?* "Quite accidentally, by noticing the pleasant sensations associated with touching the genital area while bathing, etc."

"Fifteen [and later]." *Learned?* "By accident, through inserting a tampon into the vagina."

Age Sixteen to Twenty

"Began at sixteen, still continue [5__]." *Learned?* "Reading, exploration, experimenting."

"Seventeen and later (I have no memory of infantile masturbation)." *Learned?* "Extensive petting and sex play with a boyfriend."

Age Twenty-one or Older

"Started about twenty-six and since [3__]." *Learned?* "First lover taught me at twenty-two."

"Twenty-five to present [4__]." *Learned?* "Not sure— a homosexual mutual masturbation episode is the most vivid memory, but I'm pretty sure I may have experimented tentatively before."

FINDINGS

Masturbation occurred in the life experience of 81 percent of our sample of highly intelligent women. This prevalence of autoerotic activity compares favorably with other current opinion on female sexuality. McCary observed (1967) that "from 50% to 80% of all women masturbate at one time or another, the variance in figures resulting from differences in the results of several investigations into the subject."[1] . . . Even if the sample of women studied by Kinsey et al. was more "puritanical" or simply more reticent than the women of today, these researchers did, in fact, conclude that "about 62 percent of all the females in the sample had masturbated at some time in the course of their lives. . . ."[2]

As for the relationship between masturbation by women and personality characteristics, in 1942 Maslow found a positive correlation of .41 between dominance test score (high self-esteem) and masturbation.[3] In the current study of highly intelligent women, however, there was no significant correlation between high self-esteem and masturbatory activity, a finding which in all likelihood is due to the fact that the majority of our sample of women had high self-esteem and only very few had low self-esteem.

In the detailed study of married women undertaken by Fisher, no relationship was discovered between the practice of masturbation and the "mental health" of his subjects. He did find, however, that the frequency with which the women engaged in masturbation was positively correlated with the following: "The degree of importance ascribed by each woman to sex in her own life. The extent to which movies and novels about sex provide enjoyment. The degree to which there is belief that sexual freedom in our culture should be increased. The amount of time spent

[1]From *Human Sexuality* by James Leslie McCary, © 1967 by Litton Educational Publishing, Inc. Reprinted by permission of Van Nostrand Reinhold Company, p. 213.

[2]Kinsey, A. C., et al. 1953. *Sexual Behavior in the Human Female*, p. 142. Philadelphia: Saunders. By permission of Dr. P. H. Gebhard and the Institute for Sex Research, Inc.

[3]Maslow, A. H. 1942. Self-esteem (dominance-feeling) and sexuality in women. *J. of Social Psychology*, **16**, 269. By permission of The Journal Press.

thinking about sex. The frequency of intercourse during menstruation. . . ."[4]

The women in Fisher's sample who masturbated frequently described themselves as persons who enjoy "novelty and stimulation rather than routine," a characteristic of both high intelligence and high feelings of self-esteem (Fisher, 1973, p. 336). In fact, practically all the attitudes described by Fisher which correlated positively with frequency of masturbation are characteristic of women with high feelings of self-esteem, while the attitudes correlated with limited masturbation are characteristic of women with low feelings of self-esteem (Maslow, 1942, pp. 259–294). . . .

Abramson, who studied the masturbatory experiences of undergraduate men and women, recently reported the following: "There is no significant difference in neuroticism between females who are high and females who are low in their frequency of masturbation per month. . . . What is illuminating here is the finding that females who are high masturbators are significantly higher than females who are low masturbators on the sex drive and interest scale. . . . For females, the results indicate that the only variables significantly related to the frequency of masturbation are sex drive and interests."[5]

The earliest age at which women in our sample of highly intelligent women first experienced masturbation was infancy; the oldest age reported was 57; and the median age at which masturbatory activity first began was 14. In most instances, masturbation was practiced for years, including the period of adult life. . . .

[4]From Chapter 12 of *The Female Orgasm*, pp. 330–331, by Seymour Fisher, © 1973 by Basic Books Inc., Publishers. By permission of Basic Books, Inc.

[5]Abramson, P. R. 1973. The relationship of the frequency of masturbation to several personality dimensions and behavior. *The Journal of Sex Research*, 9:139. By permission of *The Journal of Sex Research*.

By far the most frequent way in which our subjects of high intelligence learned to masturbate was through self-discovery (experimentation, exploration, accidentally). The second most commonly reported means of discovery was reading. Other stated means of discovery were boyfriends, girlfriends, husbands, and sisters. These methods of discovery, and the proportion of each to the others, are roughly borne out by the findings of Kinsey et al.

MASTURBATION: METHODS, FANTASY, ORGASM ATTAINMENT

The second part of our question on masturbation dealt with the methods our women used, whether or not they achieved an orgasm, and whether or not their masturbatory experiences were accompanied by fantasies. . . .

The . . . data show clearly that a higher percentage of women in our oldest age group (50–61), compared with any other group, reported that they had achieved an orgasm from masturbation—93 percent. The women in the 40–49 age group, with an 86 percent positive response, ranked second in this regard. The 20–29 and 30–39 age groups, with 83 percent and 80 percent positive responses, were similar to one another. As with the question of masturbation itself, the 16–19 age group is again unique; their 56 percent positive response is significantly lower than the rest of the sample. It is also apparent that a significantly higher percentage of the women in the 16–19 age group who did masturbate reported that they had *never* achieved an orgasm from the activity, as compared with any other group in our study—43 percent compared to 15 percent for the 20–29 age group, 17 percent for the 30–39 age group, 7 percent for the 40–49 age group, and 6 percent for the 50–61 age group. . . .

It is interesting to see . . . that the 40–49 age group reported the highest use of fantasy during masturbation: 79

percent. The next highest group was the 20–29 age group —70 percent—closely followed by the 30–39 and the 50–61 age groups, both with 68 percent. Once again the 16–19 age group was unusual in terms of the rest of the women: only 50 percent of the subjects in this age group indicated that they had ever fantasied during masturbation.

The following sample responses reflect the methods and fantasies used by our highly intelligent women during masturbation, as well as whether or not an orgasm was attained. Various methods of masturbation have been classified insofar as possible—for example, manual stimulation of the clitoris and external genitalia, manual stimulation of the vagina, stimulation of breasts, stimulation of genital area, use of vibrator, use of various objects, use of water, and miscellaneous methods.

Manual Stimulation of Clitoris and External Genitalia

"Manual clitoral stimulation." *Orgasm?* "Yes." *Fantasy?* "Imagining myself with different sex partners. Thoughts of seduction, sometimes forceful. Animal coitus. Group sex activity. Recalling erotic literature."

"Manual." *Orgasm?* "Yes." *Fantasy?* "Yes, incestual. My father raping me, orgy—men and women; making love to and with a girl friend; rape by boyfriend or strange man."

"As a child, clitoral stimulation by fingers. Now, that, as well as frankfurters or bananas." *Orgasm?* "Almost always." *Fantasy?* "Oh yes. I like to picture myself as similar to Catherine the Great. Imagine having so many attractive young men to pick from."

"Rubbing clitoris; tried and rejected candle." *Orgasm?* "Yes." *Fantasy?* "Imagined orgies, brutality, normal intercourse with someone never contacted but secretly admired."

"Manual manipulation; I have occasionally used objects." *Orgasm?* "Yes—scared the daylights out of me the first time." *Fantasy?* "Yes, but not at first. Fantasies now are mostly based on realistic encounters with men from the past. They mostly involve oral-genital intercourse fantasies and/or straight genital intercourse. Occasionally some fantasies of being manipulated by the male partner—in earlier years, fantasies largely involved my being forced or controlled, veiled rape."

"Manual manipulation." *Orgasm?* "Yes." *Fantasy?* "Intercourse with animals or small boys."

"Pressure on clitoris and insertion of warm, damp cloth." *Orgasm?* "Sometimes." *Fantasy?* "Always. Always a man, but not always the same man."

"Hand." *Orgasm?* "Yes." *Fantasy?* "Picturing two dogs."

"Fingers on clitoris, usually; sometimes in vagina." *Orgasm?* "From age twenty-one on." *Fantasy?* "Mentally undressed and was undressed by women or girls, engaged in every conceivable sexual activity with them. Imagined more and more revealing costumes for girls; imagined introducing girls and also sometimes little boys to sexual activities."

"Aroused by gentle stroking in general pubic area from titillation of the clitoris and finally insertion of finger into vagina. This last on a few occasions done with a candle as experimental substitute for penis." *Orgasm?* "Yes." *Fantasy?* "On occasion, if circumstances are right, it has been possible to become aroused by a bit of erotic reading and then by imagining a desirable partner and fantasizing the act itself to reach an orgasm with little or no manual manipulation."

"Rubbing beside clitoris with heel of hand." *Orgasm?* "Yes." *Fantasy?* "Being strung up and whipped, or being spanked with a leather strap."

"Rubbing clitoris; now vaginal stimulation, also breast stimulation." *Orgasm?* "Always." *Fantasy?* "No. Sometimes read erotic literature first to shorten period to orgasm."

"I am right-handed." *Orgasm?* "Yes." *Fantasy?* "Only after I had begun to engage in heterosexual sex. Involving animals or young males; nonviolent seducion.

"Foreplay; caressing of body, breasts, going down to vulva, then concentrating on clitoris." *Orgasm?* "Always." *Fantasy?* "Always. Am unable to have an orgasm without fantasy. Usual theme was of a man I was in love with who was doing this to me, having intercourse with him. Recent theme—in sex science lab, doctor is encouraging me to masturbate to orgasm quickly in order to hasten my response."

Manual Stimulation of Vagina

"Fingers in the vagina, also in the rectum. Kissing my hand (imagining it is my love interest at the time, his lips touching mine, rather than my hand touching my lips). Masturbation through the anus." *Orgasm?* "Yes." *Fantasy?* "Vaginal —imagine being with my boyfriend. Anal—being given an enema by kidnappers or by lesbians in a woman's prison. Kissing—always the imagined partner would be someone I knew and loved whom I had never kissed, so imagined over and over that it was our first kiss."

Stimulation of Breasts

"Manipulation of breasts, clitoris, and outer vaginal area." *Orgasm?* "Yes." *Fantasy?* "Usually fantasies of handsome men making love to me; fantasies of being nude in front of a large group of men who all desire me."

Stimulation of Genital Area

"Rubbing on wadded-up bedding, face down." *Orgasm?* "Always." *Fantasy?* "Always. About a chase, rape, whipping —or rather, being chased, raped, and whipped."

"Place the bedspread and pillow between my legs and

arouse my organs, even at age eight. At nineteen, remembering, I saw no reason to change my means. Writing this even raises the tingle of desire—if the fact helps any." *Orgasm?* "Yes." *Fantasy?* "I think about naked, big, heavily muscled men. A couple of years ago I'd think of them wrestling, now I dream of myself being physically overpowered and thoroughly screwed!"

"Massage of the genitals on a hard edge, a chair." *Orgasm?* "Yes." *Fantasy?* "Sometimes. The remembrance of a satisfying absent partner."

Use of Vibrator

"Hand and electrical vibrator." *Orgasm?* "Sometimes." *Fantasy?* "Particularly exciting aspect seems to have been picturing myself with an extremely voluptuous body, especially large breasts (I'm skinny), wearing extremely seductive clothing, and performing extremely exotic dances, being the seductress to one or more strange men, sometimes of opposite race—I often masturbate to excite my partner, often using electrical vibrator."

"Massaging machine, on the average, masturbation daily." *Orgasm?* "Always." *Fantasy?* "Varies, usually with more than one man. I enjoy imagining being used sexually by men after being captured."

Use of Various Objects

"I used fingers, hot dogs, a rubber hose, a banana, a Trojan (condom) filled with paper, my teddy bear, a soda bottle, wooden stick, pipe, sour pickle." *Orgasm?* "Yes." *Fantasy?* "I dreamed of having sex with my boyfriends, movie stars, my teddy bear, father, minister, the president, an animal, or a deformed monster."

"Artificial penis and clitorial friction." *Orgasm?* "Yes." *Fantasy?* "Usually a group sex experience or a rape situation."

Use of Water

"Running water in tub during bath, manual manipulation; insertion of objects." *Orgasm?* "Yes." *Fantasy?* "Seldom. Thoughts of sexual lover."

"Running water through shower hose. Manual method is too painful and lengthy to be worthwhile." *Orgasm?* "Sometimes." *Fantasy?* "Sometimes I'm a female, but more often I'm a male aggressor in fantasies. Involve rape occasionally."

Miscellaneous Methods

"At first, clenching legs together so thighs rubbed against clitoris, then fingers when a teen-ager." *Orgasm?* "Always." *Fantasy?* "None as a child, always as an adolescent. It was always someone I felt a romantic attraction for."

"Rubbing myself at first, later using silk, fur, and body gyrations." *Orgasm?* "I don't know." *Fantasy?* "Flying above crowds, watching stripteasers and belly dancers, making love to someone I liked (loved)."

"The janitor's son urinated on several of us in a park, age six or seven. As an adult, masturbation is a part of taking a bath." *Orgasm?* "Yes." *Fantasy?* "The strong wish for someone . . . to love me."

"Anal at seven years—cardboard between buttock; genital at twenty-three, manual." *Orgasm?* "Yes." *Fantasy?* "I am helpless against the invading army, men who pillage and rape."

"Electric razor." *Orgasm?* "Yes." *Fantasy?* "No."

"Manipulation of clitoris, insertion of instruments— even use of pets." *Orgasm?* "Yes." *Fantasy?* "Generally. Not true fantasy. About someone I was in love with (or when younger had a crush on). Imagine real person was present. No longer use fantasy."

"By hand. Also tried a Coke bottle filled with hot water, also running water in a tub." *Orgasm?* "Yes." *Fantasy?* "Fantasy of making love to point of becoming pregnant by dearly loved man."

FINDINGS

According to our subjects, the primary method employed during masturbatory activity was manual clitoral stimulation. The second most commonly described method involved manual manipulation of the external genitalia. Our highly intelligent women appeared to be quite inventive in their methods of masturbation. Manipulation and caressing of breasts and nipples played a minor role in our sample, a finding that may be compared with Masters and Johnson's subjects, of whom only three women were able to achieve an orgasm through stimulation of the breasts alone (1966). . . .

Of those women in our sample who had ever masturbated, 82 percent reported that they had achieved an orgasm from this activity at some point in their lives. In this connection, the Kinsey investigators reported: "About 62 percent of all females in the sample had masturbated. . . . About 58 percent had masturbated at some time to the point of orgasm. The 4 to 6 percent which had masturbated without reaching orgasm was chiefly a group of females who had made only single or desultory and infrequent trials of their capacities, for nearly all of those who had seriously experimented soon learned to reach orgasm" (Kinsey, 1953, p. 142). Masters and Johnson, moreover, have pointed out that many "well-adjusted women," when engaged in clitoral manipulation, may experience several orgasms during the course of a single act of masturbation. In view of these findings and those of the present study, there can be little doubt that the overwhelming majority of women who masturbate learn to reach orgasms through their activity.

Regarding the use of fantasy during masturbation, some 70 percent of our women who had ever masturbated stated that they at one time or another employed fantasy while masturbating. This finding is slightly higher than that revealed by Kinsey et al. . . .

In general, the responses of our sample of women agree with Maslow's remarks regarding the masturbatory activities of women with high dominance-feeling (self-esteem): "Masturbation is often (not always) found to be a highly sensual affair, protracted and making use of all sorts of titillating and stimulating thoughts, objects, and acts. In both masturbation and intercourse the whole body, rather than just the restricted genital area, is apt to be involved. Every spot or area that is erotically stimulable is apt to be enlisted in the game that the act has become, and in building up to a tremendous orgiastic climax" (Maslow, 1942, pp. 286–287).

In the current study, no significant relationship was discerned between the experiencing of fantasy and high feelings of self-esteem. Again, as in the case of the previously noted lack of correlation between the practice of masturbation and self-esteem, the lack of a significant positive correlation between the use of fantasy during masturbatory activity and feelings of self-esteem may be explained by the fact that most of our respondents were of high self-esteem while only a very small number were of low self-esteem.

Based on the various findings noted, it seems accurate to conclude that the majority of women who masturbate eventually enhance the experience by means of fantasy. There also appears to be a rather strong tendency on the part of highly intelligent women, who generally are quite imaginative, to use fantasy during masturbatory activity.

The fantasies experienced during masturbation by our

subjects were quite diverse, while naturally involving primarily sexual thoughts of desirable men. Other fantasies reported involved thoughts of being raped, having sexual intercourse, group sex, orgies, being whipped, seduction, sexuality with other females, erotic or pornographic literature, movie stars, sado-masochistic scenes, exhibitionism, voyeurism, sexuality with animals, being a prostitute, incest, an erect penis, oral-genital contacts, and being loved.

It is interesting to note that the fantasy experienced was by no means constant in content—that is, several women specifically noted the changes in fantasy content over the period of time they had masturbated. . . .

It is also noteworthy that a few women in our sample associated different fantasies with different erotic areas— another example, it would appear, of the highly imaginative masturbatory activities of our sample.

Masturbation During Marriage

The third aspect of our question on autoerotic behavior concerned the part played by masturbation in the lives of our married subjects (divorced, separated, and widowed women were included in this category). . . . Women who reported that they had masturbated after, but not during, marriage were not included.

As the . . . data indicate, women in the 50–61 age group reported the highest incidence of masturbation during marriage: 87 percent. The next highest incidence occurred in the 30–39 age group: 81 percent. Our findings in the 20–29 and 40–49 age groups were similar to one another: 78 and 75 percent, respectively. None of the subjects in the 16–19 age group had ever been married.

The following sample responses by women who masturbated during their marriages are grouped insofar as possible according to the circumstances in which masturbation occurred.

Husband Was Away

"During my marriage when separated from my husband. Since then with great frequency during periods when I had no man. Sometimes now when masturbating partner."

"When stimulated in absence of husband, either physical absence or through sleep. My husband works very hard and I can't bear to wake him though urged."

"Occasionally when alone during the day, occasionally evenings when husband is gone."

"Usually when husband is away on a long trip; sometimes in the morning when very rested, even after long sexual activity the previous evening."

"No physical masturbation. However, during my husband's business trip, I fantasized his presence and had an orgasm without masturbation."

"My husband is away ... quite often, sometimes for several weeks and [longer]. First I had sex dreams, even reaching orgasm while asleep. Later I found that by masturbating I kept my sexual desire alive and was much more eager for my husband's embrace after his return than if I had completely forgotten about sex during his absence."

After Unsatisfactory Marital Relations

"This was usually to complete satisfaction after unsuccessful sex relations with my husband."

"Marital sex has never produced orgasm, so I masturbate occasionally to relieve sexual tension."

"After a copulation when I had no orgasm but only feigned it to get rid of him. As soon as he fell asleep, I masturbated."

"Sometimes after intercourse—sometimes in the middle of the night on awakening from a dream."

Desire for More Frequent Sexual Activity

"Husband with less sex drive than mine."

"Used as a release from sexual tension due to husband's lack of interest."

"Husband's sex life was 'once a week' and not very exciting."

"I have a stronger sex drive than my husband."

"My husband thought it indecent for me to desire or take initiative in sex, yet there were times when my desire was tremendous."

When Feeling Anxious, Frustrated, Lonely

"During periods of tension and anxiety. Husband absent."

"When frustrated, diddle."

"My main outlet for sexual and emotional tensions."

"During the day to relieve tension. Occasionally after intercourse."

"Occasionally the day after a long love session with my husband, as an emotional release."

"Whenever I felt lonely or unloved. Once during analysis when the psychiatrist was on vacation."

"First year I was married—usually as a reaction to tense or adjustive situations within the new marriage situation."

After Reading Erotic Literature

"Was reading *Fanny Hill,* became aroused, husband was not at home."

"If I have been reading or watching something stimulating and happen to be alone."

During Pregnancy

"During pregnancy. Husband away. Under emotional stress due to husband's illness or absence."

Miscellaneous

"Husband was ill and I desired him."

"Husband suggested it to hasten my arousal before intercourse."

"Sudden thought and desire—unable to pinpoint what triggers this feeling, but it usually comes when I am alone."

"Very unsatisfactory, disturbed sex life within an otherwise quite happy marriage. I masturbate two or three times a week."

FINDINGS

Of those women in our sample who were married (or had been) and reported that they had masturbated, 80 percent stated that they had done so at some point in their marriage. Seymour Fisher, in a personal communication to this writer concerning his study of 300 middle-class married women between the ages of 21 and 45, stated that 50 percent of them revealed they had masturbated during marriage. Apparently, therefore, masturbation during marriage is a common occurrence.

In describing the circumstances surrounding their marital masturbation, our sample gave two main explanations: a husband's absence and the need to relieve feelings of tension following unsatisfactory intercourse (due to a lack of orgasm). Some of the other leading reasons given were the desire for more frequent sexual activity (where husband was unwilling to satisfy subject), Loneliness, boredom, depression, anxiety, frustration, marital disharmony or disruption, husband's illness, sexual excitation from erotic reading when alone, pregnancy, husband's impotence, simple pleasure from the act, and after awakening from a sexy dream.

One particularly interesting response was that of the woman who attained an orgasm simply by imagining the presence of her absent husband. In the sample of 382 women studied by Masters and Johnson, not one was able to reach an orgasm simply through fantasy without manual or physical stimulation of any kind. Kinsey et al. reported that "some 2 percent of the females in the sample had reached orgasm by fantasying erotic situations without tactilely stimulating their genitalia or other parts of their bodies" (1953, p. 163).

ACCEPTABILITY OF MASTURBATION AND EFFECT ON MARRIAGE

The fourth part of our multifaceted question on masturbation was concerned with the degree of acceptability the practice had with our sample of women, and whether or not married women who had masturbated thought the practice had any effect on their marriage. . . .

Once again, as the data indicate, the 16–19 age group shows itself to be different from the rest of the age groups: only 48 percent of the women in this group found masturbation acceptable, compared to the next lowest group, the women in the 50–61 age group with 57 percent acceptability. The 20–29 and 30–39 age groups, with 71 percent and 73 percent, respectively, were practically the same; the 40–49 age group was also similar to them, with 66 percent acceptability. Those women who found masturbation unacceptable were essentially a negative image of those who found it acceptable. That is, *more* women in the 16–19 age group found it unacceptable than any other: 29 percent. The next highest disapproving group was the 50–61 age group—21 percent—and so on, with the negative responses corresponding to the positive responses in terms of percentage rank with each age group.

After the question about general acceptability of masturbation, we asked the women who had masturbated whether they felt their masturbatory activity had any effect on their marital sex life. . . .

Of those women who were married (or had once been) and who engaged in masturbatory activity, a higher percentage of the women in the 20–29 age group than any other—30 percent—reported that such activity had a positive effect on their marital sex lives. Women in the 30–39 age group ranked second in this regard: a positive response of 26 percent. The positive responses of the 40–49 and 50–61 age groups were the same: 20 percent. The . . . data also make it clear that *none* of the women in the 50–61 age group and only 4 percent of those in the 40–49 age group stated that the practice of masturbation had a negative effect on their marital sex experiences. The negative responses noted by the 20–29 and 30–39 age groups were much higher: 12 and 15 percent, respectively. Corroborating their very low negative responses, the 40–49 and 50–61 age groups had the highest "no effect" responses: 63 percent of the 40–49 age group and 60 percent of the 50–61 age group felt that the practice of masturbation had no effect on their marital sexuality, while only 48 percent of the 20–29 age group and 53 percent of the 30–39 age group stated that their having engaged in masturbation had no effect on their marital sex lives.

The following sample responses deal with the general acceptability of masturbation and, where applicable, its effect on marriage. The responses have been divided into acceptable and nonacceptable statements.

Acceptable

"Acceptable." *Effect?* "Helped."

"Acceptable." *Effect?* "It may have been a cause of unspoken resentment in my marriage. It is no hindrance to my present sex life."

"When my husband is not around, I find it quite acceptable." *Effect?* "No effect that I notice; we have no problems with sex."

"Poor substitute for coitus, but sometimes better than nothing and definitely better than 'using' a man-or promiscuity." *Effect?* "No."

"Acceptable. Very good to relieve tension and keeps me from feeling hostile toward my husband." *Effect?* "Helped me."

"Acceptable, necessary at times; but not as good as orgasm gained through intercourse." *Effect?* "Helped on those occasions when I did not feel satisfied and when my husband was away."

"Acceptable—no moral implications." *Effect?* "Probably beneficial, kept me from being a total bitch at any rate."

"Acceptable, even therapeutic. However, should be 'controlled,' not used to extremes." *Effect?* "I am sure it has helped and kept me from seeking extramarital experiences."

"Acceptable as long as it does not affect my sexual desire toward husband." *Effect?* "No, other than perhaps making me more aware of my own reactions to certain stimulation."

"I feel that it is not only good for relieving tension, but also it is safer than having affairs with other men." *Effect?* "Yes. It has probably helped."

"Sometimes preferable to unnecessary tension adversely affecting oneself and others." *Effect?* "Filled certain gaps adequately and so helped."

"Highly acceptable, and pleasant to think of others

engaging in it." *Effect?* "It has helped in that I haven't been accusatory toward my husband because of an unsatisfactory sex life."

"I like it. It meets a need in the absence of any other sexual involvement and it does no harm." *Effect?* "Since I haven't gotten orgasms from intercourse, being able to 'come' after intercourse through masturbation has allowed me to enjoy marital sex without feeling cheated by not having an orgasm."

"O.K. if it doesn't become an obsession." *Effect?* "Hindered, since I'm not used to cooperating with another person."

"It's acceptable but lonely." *Effect?* "Helped, I suppose, in that I don't nag my husband to make love to me when he's not feeling well."

"I feel it fills a need when the normal sex act is not available." *Effect?* "It helped in that it kept me reminded that sex is pleasurable during a period when I was about to scrap it completely."

"Generally acceptable—sometimes desirable, but feel slightly guilty about occurrence after intercourse." *Effect?* "It has helped by allowing me not to pester my husband."

"It is acceptable if no suitable partner is available. It releases unnecessary tension and keeps the valuable sex drive alive. Rather masturbate than take a partner for whom one has no personal affection." *Effect?* "It has helped me a lot; I can now lead a happy marital sex life. I learned my responses, communicated them to my husband and he now tries to adjust the sex act to accommodate them and give me the most sexual satisfaction."

"Acceptable, but not really desirable." *Effect?* Hindered, perhaps at first—by setting a level of pleasure hard to achieve in conventional manner."

"I now feel it to be completely acceptable but for several years I felt guilty about it." *Effect?* "It has made me much less responsive to sexual intercourse with my husband."

"Completely acceptable. Felt great guilt during my younger years. But now feel it is pretty universally practiced; it is often healthy." *Effect?* "Made bad periods and periods of sexual deprivation bearable. Ultimately helped to complete sexual freedom of thought and action."

Not Acceptable

"It's a misuse of one's sexual powers besides being nothing like the real thing." *Effect?* "No effect whatsoever—but my husband doesn't know, I think he would be disgusted with me."

"Bad." *Effect?* "No."

"Don't believe it is good, but think it might be preferable to giving myself to a man again without benefit of marriage." *Effect?* "Hindered, because I was married for about . . . before I had an orgasm as a result of conventional sex practice."

"When I'm sensible, I know I have to accept it. But often I feel depressed, even cry after I do it—though I'm saying all the time, 'For God's sake, what else can you do?'" *Effect?* "It has helped keep me from being a sex frenzied lunatic and thus calmer once it is over with than I would be otherwise. It hurts no one but myself and leaves me better able to deal with my work and family."

FINDINGS

We were rather surprised to find that only 68 percent of our sample of highly intelligent women stated that masturbation was acceptable to them (some responses were nonscorable). In view of their intellectual levels, we had anticipated that, as a result of reading and so on, more of them would express approval, particularly since 81 percent of the women in our study had at some time practiced masturbation.

In the present study, significant positive correlations were found between an acceptance of masturbation and both high feelings of self-esteem ($r=.15$ p $<.05$) and high feelings of security ($r=.17$ p $<.05$). In the light of our findings concerning the relationships between an acceptance of masturbation and feelings of self-esteem, and security-insecurity, it would appear that acceptance of masturbatory activity in one's life is dependent more on basic personality characteristics rather than on intelligence levels or intellectual enlightenment.

Whether the practice of masturbation by a woman has a positive or negative effect on her marital sex life is a question that has still not been answered conclusively, but we can now venture some reasonably certain conjectures. Katherine B. Davis, in her well-known 1929 study of female sexuality, noted that there did not appear to be any relationship between the practice of masturbation and sexual activity during marriage. In 1953, Kinsey et al. stated:

> It has been claimed that premarital masturbatory behavior may so condition an individual that she may want to continue solitary activities in preference to having coital relations after marriage; but we have seen very few histories of this sort. There are more cases of marital relations which were disturbed by some guilt which the wives had acquired during their premarital masturbatory experience. Much more important is the evidence that premarital experience in masturbation may actually contribute to the female's capacity to respond to her coital relations in marriage. (pp. 171–172)

In the current study we found that many more of those women who were married (or had been), and who had masturbated, reported that masturbation had a positive effect on their marital sex life (26 percent) than did those who reported that the practice had a negative effect on their marital sex life (10 percent). Moreover, although some responses were nonscorable, more than half of the married participants (55 percent) said that masturbation did not have *any* influence on their marital sexual activities.

In summary, based on the findings of Davis, Kinsey et al., and the present study, it appears that while in general the practice of masturbation by women tends to have no substantial effect on their marital sexual behavior, if anything, it exerts a positive rather than a negative effect.

MASTURBATION AND NONVIRGINITY

To conclude our discussion of masturbation in our sample of highly intelligent women, we would like to mention briefly some correlations between virginity/nonvirginity and masturbation.... Since gratification through autoeroticism requires no partner, many people once considered this form of sexual activity to be immature and antisocial, holding that it augured poor prospects for heterosexual relationships.[6]

That this belief is simply untrue with respect to women (and probably to men, also) can be seen clearly from the results of both Maslow's investigation and the findings of the present study. In 1942, based on a statistical analysis of his observations, Maslow reported: "Masturbation and nonvirginity go together more than do masturbation and virginity. This indicates that masturbation in normal people need not be thought of only as a method of compensating for lack of love or heterosexual experience, nor as

[6]See: Brill, A. A. 1938. *Basic Works of Sigmund Freud,* New York: Modern Library, Random House; Jones, E. 1955. *Life and Work of Sigmund Freud,* New York: Basic Books.

solely a product of fear of heterosexuality." The results of our current study also reveal that masturbation and nonvirginity go together more than do masturbation and virginity ($r = .11$ p $<.05$). It is interesting, too, that in regard to females and males, ages 13–19, Dr. Robert C. Sorensen reported that "masturbation is less common among virgins (34%) than among nonvirgins (62%)." Moreover, Abramson stated that his results "suggest that those females who have masturbated tend to be older and have had intercourse. This finding is in accordance with the hypothesis that the disposition to use masturbation as a form of sexual outlet signifies a positive interest and attitude toward a wide range of expressions of sexuality" (1973, p. 140). . . .

Finally, in his study of married women, Fisher has pointed out that "no evidence exists that the woman who likes masturbation is deficient in her ability to enter into, and enjoy, orthodox sexual intercourse. What has been proposed is that masturbation provides such a woman with periodic opportunity to reassure herself that she can attain gratification on her own and that she retains the option of not counting on personal intimacy with another to allay her needs."[7]

[7]From Chapter 12 of *The Female Orgasm* by Seymour Fisher, p. 339, © 1973 by Basic Books Inc., Publishers. By permission of Basic Books, Inc.

Chapter 12

MASTURBATION AS MEDITATION

Betty Dodson

Masturbation is a meditation on self-love. Since so many of us are afflicted with self-loathing, bad body images, shame about body functions, and confusion about sex and pleasure, I recommend an intense love affair with yourself. We can then move into positions of self-love, strength and pleasure by discovering our own sexual response patterns, learning to turn ourselves on, and giving ourselves massive doses of love and support.

Start Now

Look into the mirror and tell yourself, right out loud, "I love you." Say it several times. Smile. Say, "I love you" and your name. It may sound strange at first, even make you feel embarrassed or foolish—but do it. Every time you are overwhelmed with negative emotions about yourself—Stop! Forgive yourself! Say, "I love you." This is an exercise in learning how to be loving. We can only give and receive love when we feel good and loving about ourselves, otherwise we operate with desperate negative needs from self-hatred.

Love Your Body

Try a hot bubble bath or hot shower. Not to be lovely for someone else—to be lovely for yourself. Place candles in the bathroom. Your favorite bath oil. Wash and touch your body tenderly all over. On a particularly difficult, stressful day, I have taken as many as three hot baths. Try singing a song or humming a tune. RELAX! After you dry yourself, stand in front of a full-length mirror. Study yourself with love and compassion. Never mind the flaws—you know them all too well. Find things about your body that you like and tell yourself you like them. If you were looking at someone you loved, you would not concentrate on the negative things—you would praise the things about them you loved. Give yourself a massage with baby or coconut oil. Go over your entire body, everywhere you can reach, lovingly massaging the oil into your skin. Listen to your breathing.

The Mirror

Use a mirror that stands by itself to free both your hands. Find a comfortable position and a good light. Look at your genitals. Give yourself a loving genital massage with oil. Pull the lips apart, look inside, pull the foreskin back and expose your clitoris, rub it gently, move your fingers all over. Explore your genitals with as much interest as you have always explored your face. Get to know how you look, smell, and taste. It's a beautiful part of you. Say hello to your source of pleasure.

MOVING YOUR BODY

Try doing some body movements. Be conscious of your breathing. Yoga postures are a perfect way to stretch and bend, always breathing deep into your stomach. Or put some music on and dance. Watch yourself dance in front of your mirror. Allow yourself to do any movement you feel like doing—be outrageous! Have fun and pleasure moving your body. Rotate your pelvis, do bumps and grinds, shimmy and shake, let it all hang out. When I first started dancing again (as an adult) I practiced for several months alone in front of a mirror until I had enough confidence to dance with my friends at a discotheque.

CREATE AN EROTIC ENVIRONMENT

How would you create a space for a very special lover? That's the same thoughtfulness you want to give yourself. Set a stage for lovemaking including soft lights, candles, incense, colors, textures, sound and whatever turns you on. We are mostly in charge of decorating the home, so you might consider designing your bedroom for sex and body tripping. I prefer my beds on the floor with a thick carpet. A mattress plus box springs are just the right height for several lovemaking positions. Lighting and color are very important. Cut loose and do your own erotic environment.

Sexual Fantasy

Think erotic thoughts. Review a memory of an experience that was a good sexual high. Tell yourself a sexy story. Go over your memory or fantasy in detail. Read an erotic book. Look at pornography or erotic art. Let your imagination go —fantasy has no limits. I fantasize as preparation for something I want to do. For instance, I have been having fantasies about making a porn movie: I am the camera, the director, the star performer, everything. You can also have fantasies that you would never expect to act out. One friend of mine was disturbed because her fantasies were not feminist. She was always being passive and helpless. I told her that it was all right to have those fantasies. She could simply experiment with new ones. She now has more assertive fantasies, yet, if she gets stuck or is in a hurry, she brings out the Five Irish Cops and the Rape Scene. However, one of her more recent fantasies is about her clitoris—as she gets excited, it becomes big and erect and she gets over her boyfriend's face and slowly moves her clitoris in and out of his mouth until she comes. Female sexual fantasy is just now emerging in our own culture. Being able to fantasize is the heart of the creative act. To have a fantasy is to have a dream or a vision about something you would like to experience or just think about. Sharing your sexual fantasies with your lover, especially during sex, is exciting.

Meditation on Self Love

Get comfortable. Place the phone off the hook or under a pillow. Breathe slowly and deeply. Stretch, luxuriate. Take your time, be a good lover. Touch yourself all over and feel good about you. Have your sexual toys available—vibrators, porno, creams or oils, perfumes. Bring yourself up slowly . . . don't think about orgasm, think about pleasure, play with yourself and your fantasies. If you feel you are getting close to coming—drop back—tease and please yourself. We have been conditioned wrongly to make love like we are rushing to catch a plane. Spend at least thirty minutes to an hour. For some women who have put tremendous pressure on themselves to achieve orgasm, I suggest spending several self-lovemaking sessions without performance demands.

If you are brand new to masturbation, don't expect immediate results. Be as gentle and tender with yourself as you would be towards a virgin lover. When you have your orgasm—don't stop stimulation, just lighten up and stay with the good feelings. Ride the waves of pleasure. Let the pleasure come out with sound, sighs, words, breathing and movement. If you feel like it, go on to a second buildup and another orgasm. Pleasure is pure healing. ENJOY YOURSELF.

PRESSURE

Some women achieve orgasm by pressing the thighs together and squeezing and tensing the muscles. This is done in different positions, squeezing and pressing rhythmically. It is impossible for me to experience orgasm this way, but some women do. I require more direct stimulation. The pressure technique is great for buses and planes and sitting in waiting rooms.

WATER

Some women have orgasms by letting water run on their genitals. The amount of pressure can be controlled and the water is symbolically pleasing. This is especially good for women who find it difficult to touch their genitals, and the bathroom offers privacy and security. *Never use your vibrator in the tub or shower.* Water and electricity, as you know, do not mix.

HAND

This is perhaps the most common form of self-love. I always use an oil or cream. Saliva works but it dries too quickly. Also, reaching inside and using your own lubrication is fine. For me the slippery, moist feeling of oil on my genitals is a turn on. You can use one finger or your whole hand. Try circular motions, above the clitoral body, below, on top, or to the side. Every woman is different, so different strokes for different folks. Experiment with several techniques, observing the arousal potential of each—going slow, fast, soft, firm. You can lie on your stomach, your side, your back. Try putting your legs up and also stretching them out. Try sitting up, standing up, watching in a mirror.

VIBRATOR

The vibrator has proven to be an excellent erotic toy for women. Many women who have never had orgasm after years of lovemaking, have their first one with the vibrator. The advantage of the vibrator is its strong and consistent stimulation. If a woman has had little or no experience with childhood, adolescent or adult masturbation, she needs to train the nerve pathways from her genitals to her brain. She has literally CUT OFF sensations from her genitals in her desire to be "a good girl." Learning how to say "NO" to genital sensations. A woman can reverse that conditioning at any stage of her life—by saying "YES" to her body, her genitals, her pleasure. The physical reconditioning is positive, joyful orgasmic masturbation. I have worked with women in their 20's, 30's, 40's and 50's, and have seen many experience their first orgasm with the vibrator. By the way, the vibrator is great for your entire body. Use it for scalp and facial massage to relieve all the tension at the temples and around the eyes, mouth and clenched jaw. Go on to the neck and shoulders where most of us carry an abundance of tension and holding patterns, and on down to your feet. Feels great!

VIBRATING WITH MUSIC

I have had some women complain that the vibrator simply makes them go numb. Of course, if you put the vibrator directly on your clitoris and don't move either the vibrator or your body, you will numb out. I always use a bit of material between me and the vibrator—a piece of velvet, satin, fur, or a towel. I move the vibrator back and forth as well as rocking my pelvis forward and back and around. It's very much like dancing with my vibrator. I love to masturbate to music and do sensate focus. It's as if the music is on my clitoris—a particular instrument or the drums. I follow the rhythmic build-up. It's a great way to find out which music and musicians are having orgasms. Many of the rock groups generate a lot of energy and orgasms. The Indian Ragas are beautiful to come by. Classical music and jazz work also. Pick a musical lover. You can masturbate to music while having any fantasy you want.

VIBRATOR OR HAND PLUS PENETRATION

I have experimented with dildos (rubber penises) and have decided that as soon as the novelty wears off, they are really not so good. They are made too big and hard. The plastic penis-shaped battery vibrator is also too hard and uncomfortable and has weak vibrations. If a woman desires penetration she can use her fingers or a peeled cucumber. I heard one woman say she preferred a wilted carrot. Many women don't want huge things inside their vagina, contrary to male fantasy.

A Partner and a Vibrator

Most of the women I have talked with give me very positive feedback about using the vibrator with their partners. It's very much like going exploring together sexually. Remember, when you bring out your vibrator it separates the "chauvinists" from the "lovers." Every good lover I have ever known has always been interested, turned on, and curious about pleasure from a vibrator and they want to try it also. That's one of the reasons I keep several vibrators around, that way we can do it together or experiment with the different vibes each one has. It's ridiculous for a man to feel competitive with the vibrator . . . it's like competing with CON ED, you plug it in and it's there forever. (With only one major power failure that I know of.) I suggest cooperation not competition. Actually vibrators at this stage are very primitive. I would like to design pleasure appliances for the whole family. . . .

Denial of the woman's phallus has for centuries been the essence of male dominance and female subjugation. Therefore, our whole society, as long as it tries to maintain its highly male authoritarian posture, has a vested interest in the continuance of this mystification and denial of sexual liberation for women.

Masturbation holds the key to breaking this socially approved bondage simply because it reverses the whole process of repression. With sexual independence, we gain control of our bodies and stand up straight and strong. By making no secret of our masturbation, we challenge those who have a stake in our repression, who perpetuate the conspiracy of grim silence. By openly advocating masturbation and debunking myths about it, we become less intimidated and more confident about ourselves and our bodies.

We must have access to information. Since our present society has no interest in enlightening women about sex or encouraging them to grow and be independent, women must teach women.

I would like to point out that in addition to heterosexuality, homosexuality, bisexuality, and group sexuality, that self sexuality as a total sex life is absolutely valid. Some of my sisters have been so hurt and turned off by heterosex and male insensitivity that they prefer masturbation to intercourse. A lot of women out of long-term marriages find it just too painful to try to re-establish themselves sexually in a youth market. Relations with another woman can be a reasonable alternative for some women. It is important to know that there are all kinds of people who are not in relationships with others. Some because of personal preference, lack of confidence or physical disability. Others are alone because they are in prisons, nursing homes, mental institutions, boarding schools or the military. Acceptance of masturbation can make these lifestyles more fulfilling and sexually liberated.

Masturbation is our primary sex life. It is our sexual base. Everything we do beyond that is simply how we choose to socialize our sex life. Under ideal circumstances, there would be no set or prescribed way in which we would sexualize. Our sexual preferences would naturally be multifaceted, varied and independent, and would include a combination of all living things. Socially institutionalized dependent sex is depersonalizing. Masturbation can help return sex to its proper place—to the individual.

Part IV

AUTOEROTICISM IN WOMEN AND MEN

INTRODUCTION

The chapters in this section deal with the autoerotic experiences of both women and men from a number of different viewpoints. And, as will be seen, some of the autoerotic practices of women reported here date as far back as the Babylonian sculptures. Reference is also made in Chapter 13 of the masturbatory behavior of nuns, a subject that is very rarely discussed.

Aside from Sigmund Freud, one of the earliest pioneers in the field of human sexuality and one of the most famous was Havelock Ellis. Pomeroy, in referring to Ellis, has aptly described him as one of "the founding fathers of sex research" (Pomeroy, 1972, p. 66). While the name Havelock Ellis is synonomous with sex research, his method of collecting data, it will be remembered, was unique in that this English researcher with a medical degree acquired his sexual information for the most part from letters that were written to him by various persons. In Chapter 13, which is from Volume 1 of his classic work,

"Studies in the Psychology of Sex," Ellis points out that masturbation is practiced by men and women of almost "every race" about which intimate data are available. To illustrate the universality of masturbation among human beings, he specifically refers to the masturbatory behavior of women and men from different parts of the world including Bali, Egypt, India, China, and Japan, and also mentions that some women used such devices as an artificial penis, a wax penis, and two small hollow balls called *rin-no-tama* (which were experienced especially by Japanese women). In addition to using *rin-no-tama,* Japanese women also frequently employed an artificial penis made of paper or clay, and Chinese women utilized a rose-colored penis made of rosin. The use of an artificial penis for masturbatory activity as reported by Ellis was in existence "in the very earliest human civilization" and was represented in the Babylonian sculptures. Interestingly, too, lesbians were noted to have used artificial penises made of ivory or gold and Milesian women employed an artificial penis made of leather. In the sixteenth century, according to Ellis, a "glass object filled with warm water" was said to have been used by nuns and other women during autoerotic activity. By the eighteenth century in London the use of dildos was common and they were sold openly. In France in the eighteenth century dildos were called *consalateurs* and many nuns appear to have used them. Ellis also refers to the penis substitute utilized in France, consisting of hardened red rubber and being "capable of holding warm milk or other fluid for injection at the moment of orgasm," and to the use of an artificial penis by Turkish women. In regard to the "ordinary objects and implements" that were employed by women during autoerotic activity, Ellis comments on the use of bananas, cucumbers, turnips, carrots, and beet roots. And some of the objects that were known to have been found in the vagina or female bladder include pencils, hairpins (these were frequently found in the female bladder), bonepins

used in the hair (especially in Italy), knitting needles, candles, corks, toothbrushes, and a hen's egg. Ellis also describes some of the techniques females were known to have
engaged in to produce erotic arousal: for example, rubbing
against a chair, rubbing against a knot in one's chemise,
sitting on one's naked heel and rubbing against it, riding
on hobby-horses, swinging in a swing, and standing before
a mirror and rubbing against a key in a bureau drawer. Ellis
further states that in the case of boys climbing up a pole,
as well as swinging around a pole may produce a sense of
sexual excitement and horseback riding particularly by
women is also described as possibly resulting in orgasm.
Very noteworthy, as Ellis reveals, in France women were
known to experience orgasms while working sewing machines with great rapidity. Reports of women attaining an
orgasm while riding bicycles are also referred to and mention is made of the tightlacing of corsets as a "method of
masturbation." Finally, Ellis discusses the use of thigh pressure by both women and men while sitting or standing as
a method of producing orgasms.

Chapter 14, by Dr. Clelland S. Ford (anthropologist)
and Dr. Frank A. Beach (psychologist), two of the foremost
researchers in their respective fields, has long been viewed
as a classic. In this chapter, in addition to reviewing the
important research pertaining to masturbation by American men and women up until the R. L. Dickinson report of
1949, Ford and Beach discuss the attitudes held toward
masturbation as well as the masturbatory practices engaged
in by men and women in America and other societies, for
example, Lesu, Lepcha, Siriono, Crow Indians, Trobrianders, Polynesians, etc. The use of autoeroticism by male and
female animals is also described, for example, apes, monkeys, porcupines, elephants, dogs, cats, and dolphins. And
some attention is devoted to the experiencing of "spontaneous" orgasms and nocturnal emissions by men and
women. Among the various important conclusions drawn

by Ford and Beach are the following: "The basic mammalian tendencies toward self-stimulation seem sufficiently strong and widespread to justify classifying human masturbation as a normal and natural form of sexual expression. . . .We believe that the relative infrequency of self-stimulation among mature people in most societies is a consequence of social conditioning. In the absence of cultural rules against it, such behavior probably would occur much more frequently than it actually does."

Dr. William H. Masters and Virginia E. Johnson, in Chapter 15, in addition to commenting on the occurrence of genital manipulation by both males and females during "earliest infancy," the continuance of masturbation by most males during adolescence, as well as the age most frequently reported by their 312 male subjects when "active" autoerotic activity was first initiated (around 14 or 15 years), describe in detail the masturbatory techniques experienced by men. Although there are exceptions, as stated by Masters and Johnson "most men manipulate the shaft of the penis with stroking techniques that encompass the entire organ." The particular manner, however, in which males do this, that is, the speed, tightness of grip, and so on, varies. Masters and Johnson further point out that "with the onset of the ejaculatory process marked variation has been observed in the male manipulative technique," and present a detailed analysis of the actions of their male subjects during this stage of their masturbatory activity. Attention is also devoted to emphasizing the "sensitivity of the penis glans" immediately following ejaculation.

In Chapter 16, Dr. James Leslie McCary, the well-known author, psychologist, and sex therapist recounts the ancient attitudes held toward masturbation, refers to the literature as it pertains to certain aspects of autoerotic behavior by males and females, and makes a number of important clinical observations concerning the use of autoeroticism. He also refutes several myths regarding the

practice of masturbation and describes some of the masturbatory methods employed by males and females. Consistent with other sex therapists, McCary stresses the fact that
through the use of autoerotic activity a woman can learn
about her own sensuality as well as how to heighten her
sexual responsiveness. As for specific exercises in this behalf, detailed reference is made to the suggestions
recorded by "J" in her book *The Sensuous Woman* (1969).
McCary's observations relative to the practice of autoeroticism include the following: "Probably the most successful
way of learning to respond to one's full sexual capacity is
through self-stimulation. Masturbation is a perfectly normal, healthy act in boys and girls and in men and women,
young and old. . . .Only under extremely rare circumstances can masturbation be considered a sexual abnormality. . . . Indeed, those who do not practice masturbation, or
have never done so, are far more likely to be suffering from
an emotional or sexual problem than those who have masturbatory experience. . . . Masturbation is frustrating only
when the person feels guilt or shame about it. . . . Learning
to masturbate successfully is probably the most important
step for the woman in learning to come to orgasm easily
and quickly. . . ."

In Chapter 17, Morton Hunt, a prominent professional writer, reports some of the findings uncovered in a
very important national sex survey commissioned by the
Playboy Foundation. The research data for this study were
gathered in 1972 by the Research Guild, Inc., and the sample of subjects included 982 males and 1044 females ranging in age from 18 to 77. During the past generation, as
Hunt states, marked changes have occurred not only in the
attitudes held concerning masturbation but also in the frequency with which it is practiced as well as in regard to the
"feelings of most masturbators about their own behavior."
While more males and females of 34 years of age and
younger are accepting of masturbatory activity than those

who are 35 and over, even those individuals in the latter group appear to be moving toward a greater acceptance of autoeroticism. And as in the past, Hunt notes that in the Playboy study there was less acceptance of masturbation by people of the lower social classes and the noncollege educated than by those of the higher social classes and the college educated. Although 94% of the male and 63% of the female participants indicated having masturbated, findings that are almost the same as those disclosed by Kinsey et al. (1948, 1953), Hunt in referring to them states "but this is not an accumulative incidence; it represents what has happened up to this time, in the lives of the respondents. Presumably, some of the younger people in the sample and at least a few of the more mature people who have not yet experienced masturbation will do so during their lifetimes. Accordingly, our incidence data suggest at least a small overall increase since Kinsey's time." Hunt also reveals that both males and females are starting to masturbate at earlier ages than previously, with males beginning at much younger ages than females. Nevertheless, as before, the factor of religion, especially in the case of women, continues to exert a restraining force on the use of masturbation. In comparing the Kinsey et al. (1948) findings relating to males, with those uncovered in the Playboy survey, Hunt concludes that in reference to his sample of single males ranging in age from 18 to 24, an increase had occurred in "the active incidence of masturbation." Furthermore, many more of the young single males in the Playboy sample were found to continue the practice of masturbation beyond adolescence and into early adulthood than was the case in the investigation by the Kinsey group. And the frequency with which masturbatory activity was experienced by the single male young adults in the Playboy study was significantly higher than that revealed in the Kinsey et al. report. With respect to single women, Hunt's findings show that some of the changes that have occurred in terms of the active incidence of masturbation as well as frequency, since the Kinsey et al. study of 1953, have been even greater than in the case of single males. For instance, more than four-fifths of the single women in their late twenties and early thirties in the Playboy study were known to be masturbating as compared to about half of those single women of comparable age in the undertaking by Kinsey and his co-workers. Among the most dramatic findings reported by Hunt are those which show a "greatly increased use of masturbation by younger married men and women." Although "religious devoutness" was observed by Hunt to have an inhibitory effect on the practice by married persons, younger people were less affected by this factor than were older ones. Interesting too, while the Catholics in the sample were the most devout of all the subjects (followed by Protestants and Jews), Catholics who were active masturbators did so more frequently than Protestants. Moreover, a much higher proportion of Jewish males than either Catholics or Protestants were actively engaged in masturbation and more Jewish women than non-Jewish women.

Dr. Albert Ellis, in Chapter 18, covers a wide range of topics related to masturbatory behavior including those of a theoretical and practical nature. He first observes that while a much greater acceptance of autoeroticism has occurred in our society during the past half century, very few writers deal with masturbation on a "completely objective" and nonmoralistic basis. Only among a small number of primitive people (e.g., Marquesan Islanders, Mohave Indians) does there appear to be complete acceptance by society of autoerotic activity, according to Ellis. After criticizing psychoanalysts for regarding masturbation as "self-destructive" even though no scientific evidence exists to support this view, Ellis cites the research of Hunt conducted in the 1970s that shows that strong and widespread feelings of guilt relating to the use of masturbation still exist. Especially in regard to the single adult male (but also with respect to females and married persons), Ellis presents evidence that disproves a number of the objections leveled against the use of autoeroticism. Following this, some of the advantages of masturbation are listed. Ellis further discusses the attitudes one must have in order to enjoy autoerotic activity, the importance of fantasizing while engaged in such behavior, and the techniques men and women may employ during autoeroticism. A number of masturbatory embellishments are also suggested, which include the use of sex talk and sounds, scenic aids, the presence of another person, use of coital movement, use of various lubricants, changes in methods employed, changes in speed and pressure, experimentation of different "sensitive genital zones," use of a variety of positions and physical locations, and the extended use of time. Moreover, Ellis notes some of the mechanical devices that have long been employed for masturbatory purposes by men and women. Specific reference is made of the electric vibrator as being "most useful and harmless" as a device for enhancing sexual stimulation in the case of both men and women, but particularly for women. However, Ellis also mentions the problems that may result from the use of vibrators. With respect to the use of masturbation and mechanical aids Ellis stresses the point that one should *not* experience them in a compulsive manner. As he states, "So try, if you want, all kinds of sex, and all kinds of mechanical devices to aid you in your masturbatory and interpersonal practices. But not compulsively! Not desperately!" Ellis concludes his observations on the practice of masturbation and the removal of possible accompanying feelings of shame and humiliation by recommending rational-emotive procedures.

Chapter 13

AUTO-EROTISM: A STUDY OF THE SPONTANEOUS MANIFESTATIONS OF THE SEXUAL IMPULSE

Havelock Ellis, M.D.

To whatever extent masturbation may have been developed by the conditions of European life, which carry to the utmost extreme the concomitant stimulation and repression of the sexual emotions, it is far from being, as Mantegazza has declared it to be, one of the moral characteristics of Europeans.[1] It is found among the people of

From *Studies in the Psychology of Sex,* by Havelock Ellis. Copyright 1936 by The Modern Library, Inc. Copyright 1941, 1942 by the Executrixes of the author, Havelock Ellis. Reprinted by permission of Random House, Inc.

[1]Dr. J. W. Howe (*Excessive Venery, Masturbation, and Continence,* London and New York, 1883, p. 62) writes of masturbation: "In savage lands it is of rare occurrence. Savages live in a state of Nature. No moral obligations exist which compel them to abstain from a natural gratification of their passions. There is no social law which prevents them from following the dictates of their lower nature. Hence, they have no reason for adopting onanism as an outlet for passions. The moral trammels of civilized society, and ignorance of physiological laws, give origin to the vice." Every one of these six sentences is incorrect or misleading. They are worth quoting as a statement of the popular view of savage life.

nearly every race of which we have any intimate knowledge, however natural the conditions under which men and women may live.[2] Thus among the Nama Hottentots, among the young women at all events, Gustav Fritsch found that masturbation is so common that it is regarded as a custom of the country; no secret is made of it, and in the stories and legends of the race it is treated as one of the most ordinary facts of life. It is so also among the Basutos, and the Kaffirs are addicted to the same habit.[3] The Fuegians have a word for masturbation, and a special word for masturbation by women.[4] When the Spaniards first arrived at Vizcaya, in the Philippines, they found that masturbation was universal, and that it was customary for the women to use an artifical penis and other abnormal methods of sexual gratification. Among the Balinese, according to Jacobs (as quoted by Ploss and Bartels), masturbation is general; in

[2] I can recall little evidence of its existence among the Australian aborigines, though there is, in the Wiradyuri language, spoken over a large part of New South Wales, a word (whether ancient or not, I do not know) meaning, masturbation (*Journal of the Anthropological Institute*, July-Dec. 1904, p. 303). Dr. W. Roth (*Ethnological Studies Among the Northwest-Central Queensland Aborigines*, p. 184), who has carefully studied the blacks of his district, remarks that he has no evidence as to the practice of either masturbation or sodomy among them. More recently (1906) Roth has stated that married men in North Queensland and elsewhere masturbate during their wives' absence. As regards the Maori of New Zealand, Northcote adds, there is a rare word for masturbation (as also at Rarotonga), but according to a distinguished Maori scholar there are no allusions to the practice in Maori literature, and it was probably not practiced in primitive times. The Maori and the Polynesians of the Cook Islands, Northcote remarks, consider the act unmanly, applying to it a phrase meaning "to make women of themselves." (Northcote, *loc. cit.*, p. 232).

[3] Greenlees, *Journal of Mental Science*, July, 1895. A gentleman long resident among the Kaffirs of South Natal told Northcote, however, that he had met with no word for masturbation, and did not believe the practice prevailed there.

[4] Hyades and Deniker, *Mission Scientifique du Cap Horn*, vol. vii, p. 295.

the boudoir of many a Bali beauty, he adds, and certainly in every harem, may be found a wax penis to which many hours of solitude are devoted. Throughout the East, as Eram, speaking from a long medical experience, has declared, masturbation is very prevalent, especially among young girls. In Egypt, according to Sonnini, it is prevalent in harems. In India, a medical correspondent tells me, he once treated the widow of a wealthy Mohammedan, who informed him that she began masturbation at an early age, "just like all other women." The same informant tells me that on the *facade* of a large temple in Orissa are bas-reliefs, representing both men and women, alone, masturbating, and also women masturbating men. Among the Tamils of Ceylon masturbation is said to be common. In Cochin China, Lorion remarks, it is practiced by both sexes, but especially by the married women.[5] Japanese women have probably carried the mechanical arts of auto-erotism to the highest degree of perfection. They use two hollow balls about the size of a pigeon's egg (sometimes one alone is used), which, as described by Joest, Christian, and others,[6] are made of very thin leaf of brass; one is empty, the other (called the little man) contains a small heavy metal ball, or else some quicksilver, and sometimes metal tongues which vibrate when set in movement; so that if the balls are held

[5] *La Criminalite en Cochin-Chine,* 1887, p. 116; also Mondiere, "Monographie de la Femme Annamite," *Memoires Societe d'Anthropologie,* tommi ii, p. 465.

[6] Christian, article on "Onanisme," *Dictionnaire encyclopedique des sciences medicales;* Ploss and Bartels, *Das Weib;* Moraglia. "Die Onanie beim normalen Weibe," *Zeitschrift fur Criminal-Anthropologie,* 1897; Dartigues, *De la Procreation Volontaire des Sexes,* p. 32. In the eighteenth century, the rin-no-tama was known in France, sometimes as "pommes d'amour." Thus Bachaumont, in his Journal (under date July 31, 1773), refers to "a very extraordinary instrument of amorous mystery," brought by a traveler from India; he describes this "boule eretique" as the size of a pigeon's egg, covered with soft skin, and gilded. Cf. F. S. Krauss, *Geschlechtsleben in Brauch und Sitte der Japaner,* Leipzig, 1907.

in the hand side by side there is continuous movement. The empty one is first introduced into the vagina in contact with the uterus, then the other; the slightest movement of the pelvis or thighs, or even spontaneous movement of the organs, causes the metal ball (or the quicksilver) to roll, and the resulting vibration produces a prolonged voluptuous titillation, a gentle shock as from a weak electric inductive apparatus; the balls are called *rin-no-tama,* and are held in the vagina by a paper tampon. The women who use these balls delight to swing themselves in a hammock or rocking-chair, the delicate vibration of the balls slowly producing the highest degree of sexual excitement. Joest mentions that this apparatus, though well known by name to ordinary girls, is chiefly used by the more fashionable *geishas,* as well as by prostitutes. Its use has now spread to China, Annam, and India. Japanese women also, it is said, frequently use an artificial penis of paper or clay, called *engi.* Among the Atjeh, again, according to Jacobs (as quoted by Ploss), the young of both sexes masturbate and the elder girls use an artificial penis of wax. In China, also, the artificial penis— made of rosin, supple and (like the classical instrument described by Herondas) rose-colored—is publicly sold and widely used by women.[7]

It may be noticed that among non-European races it is among women, and especially among those who are subjected to the excitement of a life professionally devoted to some form of pleasure, that the use of the artificial instruments of auto-erotism is chiefly practiced. The same is markedly true in Europe. The use of an artificial penis in solitary sexual gratification may be traced down from classic times, and doubtless prevailed in the very earliest hu-

[7]It may be worth mentioning that the Salish Indians of British Columbia have a myth of an old woman having intercourse with young women, by means of a horn worn as a penis (*Journal of the Anthropological Institute,* July-Dec., 1904, p. 342).

man civilization, for such an instrument is said to be represented in old Babylonian sculptures, and it is referred to by Ezekiel (Ch. XVI, v. 17). The Lesbian women are said to have used such instruments, made of ivory or gold with silken stuffs and linen. Aristophanes (Lysistrata, v. 109) speaks of the manufacture of the Milesian women of a leather artificial penis, or olisbos. In the British Museum is a vase representing a *hetaira* holding such instruments, which, as found in Pompeii, may be seen in the museum at Naples. One of the best of Herondas's mimes, "The Private Conversation," presents a dialogue between two ladies concerning a certain olisbos (or *υβην*), which one of them vaunts as a dream of delight. Through the Middle Ages (when from), time to time the clergy reprobated the use of such instruments[8]) they continued to be known, and after the fifteenth century the references to them became more precise. Thus Fortini, the Siennese novelist of the sixteenth century, refers in his *Novelle dei Novizi* (7th Day, Novella XXXIX) to "the glass object filled with warm water which nuns use to calm the sting of the flesh and to satisfy themselves as well as they can"; he adds that widows and other women anxious to avoid pregnancy availed themselves of it. In Elizabethan England, at the same time, it appears to have been of similar character and Marston in his satires tells how Lucea prefers "a glassy instrument" to "her husband's lukewarm bed." In sixteenth century France, also, such instruments were sometimes made of glass, and Bran-

---

[8]In Burchard's Penitential (cap. 142–3), penalties are assigned to the woman who makes a phallus for use on herself or other women. (Wasserschleben, *Bussordnungen der abendlandlichen Kirche*, p. 658). The *penis succedancus,* the Latin *phallus* or *fascinum,* is in France called *godemiche;* in Italy, *passatempo,* and also *diletto,* whence *dildo,* by which it is most commonly known in England. For men, the corresponding cunnus succedaneus is, in England, called *merkin,* which meant originally (as defined in old editions of Bailey's *Dictionary*) "counterfeit hair for women's privy parts."

tome refers to the godemiche; in eighteenth century Germany they were called *Samthanse,* and their use, according to Heinse, as quoted by Duhren, was common among aristocratic women. In England by that time the dildo appears to have become common. Archemholtz states that while in Paris they are only sold secretly, in London a certain Mrs. Philips sold them openly on a large scale in her shop in Leicester Square. John Bee in 1835, stating that the name was originally dil-dol, remarks that their use was formerly commoner than it was in his day. In France, Madame Gourdan, the most notorious brothel-keeper of the eighteenth century, carried on a wholesale trade in *consolateurs,* as they were called, and "at her death numberless letters from abbesses and simple nuns were found among her papers, asking for a 'consolateur' to be sent."[9] The modern French instrument is described by Garnier as of hardened red rubber, exactly imitating the penis and capable of holding warm milk or other fluid for injection at the moment of orgasm; the compressible scrotum is said to have been first added in the eighteenth century.[10]

In Islam the artificial penis has reached nearly as high a development as in Christendom. Turkish women use it and it is said to be openly sold in Smyrna. In the harems of Zanzibar, according to Baumann, it is of considerable size, carved out of ebony or ivory, and commonly bored through so that warm water may be injected. It is here regarded as an Arab invention.[11]

Somewhat similar appliances may be traced in all centres of civilization. But throughout they appear to be frequently confined to the world of prostitutes and to those women who live on the fashionable or semi-artistic verge

[9]Duhren, *Der Marquis de Sade und Seine Zeit,* 3d ed., pp. 130, 232; id. *Geschlechtsleben in England,* Bd. II, pp. 284, *et seq.*

[10]Garnier, *Onanisme,* p. 378.

[11]*Zeitschrift fur Ethnologie,* 1899, p. 669.

of that world. Ignorance and delicacy combine with a less versatile and perverted concentration on the sexual impulse to prevent any general recourse to such highly specialized methods of solitary gratification.

On the other hand, the use, or rather abuse, of the ordinary objects and implements of daily life in obtaining auto-erotic gratification, among the ordinary population in civilized modern lands, has reached an extraordinary degree of extent and variety we can only feebly estimate by the occasional resulting mischances which come under the surgeon's hands, because only a certain proportion of such instruments are dangerous. Thus the banana seems to be widely used for masturbation by women, and appears to be marked out for the purpose by its size and shape;[12] it is, however, innocuous, and never comes under the surgeon's notice; the same may probably be said of the cucumbers and other vegetables more especially used by country and factory girls in masturbation; a lady living near Vichy told Pouillet that she had often heard (and had herself been able to verify the fact) that the young peasant women commonly used turnips, carrots, and beet-roots. In the eighteenth century Mirabeau, in his *Erotika Biblion*, gave a list of the various objects used in convents (which he describes as "vast theatres" of such practices) to obtain solitary sexual excitement. In more recent years the following are a few of the objects found in the vagina or bladder whence they

[12]The mythology of Hawaii, one may note, tells of goddesses who were impregnated by bananas they had placed beneath their garments. B. Stern mentions (*Medizin in der Turki,* Bd. II, p. 24) that the women of Turkey and Egypt use the banana, as well as the cucumber, etc., for masturbation. In a poem in the *Arabian Nights,* also ("History of the Young Nour with the Frank"), we read: "O bananas, of soft and smooth skins, which dilate the eyes of young girls . . . you, alone among fruits are endowed with a pitying heart. O consolers of widows and divorced women." In France and England they are not uncommonly used for the same purpose.

could only be removed by surgical interference[13]: Pencils, sticks of sealing wax, cotton-reels, hair-pins (and in Italy very commonly the bone-pins used in the hair), bodkins, knitting-needles, crochet-needles, needle-cases, compasses, glass stoppers, candles, corks, tumblers, forks, tooth-picks, tooth-brushes, pomade-pots (in a case recorded by Schroeder with a cockchafer inside, a makeshift substitute for the Japanese *rin-no-tama*), while in one recent English case a full-sized hen's egg was removed from the vagina of a middleaged married woman. More than nine-tenths of the foreign bodies found in the female bladder or urethra are due to masturbation. The age of the individuals in whom such objects have been found is usually from 17 to 30, but in a few cases they have been found in girls below 14, infrequently in women between 40 and 50; the large objects, naturally, are found chiefly in the vagina, and in married women.[14]

Hair-pins have, above all, been found in the female bladder with special frequency; this point is worth some

[13]See e.g., Winckel, *Die Krankheiten der weiblichen Harnohre and Blase,* 1885, p. 211; and "Lehrbuch der Frauenkrankheiten," 1886, p. 210; also Hyrtl, *Handbuch du Topographischen Anatomie,* 7th ed., Bd. II pp. 212–214. Grunfeld (*Wiener medizinische Blatter,* November 26, 1896), collected 115 cases of foreign body in the bladder—68 in men, 47 in women; but while those found in men were usually the result of a surgical accident, those found in women were mostly introduced by the patients themselves. The patient usually professes profound ignorance as to how the object came there; or she explains that she accidentally sat down upon it, or that she used it to produce freer urination. The earliest surgical case of this kind I happen to have met with, was recorded by Piazzon, in Italy, in 1621 (*De Partibus Generationi Inservientibus* lib. ii, Ch. XIII): it was that of a certain honorable maiden with a large clitoris, who, seeking to lull sexual excitement with the aid of a bone needle, inserted it in the bladder, whence it was removed by Aquapendente.

[14]A. Poulet, *Traite des Corps etrangers en Chirurgie,* 1879. English translation, 1881 vol. ii, pp. 209, 230. Rohleder (*Die Masturbation,* 1899, pp. 24–31) also gives examples of strange objects found in the sexual organs.

consideration as an illustration of the enormous frequency of this form of auto-erotism. . . .

There is, however, another class of material objects, widely employed for producing physical auto-erotism, which in the nature of things never reaches the surgeon. I refer to the effects that, naturally or unnaturally, may be produced by many of the objects and implements of daily life that do not normally come in direct contact with the sexual organs. Children sometimes, even when scarcely more than infants, produce sexual excitement by friction against the corner of a chair or other piece of furniture, and women sometimes do the same.[15] Guttceit, in Russia, knew women who made a large knot in their chemises to rub against, and mentions a woman who would sit on her naked heel and rub it against her. Girls in France, I am informed, are fond of riding on the chevaux-de-bois, or hobby-horses, because of the sexual excitement thus aroused; and that the sexual emotions play a part in the fascination exerted by this form of amusement everywhere is indicated by the ecstatic faces of its devotees.[16] At the temples in some parts of Central India, I am told, swings are hung up in pairs, men and women swinging in these until sexually excited; during the months when the men in these districts have to be away from home the girls put up swings to console themselves for the loss of their husbands. . . .

[15]"One of my patients," remarks Dr. R. T. Morris, of New York (*Transactions of the American Association of Obstetricians,* for 1892, Philadelphia, vol. v), "who is a devout church-member, had never allowed herself to entertain sexual thoughts referring to men, but she masturbated every morning, when standing before the mirror, by rubbing against a key in the bureau-drawer. A man never excited her passions, but the sight of a key in any bureau-drawer aroused erotic desires."

[16]Freud (*Drei Abhandlungen zur Sexualtheorie,* p. 118) refers to the sexual pleasure of swinging. Swinging another person may be a source of voluptuous excitement, and one of the 600 forms of sexual pleasure enumerated in De Sade's *Les 120 Journees de Sodome* is (according to Duhren) to propel a girl vigorously in a swing.

Somewhat similarly sensations of sexual character are sometimes experienced by boys when climbing up a pole. It is not even necessary that there should be direct external contact with the sexual organs, and Howe states that gymnastic swinging poles around which boys swing while supporting the whole weight on the hands, may suffice to produce sexual excitement.

Several writers have pointed out that riding, especially in women, may produce sexual excitement and orgasm.[17] It is well-known, also, that both in men and women the vibratory motion of a railway-train frequently produces a certain degree of sexual excitement, especially when sitting forward. Such excitement may remain latent and not become specifically sexual.[18] I am not aware that this quality of railway traveling has ever been fostered as a sexual perversion, but the sewing-machine has attracted considerable attention on account of its influence in exciting autoerotic manifestations. The early type of sewing-machine, especially, was of very heavy character and involved much up and down movement of the legs; Langdon Down pointed out many years ago that this frequently produced great sexual erethism which led to masturbation.[19] According to one French authority, it is a well-recognized fact that

[17]The fact that horse exercise may produce pollutions was well recognized by Catholic theologians, and Sanchez states that this fact need not be made a reason for traveling on foot. Rolfincius, in 1667, pointed out that horse-riding in those unaccustomed to it, may lead to nocturnal pollutions. Rohleder (*Die Masturbation,* pp. 133–134) brings together evidence regarding the influence of horse exercise in producing sexual excitement.

[18]A correspondent, to whom the idea was presented for the first time, wrote: "Henceforward I shall know to what I must attribute the bliss—almost the beatitude—I so often have experienced after traveling for four or five hours in a train." Penta mentions the case of a young girl who first experienced sexual desire at the age of twelve, after a railway journey.

[19]Langdon Down, *British Medical Journal,* January 12, 1867.

to work a sewing-machine with the body in a certain position produces sexual excitement leading to the orgasm. The occurrence of the orgasm is indicated to the observer by the machine being worked for a few seconds with uncontrollable rapidity. This sound is said to be frequently heard in large French workrooms, and it is part of the duty of the superintendents of the rooms to make the girls sit properly.[20]

"During a visit which I once paid to a manufactory of military clothing," Pouillet writes, "I witnessed the following scene. In the midst of the uniform sound produced by some thirty sewing machines, I suddenly heard one of the machines working with much more velocity than the others. I looked at the person who was working it, a brunette of 18 or 20. While she was automatically occupied with the trousers she was making on the machine, her face became animated, her mouth opened slightly, her nostrils dilated, her feet moved the pedals with constantly increasing rapidity. Soon I saw a convulsive look in her eyes, her eyelids were lowered, her face turned pale and was thrown backward; hands and legs stopped and became extended; a suffocated cry, followed by a long sigh, was lost in the noise of the workroom. The girl remained motionless a few seconds, drew out her handkerchief to wipe away the pearls of sweat from her forehead, and, after casting a timid and ashamed glance at her companions, resumed her work. The forewoman, who acted as my guide, having observed the direction of my gaze, took me up to the girl, who blushed, lowered her face, and murmured some incoherent words before the forewoman had opened her mouth, to advise her to sit fully on the chair, and not on its edge.

"As I was leaving, I heard another machine at another part of the room in accelerated movement. The forewoman

[20]Pouillet, *L'Onanisme chez la Femme*, Paris, 1880; Fournier, *De L'Onanisme*, 1885; Rohleder, *Die Masturbation*, p. 132.

smiled at me, and remarked that that was so frequent that it attracted no notice. It was specially observed, she told me, in the case of young work-girls, apprentices, and those who sat on the edge of their seats, thus much facilitating friction of the labia.". . .

Sexual irritation may also be produced by the bicycle in women. Thus, Moll[21] remarks that he knows many married women, and some unmarried, who experience sexual excitement when cycling; in several cases he has ascertained that the excitement is carried as far as complete orgasm. This result cannot, however, easily happen unless the seat is too high, the peak in contact with the organs, and a rolling movement is adopted. . . .

Reference may be made at this point to the influence of tight-lacing. This has been recognized by gynaecologists as a factor of sexual excitement and a method of masturbation.[22] Women who have never worn corsets sometimes find that, on first putting them on, sexual feeling is so intensified that it is necessary to abandon their use.[23] The reason of this (as Siebert points out in his *Buch für Eltern*) seems to be that the corset both favors pelvic congestion and at the same time exerts a pressure on the abdominal muscles which brings them into the state produced during coitus. It is doubtless for the same reason that, as some women have found, more distension of the bladder is possible without corsets than with them.

In a further class of cases no external object whatever is used to procure the sexual orgasm, but the more or less voluntary pressure of the thighs alone is brought to bear upon the sexual regions. It is done either when sitting or

[21]*Das Nervose Weib,* 1898, p. 193.

[22]In the Appendix to volume iii of these *Studies,* I have recorded the experience of a lady who found sexual gratification in this manner.

[23]Dr. J. G. Kiernan, to whom I am indebted for a note on this point, calls my attention also to the case of a homosexual and masochistic man (*Medical Record,* vol. xix), whose feelings were intensified by tight-lacing.

standing, the thighs being placed together and firmly crossed, and the pelvis rocked so that the sexual organs are pressed against the inner and posterior parts of the thighs.[24] This is sometimes done by men, and is fairly common among women, especially, according to Martineau,[25] among those who sit much, such as dressmakers and milliners, those who use the sewing-machine, and those who ride. Vedeler remarks that in his experience in Scandinavia, thigh-friction is the commonest form of masturbation in women. . . .

[24]Some women are also able to produce the orgasm, when in a state of sexual excitement, by placing a cushion between the knees and pressing the thighs firmly together.

[25]*Lecons sur les Deformations Vulvaires,* p. 64. Martineau was informed by a dressmaker that it is very frequent in workrooms and can usually be done without attracting attention. An ironer informed him that while standing at her work, she crossed her legs, slightly bending the trunk forward and supporting herself on the table by the hands; then a few movements of contraction of the adductor muscles of the thigh would suffice to produce the orgasm.

Chapter 14

SELF-STIMULATION

Clelland S. Ford, Ph.D.
and Frank A. Beach, Ph.D.

At this point we wish to analyze sexual activity in which a person or animal can indulge alone. Masturbation, for example, may be practiced in solitude and for that reason it is discussed in this chapter even though the same response often occurs when several individuals are together.

MASTURBATION

We define masturbation as any sort of bodily stimulation that results in excitation of the genitals. It commonly involves handling, rubbing or mouthing of the sexual organs, or bringing them into contact with some foreign object. Deliberate excitation of one's own genitals is considered a perversion by many members of our society. The majority

Abridgment of "Self-Stimulation" from *Patterns of Sexual Behavior* by Dr. Clelland S. Ford and Dr. Frank A. Beach. Copyright 1951 by Clelland Stearns Ford and Frank Ambrose Beach. Reprinted by permission of Harper & Row, Publishers, Inc.

of adults condemn masturbation among contemporaries and attempt to prevent children from engaging in such activities. Nevertheless, the behavior is extremely common.

American Men

Kinsey, Pomeroy, and Martin report that 92 percent of American men masturbate to the point of orgasm at least once during their lifetime. Various other workers have estimated that the same statement applies to 85 to 96 percent of males in European countries. Self-masturbation is responsible for the first ejaculation experience by most American boys, and this form of stimulation furnishes the chief source of sexual outlet during the early years of adolescence, during which period it occurs an average of 2.4 times per week. The frequency of masculine masturbation is progressively reduced in post-adolescent years, although it may continue throughout adult life. Kinsey and his collaborators found that 69 percent of American husbands who have graduated from college masturbate at least occasionally. However, males of lower educational levels are apt to stop masturbating at some point in adolescence. They are more likely to consider this practice "unnatural" or "perverted." Men who do not go beyond grade school usually begin to indulge in heterosexual intercourse much earlier than those who are going to college. They have, accordingly, a different source of sexual satisfaction and can dispense with masturbation without becoming sexually inactive. According to Hamilton, autogenital stimulation tends to increase in men during their sixties and may at this time be more frequent than during the preceding two decades. This statement is at variance with the findings of Kinsey and his co-workers.

By far the most common method of masturbation in our society involves manual stimulation of the penis. In a very small proportion of the cases foreign objects are inserted in the urethra or anus as a means of self-stimulation, and a fraction of one percent of the males studied by Kinsey and his collaborators were capable of taking their own penis in their mouth and thus inducing ejaculation.

American Women

Self-stimulation is not limited to the masculine sex in our society. Landis and his co-workers questioned 295 American women and found that 54 percent of them had indulged in masturbation at one time or another. One-quarter of these individuals practiced the habit at least once per week during the period when they were masturbating, and 25 percent of the positive cases had indulged in genital stimulation regularly "over a period of time." The majority of masturbators had begun self-stimulation early in life and tended to cease after adolescence when heterosexual interests became predominant. Hamilton found that 74 percent of a selected group of married women had some experience in masturbation, and Dickinson found the habit to be almost universal in widows over forty years of age. Davis examined 1183 unmarried women with college education and discovered that two-thirds of this number had masturbated at one time or another, although many of these had never induced orgasm in this fashion. One-third of the masturbating individuals ceased the behavior within one year of its inception and one-half of them continued for ten to twenty years.

American men who begin to masturbate and then discontinue the practice usually do so because self-stimulation is replaced by heterosexual intercourse. The same does not appear to hold true for women. Davis analyzed the records of nearly 300 unmarried women who had indulged in masturbation and then given up the practice. Of this total, 230 individuals said they had experienced orgasm, and 65 said they had not. Reasons given for discontinuation of masturbation by the two groups were compared, and the occurrence or nonoccurrence of climax was rarely mentioned. The most common explanation in both groups was fear of the results in terms of physical or mental deterioration. Among the women who had experienced orgasm the second most common reason advanced was that the self-manipulation engendered feelings of shame and disgust. This particular explanation was less often mentioned by individuals lacking the orgasmic experience. Instead, they said that they had "outgrown the habit," "no longer needed" the stimulation, or "had lost desire for it."

The apparent unimportance of orgasm as a determining factor in the decision to stop masturbating may be deceiving. We wonder whether in the one group the actual occurrence of climax was not sufficiently upsetting to evoke inhibitions (e.g., "shame," "disgust," etc.) that prevented complete enjoyment of self-stimulation, thus leading to discontinuation of the practice. And in the other group, the so-called "loss of desire" may very well represent a reaction against the inability to achieve satisfactory orgasm. Although many women who can induce orgasm by masturbating do give up the habit, there is some reason to believe that ability to reach climax in this fashion increases the probability that the masturbation will be continued. Comparison of those women in the Davis study who had stopped with those who persisted in masturbatory practices shows that 97.1 percent of the latter group experienced orgasm, whereas only 74.8 percent of the former reached climax while masturbating.

Additional evidence pointing to the importance of orgasm as a factor affecting duration of masturbatory habits is seen in the fact that 48.8 percent of the women who had never experienced climax stopped masturbating within one year or less after the habit began. But among women who were capable of orgasm as a result of masturbation, only 26.2 percent ceased to indulge in this activity within less than a year from its inception.

At least a few women derive sufficient satisfaction from self-stimulation without climax to continue the practice for long periods of time. Davis describes six long-term masturbators who said they never had an orgasm and two others who were uncertain as to its occurrence. The duration of the habit in these cases ranged from four to 27 years. One 28-year-old woman who had been masturbating for several years wrote, "I believe I have never experienced the orgasm. I have tried in vain to produce it and am still trying."

Masturbatory techniques employed by American women center in most cases around stimulation of the clitoris by means of vulvar friction. Sixty-seven percent of 419 women reporting to Dickinson stated that this was the preferred means of self-stimulation. In 20 percent of the group vaginal sensation was preferred and was evoked by insertion of a foreign object into this organ. For 11 percent of these women masturbation depended upon stimulation of the urethral meatus (external opening of the urinary tract), and in 2 percent of the cases orgasm was regularly induced by pressing the thighs together rhythmically or it occurred spontaneously during sleep.

Evidence concerning the relationship between technique of self-stimulation, and incidence of orgasm is not currently available. Nevertheless, it is probably of considerable significance that clitoris stimulation was stressed by the majority of the women whose masturbatory methods are specified by Dickinson. It might be expected that the most gratifying technique would be the one used by the largest percentage of the women studied.

Attitudes of People in Other Societies

The cross-cultural evidence suggests that adults in other societies rarely engage in autogenital stimulation. But in evaluating ethnological reports it is necessary to hold in mind the fact that some social pressure is leveled against masturbation in nearly all the societies on which we have information, and that informants are likely to underestimate the frequency or to deny the occurrence of behavior that is socially condemned. For most peoples masturbation represents an inferior form of sexual activity in which adults should never participate. An apparent exception are the Lesu of New Ireland, who expect the adult woman to engage in a form of masturbation when sexually excited and lacking a sex partner.

Even among some of the peoples whose sex mores are very free, masturbation on the part of mature persons is considered undesirable. Lepcha men say that they never masturbate; they regard semen as a soiling substance. Siriono men are reported never to engage in autogenital stimulation. They may be observed standing and tugging at the foreskin when preoccupied or worried, but the genital manipulation is not accompanied by erection. The Crow Indians interpret masturbation by an adult as a confession of inability to obtain a lover and therefore something of which a man or woman should be ashamed. Malinowski writes of the Trobrianders:

> Masturbation (*ikivayni kwila:* "he manipulates penis," *isulumomoni:* "he makes semen boil over") is a recognized practice often referred to in jokes. The natives maintain, however, that it would be done only by an idiot . . . or one of the unfortunate albinos, or one defective in speech; in other words, only by those who cannot obtain favors from women. The practice is therefore regarded as undignified and unworthy of a man, but in a rather amused and entirely indulgent manner. Exactly the same attitude is adopted towards female masturbation (*ikivayni wila:* "she manipulates cunnus"; *ibasi wila o yamala:* "she pierces vagina with her hand"). (Malinowski, 1929, pp. 475–476.)

While adult masturbation is generally frowned upon in most societies, a different attitude is often taken toward autogenital stimulation on the part of youngsters and adolescents. There are some peoples, in addition to ourselves, who condemn masturbation regardless of the individual's age, but many societies believe that for the young boy or girl masturbation is a natural and normal activity. Wherever this permissive attitude prevails it appears that autogenital stimulation occurs early in life and is then gradually replaced by other sexual activities.

Masturbatory Behavior in Other Societies

Despite societal disapproval, there is evidence that adult males masturbate, at least occasionally, in a few societies other than our own. Although this behavior is apparently rare, Trukese men are reported to masturbate secretly, particularly while watching women bathe. The Polynesian peoples of Tikopia express distaste for masturbation, but men do induce orgasm manually, and this sometimes takes place in the company of other men. Although the Dahomeans condemn adult masturbation and it is reported to be rare, men occasionally masturbate in secret. Adult natives of the Marianas are said to stimulate themselves, but for fear of public ridicule they do so only in solitude.

The data available indicate that some women in a few societies other than our own occasionally masturbate, although the practice generally meets with social disapproval. The evidence is too fragmentary to permit generalization, but it is of interest to note that in a few cases vaginal insertion of a penis substitute appears to be more common than manipulation of the clitoris, although there is, of course, no assurance that the latter form of stimulation is not combined with insertion. African Azande women use a phallus fashioned from a wooden root; but if she is caught by her husband while masturbating, a wife may be severely beaten. In Siberia, Chukchee women masturbate with the large calf muscle of a reindeer. Tikopia women occasionally insert a manioc root or a banana for self-stimulation, and Crow women rub the clitoris or insert a finger into the vagina in the attempt to obtain sexual satisfaction. Among the Aranda of Australia, women apparently quite often finger the clitoris as a means of erotic stimulation. Powdermaker makes the following interesting statement concerning Lesu women, the one society in which there appears to be no sanction levied against female masturbation:

> A woman will masturbate if she is sexually excited and there is no man to satisfy her. A couple may be having intercourse in the same house, or near enough for her to see them, and she may thus become aroused. She then sits down and bends her right leg so that her heel presses against her genitalia. Even young girls of about six years may do this quite casually as they sit on the ground. The women and men talk about it freely, and there is no shame attached to it. It is a customary position for women to take, and they learn it in childhood. They never use their hands for manipulation. (Powdermaker, 1933, pp. 276–277.)

In this connection it is interesting to note that similar behavior sometimes occurs in American society. After describing certain physical changes in the sexual organs that he considers reliable proof of habits of self-stimulation, R. L. Dickinson adds that puzzling exceptions sometimes occur. Extreme enlargement of the labia minora, which he regards as a sign of masturbatory habits, may occur in female patients who categorically deny that they have ever handled the sex organs or inserted anything in the vagina. The solution is sometimes fairly simple. "For example, there was the patient who constituted a baffling problem because of the extreme frequency of reported orgasm, but without pressure by finger, thighs, pillow or mattress; she was finally observed at one visit to the office to be sitting on her heel" (Dickinson, 1949, p. 55).

Masturbation in Male Animals

Many animals other than man engage in activities that result in stimulation of their own sexual organs. And in at least a few species it is obvious that masturbation is undertaken with the specific purpose of producing an orgasm. This is particularly true of some subhuman primates. It is well known that some captive male apes and monkeys form habits of self-stimulation. The penis is manipulated with a hand or foot, or is taken into the mouth. . . .

Hamilton described masturbation on the part of one of his adult male monkeys but tended to consider this kind of behavior abnormal, and blamed its occurrence upon the "unnatural conditions" under which the animal had lived. Carpenter's field studies of New and Old World monkeys suggest that Hamilton's interpretation was incorrect. Free-living spider monkeys manipulate their sexual organs with the tip of the exceedingly prehensile tail; and comparable reactions occur in several other species.

When he began his observations on free-living rhesus monkeys Carpenter anticipated that some masturbatory behavior would be seen, but only under special conditions. "By *a priori* reasoning it was expected that masturbation would be observed in isolated males or immature males. . . . [However] during this study three observed instances of self-stimulation to the point of ejaculation occurred in adult, mature males during association with females!" (Carpenter, 1942, p. 152).

Case histories which are presented in conjunction with the foregoing quotation show that at least some males that have ample opportunity to copulate with receptive females will nevertheless occasionally indulge in masturbatory behavior. . . .

Male mammals of many subprimate species manipulate the penis with their forepaws or mouths and sometimes employ inanimate objects as a source of genital stimulation.

Sexually excited male porcupines, for example, walk about on three legs while holding one forepaw on the genitals. They also rub the penis and scrotum vigorously against the ground or against any projecting objects that are conveniently placed. . . .

Male elephants sometimes manipulate their semi-erect penis with the trunk. Before and after coitus male dogs and cats regularly lick the phallic organ, often showing convulsive pelvic movements which indicate the stimulatory value of the resulting sensations. . . .

Some male mammals possessing no prehensile appendages are known to stimulate their own genitals. McBride and Hebb recorded a good deal of masturbatory behavior on the part of captive dolphins. One male had a habit of holding his erect penis in the jet of the water intake, and other individuals characteristically rubbed the tumescent organ against the floor of the tank. . . .

Masturbatory Behavior in Female Animals

It is of considerable evolutionary significance that female mammals of most subprimate species indulge in self-stimulation much less frequently than do males. Exceptions do occur. For example, during the breeding season females may rub the swollen vulva against available objects or manipulate the labia with forepaws and mouth. And when they are in heat some females drag the vulva over sticks, stones, or bare patches of ground, depositing odoriferous material that serves to attract and excite the male. . . .

As far as female primates of infra-human species are concerned, three generalizations seem justified. First, as in lower mammals, masturbatory behavior is less frequent in this sex than in the male. Second, such genital stimulation as can be observed in females never produces the clear-cut climactic results that are seen in masturbating males. And, third, when it does occur, feminine masturbation in subhu-

man primates, particularly chimpanzees, more nearly resembles the self-stimulatory activity of women than does
the similar behavior pattern shown by infra-primate
females.

Autogenital manipulation is quite infrequent among
female monkeys. . . . Self-stimulation appears to be equally
rare in wild female monkeys. The female spider monkey
may manipulate her elongated clitoris with the prehensile
tail, but the reaction is neither frequent, vigorous, nor prolonged. . . .

In the great apes, as in monkeys, the tendency toward
autogenital behavior is much weaker in females than in
males. Nevertheless, recognizable attempts at masturbation do appear occasionally; and when this occurs the techniques may be similar to the methods adopted by some
women. . . .

Adult female apes sometimes devote considerable energy and ingenuity to the achievement of vulvar stimulation. . . .

Interpretation of Human Masturbation

In view of the extremely widespread occurrence of autogenital stimulation throughout the class Mammalia it
seems illogical to classify human masturbation as "abnormal" or "perverted." This form of sexual expression appears to have its evolutionary roots in the perfectly normal
and adaptive biological tendency to examine, to manipulate, to clean, and incidentally to stimulate the external
sexual organs. In the course of evolution, as learning ability
increased and individual experience and experimentation
became progressively more important, these reactions assumed a more frankly sexual nature. For many male monkeys and apes, and for some female chimpanzees,
masturbation constitutes a supplement to or a substitute
for coitus. The human capacity for symbolic behavior has

permitted marked increase in the sexual significance of masturbation by linking it with fantasy and imagination. But the basic potentialities are a part of the biological inheritance of the species.

"Spontaneous Orgasm"

One other type of sexual response that occurs without the presence or participation of a second individual is the so-called "spontaneous orgasm." The phrase is set in quotation marks to indicate the difficulty of proving the complete absence of external stimulation. There are a few women and men who say they are capable of inducing a complete sexual climax in themselves by indulging in sexual fantasies. A more common illustration of spontaneous orgasm is the nocturnal emission or "wet dream." Here, however, one cannot entirely rule out the possibility that the genitals have been stimulated to a certain extent by contact with the bedding or night clothes. Nevertheless, the amount of such stimulation probably is not sufficient to account for the resulting phenomenon.

Nocturnal ejaculation occurs in men whose spinal cords have been completely severed. Under such conditions the lower nerve centers responsible for the phenomenon are completely disconnected from the brain. Therefore, erotic dreams are not an essential complement of this response. It seems more probable that sexual dreams associated with genital reflexes are a product of sensations arising in the tumescent phallus.

According to Kinsey, Pomeroy, and Martin, 83 percent of the postpuberal males in our society have ejaculated during sleep at least once in their lives. Individual differences are great, but during the late teens nocturnal emissions occur on an average of once every four weeks. From this age onward they become progressively less frequent and are rare after the age of forty. Relatively few women experience sexual climax during sleep. But spontaneous orgasm can occur in adult females in the absence of any apparent bodily stimulation. As noted above, they sometimes take place in a few extremely responsive women in connection with sexual fantasy, and they are reported to be common in female morphine addicts during periods of enforced withdrawal.

Nocturnal emissions occur in men of other societies, but information as to their frequency is scarce. . . . Dreams involving sexual climax in women, however, are only rarely referred to in the anthropological literature. . . .

Actual ejaculation can occur in some animals while they are asleep. L. R. Aronson has observed erection in sleeping male house cats. Genital tumescence is often accompanied by pelvic movements similar to those occurring in coitus, and fluid collected from the tip of the penis contains large numbers of motile sperm, proving that ejaculation has taken place.

Summary

In this chapter we have considered those forms of sexual behavior that can be indulged in by the individual alone. The activities involved are masturbation and "spontaneous orgasm." It has been shown that societies differ with respect to their attitudes toward self-stimulation; but regardless of the cultural ideals at least a few members of every society do indulge in masturbatory practices. It appears universally true that men are more likely to practice self-stimulation than are women.

Examination of the cross-species evidence has revealed that self-stimulation occurs in many subhuman mammals. In the case of some other primates the behavior is frankly sexual. Male monkeys and apes sometimes induce ejaculation and orgasm by masturbating themselves. It is considered particularly significant that such behavior occurs in wild male primates despite ample opportunity for heterosexual coitus. Equally important is the fact that female monkeys and apes stimulate their own genitals much less frequently than do males.

Among the lower mammals, nibbling, licking, and pawing of the genitals is extremely common, although perhaps more so for males than for females. At this level of the evolutionary scale, however, the behavior has the appearance of self-cleaning, or grooming rather than deliberate self-stimulation. Nevertheless, the genital manipulations of lower mammals probably constitute the prototype of genuine masturbatory behavior which appears at the primate level.

Males of at least a few lower mammalian species sometimes develop a full genital erection during sleep. This reflexive response may be accompanied by copulatory movements and in at least one species it includes the ejaculation of seminal fluid.

The basic mammalian tendencies toward self-stimulation seem sufficiently strong and widespread to justify classifying human masturbation as a normal and natural form of sexual expression. Nevertheless, members of most human societies consider masturbation by adults to be undesirable. We believe that the relative infrequency of self-stimulation among mature people in most societies is a consequence of social conditioning. In the absence of cultural rules against it, such behavior probably would occur much more frequently than it actually does. These generalizations apply particularly to males. The lower frequency of feminine masturbation may well have an evolutionary or biological explanation. The cross-species comparisons strongly suggest that this is the case. . . .

REFERENCES[1]

Aronson, L. R. Behavior resembling spontaneous emissions in the domestic cat. *Journal of Comparative Physiology,* 1949, Vol. XL II, 226–227.

Bingham, H. C. Sex development in apes. *Comparative Psychological Monographs,* 1928, Vol. V., 1–165.

Carpenter, C. R. Sexual behavior of free ranging rhesus monkeys (*Macca mulatta*). I. Specimens, procedures and behavioral characteristics of estrus. II. Periodicity of estrus, homosexual, autoerotic and nonconformist behavior. *Journal of Comparative Psychology,* 1942, Vol. XXXIII, 113–142 and 143–162.

Davis, K. B. *Factors in the sex life of twenty-two hundred women.* New York: Harper, 1929.

Dickinson, R. L. *Human sex anatomy.* (2nd ed.) Baltimore: Williams and Wilkins, 1949.

Dickinson, R. L., & Beam, L. *A thousand marriages.* Baltimore: Williams and Wilkins, 1931.

Firth, R. *We, the Tikopia.* London: Allen and Unwin, Ltd., 1936.

Hamilton, G. V. A study of sexual tendencies in monkeys and baboons. *Journal of Animal Behavior,* 1914, Vol. IV, 295–318.

[1]These references represent only a few of the many listed by Ford and Beach in their book, *Patterns of Sexual Behavior.*

Hamilton, G. V. *A research in marriage.* New York: Boni, 1929.

Kempf, E. J. The social and sexual behavior of infra-human primates with some comparable facts in human behavior. *Psychoanalytic Review,* 1917, Vol. IV, 127–154.

Kinsey, A. C., Pomeroy, W. B., & Martin, C. E. *Sexual behavior in the human male.* Philadelphia: W. B. Saunders, 1948.

Landis, C., Landis, A. T., Bolles, M. M., Metzger, H. F., Pitts, M. W., D'Esopo, D. A., Moloy, H. C., Kleegman, S. J., & Dickinson, R. L. *Sex in development.* New York: Hoeber, 1940.

Malinowski, B. *The sexual life of savages in North Western Melanesia.* 2 Vols. New York: Harcourt, Brace, 1929.

McBride, A. F., & Hebb, D. O. Behavior of the captive bottlenose dolphin, Tursiops truncatus. *Journal of Comparative and Physiological Psychology.* 1948, Vol. XLI, 111–123.

Powdermaker, H. *Life in Lesu.* New York: Norton, 1933.

Shadle, A. R. Copulation in the porcupine. *Journal of Wildlife Management,* 1946, Vol. X, 159–162.

Zuckerman, S. *The social life of monkeys and apes.* London: Kegan Paul, Trench, Truborer, Ltd., 1932.

Chapter 15

THE PENIS

William H. Masters, M.D. and Virginia E. Johnson

Automanipulation

Genital manipulation occurs in earliest infancy in both sexes. The pleasing sensation of genital play in infancy is translated by most men into the active pleasure of tension release engendered by genital manipulation during puberty or the teenage years. The instance of a positive masturbatory history was placed at 92 percent of the total male population by Kinsey and his associates (1948). Their figures generally have been supported in this country and abroad by many similar reports (Dickinson & Beam, 1931; Haire, 1937; Hohman & Schaffner, 1947; Ramsey, 1943; Rohleder, 1902). The age most frequently recalled by the 312 members of the male study-subject population for on-

Abridged from *Human Sexual Response* by William H. Masters and Virginia E. Johnson. Boston: Little Brown and Co., 1966. By permission of Dr. W. H. Masters and the publisher.

set of active masturbatory practices centered around the fourteenth or fifteenth year. Some men described masturbatory patterns starting at the age of 9 or 10, others not until 16 or 18 years. However, by far the greatest onset frequency was concentrated during the immediate post-pubertal years. It may be recalled that all members of both study-subject populations described a positive history of masturbatory facility. . . .

Just as the female, males develop completely individual masturbatory techniques and overt response patterns. This despite the fact that a much higher percentage of boys observe their friends in masturbatory activity than do girls of similar age groups. Some men use the lightest touch on the ventral surface of the penis, some use strong gripping and stroking techniques that for many individuals would be quite objectionable, if not painful. Frequently men prefer stimulation of the glans alone, either confining manipulation to the ventral surface of the penis on or near the frenulum or using the simple finger technique of pulling at or stimulating the entire glans area. These are the exceptions, however, since most men manipulate the shaft of the penis with stroking techniques that encompass the entire organ and vary from man to man in desired rapidity, excursion, and tightness of manual constriction.

Uncircumcised males have not been observed to concentrate specifically on the glans area of the penis. Normally they follow the usual pattern of confining manipulative activity entirely to the penile shaft. Stroking techniques rarely move sufficiently distal on the shaft of the penis to encounter more than the coronal ridge of the glans even late in plateau phase just before ejaculation. For this reason the foreskin (even in those males with marked mobility of this tissue over the subjacent glans) rarely is retracted from the total glans area. Usually only that area of the glans immediately surrounding the urethral meatus is exposed prior to ejaculation. This is obviously a different picture from that occasioned by active intercourse. With full vaginal containment the foreskin not tightly attached to subjacent tissue usually retracts freely from a major portion of the glans during active male coital thrusting before ejaculation.

As the male reaches late plateau levels of sexual tension, the rapidity of manipulative excursion increases, until most men are stroking the penile shaft as rapidly as possible. However, with the onset of the ejaculatory process marked variation has been observed in male manipulative technique. During ejaculation most of the study subjects either cease completely or markedly slow the manual excursion along the penile shaft. Many of the study subjects grip the penile shaft spastically (usually just beneath the glans) and continue this spastic constrictive pressure during the entire ejaculatory process. This reaction may represent an involuntary response pattern similar to that developed during active coition. Many men plunge the penis into deepest possible vaginal containment as ejaculation develops and cease all active pelvic thrusting during the ejaculatory process.

A few study subjects manipulate the penile shaft actively during the ejaculatory process, although almost universally slowing the rapidity of and easing the constrictive tension of the stroking techniques. These men observed during active coition usually avoid spasmodic, deep vaginal containment of the penis with onset of ejaculation and continue coital thrusting during their entire ejaculatory process. No accurate check has been made of this reactive mannerism, but it is estimated that not more than 10 percent of the male study-subject population continued active stroking, either manipulative or coital in origin, during their ejaculatory response.

Many men have reported the penile glans to be quite sensitive to any pressure or containment immediately subsequent to ejaculation. A few of the study subjects develop such a degree of glans sensitivity that they involuntarily protect it against any form of stimulation. These men reject any pattern of continued intravaginal containment after ejaculation because even the low-grade exteroceptive stimulation of the static vaginal barrel is sufficient to distress. Certainly, care is taken by males with postejaculatory glans sensitivity to avoid any continuation of penile stroking after automanipulative orgasm. The sensitivity of the penile glans (like the sensitivity of the clitoral glans) in the immediate postorgasmic period rarely is appreciated by the opposite sex.

REFERENCES[1]

Dickinson, R. L., & Beam, L. *A thousand marriages.* Baltimore: Williams & Wilkins, 1931.

Haire, N. (Ed.) *Encyclopedia of sexual knowledge.* New York: Eugenics Pub. Co., 1937.

Hohman, L. B., & Schaffner, B. The sex lives of unmarried men. *American Journal of Sociology,* 1947, **52,** 501–507.

Kinsey, A. C. et al. *Sexual behavior in the human male.* Philadelphia: W. B. Saunders, 1948.

Ramsey, G. V. The sexual development of boys. *American Journal of Psychology,* 1943, **56,** 217–234.

Rohleder, H. *Die masturbation: Eine monographie für ärzte, pädagogen und gebildete eltern.* (2nd ed.) Berlin: Fischers medizinische Buchhandlung, 1902.

[1]Included here are only a few of the many references which appear in Masters and Johnson's book.

Chapter 16

TECHNIQUES IN SEXUAL AROUSAL

James Leslie McCary, Ph.D.

Probably the most successful way of learning to respond to one's full sexual capacity is through self-stimulation. Masturbation is a perfectly normal, healthy act in boys and girls and in men and women, young and old. Nevertheless, it has long been a subject of great contention, and discussions of it are often rife with ignorance, misinformation, superstition and shame. It is hence scarcely surprising that many people, especially the naive, come to believe that masturbation is an evil, abnormal, or, at best, infantile practice.

Only under extremely rare circumstances can masturbation be considered a sexual abnormality, especially since well over 95% of men and about 70% of women practice it at one time or another (Kinsey et al. a, c). It should be viewed as a sexual problem only when it becomes, as it

Abridged from McCary, J. L., *Human Sexuality,* Second Edition, (New York: D. Van Nostrand Company, 1973), 156–162. *Reprinted by permission of the publisher.*

occasionally does, part of the behavior pattern of psychotic patients, or is utilized as the sole method of sexual outlet when other outlets are readily available. Indeed, those who do not practice masturbation, or have never done so, are far more likely to be suffering from an emotional or sexual problem than those who have masturbatory experience. Suppression of the tendency to masturbate usually occurs when the individual's thinking regarding sexual matters is beclouded with guilt, fear, and perplexity (Ellis a, b).

Long prior to the birth of Hippocrates, the "Father of Medicine," down through the ages to 1900, the medical world remained largely ignorant of cause and effect in sexual behavior. Objectivity and a scientific approach were notoriously lacking in those paltry investigations that were made. Occasionally some brave scientific soul would reach out for enlightenment, but such men were few. Struggles through these dark ages toward an understanding of human sexuality were dealt a near deathblow in the mid-eighteenth century when S. A. D. Tissot of France wrote his Onana, a Treatise on the Diseases Produced by Onanism. Projecting his personal problems, to say nothing of his superabundance of ignorance, into his writings, Tissot wrote of the viciousness of "self-abuse," attributing most of the known medical disorders—including consumption, epileptic seizures, gonorrhea, and insanity—to the loss of semen through masturbation. It was Tissot who introduced the fatuous and totally unscientific idea that the loss of one drop of seminal fluid causes more bodily damage and weakness than the loss of 40 drops of blood (Dearborn).

Tissot's theories captured the attention of many, influencing medical men and laymen alike. Other "authorities" added their views to his until even today there still persist irrational social prohibitions against the perfectly normal, and probably beneficial, act of masturbation (Ellis b). Fortunately, the vast majority of people seem almost ready to accept masturbation for what it is—a not immoral and certainly harmless act of sexual stimulation and relief. The tide of ignorance concerning masturbation began turning in 1891 when Dr. E. T. Brady became one of the first authorities to challenge the concept of masturbation as a pernicious act, but even Brady considered self-stimulation somewhat dangerous (Dearborn).

The hysteria over masturbation reached such a pitch in the late nineteenth century that "depraved" women who resorted to it were frequently forced by their families to submit to a clitoridectomy (the surgical removal of the clitoris) as a method of control. French medical men, furthermore, expressed their dismay at an occupational hazard peculiar to seamstresses: the masturbatory up-and-down movements of their legs as they treadled their sewing machines were wont to cause orgasms. In at least one establishment, a matron was appointed to circulate among the seamstresses to detect runaway machines as the women became caught up in this "horrible" by-product of their profession (Duffy a, b).

Only where abnormality already exists, as in the instance of severely disturbed schizophrenic patients, does the possibility exist that masturbation could be carried to extremes. Nature carefully regulates each individual's sexual activity, and any form of it becomes unpleasant to him when it is overdone. Even in the case of, say, acute schizophrenia, any sexually excessive activity may just as easily involve coitus as masturbation. In either case, the excessive behavior is a symptom of the mental disorder, not the cause of it (Ellis m).

Problems that people tend to consider outgrowths of masturbation in fact existed before masturbation ever occurred. The only conflicts that masturbation generates stem from poor sex education and guilt on the part of parents, teachers, peers, and others who pass on their own disturbed attitudes toward a perfectly normal act (Ellis a, m).

The arguments against masturbation are legion, time-worn and invalid. These are some of the more hackneyed ones:

Only the immature person masturbates. Refutation: Masturbation provides about 50% of the total sexual outlet of unmarried college-educated men between the ages of 26 and 30. Among women, the incidence of masturbation to orgasm increases until middle age, after which time it remains about the same (Kinsey, et al. a, c). The act of masturbation, therefore, can hardly be called immature.

Masturbation is unsocial or antisocial. Refutation: It is true, of course, that masturbation usually takes place when the person is alone. But other forms of sexual behavior, including coitus, likewise are rarely carried out in public view. If a shy or withdrawn person masturbates, he does not become introverted because of masturbation any more than an outgoing popular person who masturbates becomes extroverted because of it.

Masturbating too frequently causes fatigue and physical debilitation. Refutation: The human body exerts excellent control over the amount of sexual activity that the individual engages in. When he has reached the point of satiation, further sexual activity becomes physically unpleasant, so that it is virtually impossible for him to indulge in "too much sex." In any case, there is no logic in the premise that one form of sexual functioning more than another generates debility and fatigue. An orgasm is an orgasm, whether it is the result of coitus, heavy petting, or masturbation. When the body is orgasmically surfeited from any sexual activity, further sexual functioning is most unlikely to occur, if not altogether impossible.

Sexual fantasies associated with masturbation are emotionally unhealthy. Refutation: Fantasy is inescapably a part of human existence; few today would argue with the postulate that what is universal in human nature is also normal and acceptable. Our conscious mental state involves a continuous flow of fantasy, sexual and otherwise, whether of fleeting images or protracted, volitional daydreams.

Daydreams that are not purely fanciful play, in fact, an extremely important role in planning for the future, as we imagine ourselves in a series of life situations. We reject some prospects and accept others, according to our reactions to the imagined conditions. Erotic fantasies are no less important in planning for a satisfying future sexual life. Indeed, they can help the individual to formulate his code of behavior by providing him some advance perception of the negative consequences of certain actions—e.g., the guilt feelings or pregnancy that might result from premarital coitus.

Sexual fantasy does not occur only during masturbation. It can take place in the absence of any sexual activity whatever, in the course of coition, and in homosexual contact, as well as during masturbation (Sullivan). Its effects can be beneficial, indifferent, or detrimental, regardless of what form of sexual activity (or inactivity) it accompanies. Thus the married couple who have been titillated by sexual fantasies during the day will quite likely find coitus more exciting than usual that night. But when a shy, inhibited young person allows his endless romantic or sexual fantasy to impede him from facing actual encounters with members of the opposite sex, the daydreaming cannot be called healthy.

A woman may fantasize, quite normally, of being wooed and seduced by her church's choir director while she is, in fact, masturbating (or having sexual intercourse with her husband). To allow herself actually to be seduced by the choir director might well be a self-defeating, unhealthy act—and even a dangerous one should the husband learn of it. While it is quite normal, and actually rather common, for a woman to fantasy being made love to simultaneously by several men, and perhaps by a woman or two, it may well be a sign of maladjustment if she permits such an act to actually occur, for she then must contend not merely with her psyche, but with the law and her reputation as well.

As a further example, a young soldier separated from his wife may fantasy sex relations with a voluptuous bar-girl while masturbating, thereby preserving his ideal of marital fidelity. Yet another young husband separated from his wife may indulge in the same fantasies, but not masturbate, because masturbation violates his religious principles. Since his sexual tensions heighten his irascibility and interfere with his attending to his duties, sexual fantasy in his case cannot be considered beneficial.

All in all, it would seem more healthy than unhealthy that fantasy accompany masturbation; otherwise, masturbation becomes a mechanical, somewhat dehumanized form of sexual release. On the other side of the coin, fantasy—with or without masturbation—would appear detrimental to a young person (particularly) if so much time is invested in its pursuit that schoolwork is left undone and grades drop.

Another negative aspect of sexual fantasy lies in the person's attitude toward it. If he regards it as the equivalent of "dirty thoughts," it can only produce guilt feelings and anxiety. Rather than give up fantasy, however, it would seem more appropriate for the individual to attempt to break down his inhibitions against it.

As already suggested, a further danger—although, statistically, a remote one—is that the fantasy could become harmful or even dangerous if the individual were to attempt to translate daydreams of unacceptable behavior into actuality. But the chicken-or-egg controversy immediately arises: do the unacceptable desires arise from the subject matter of the fantasy, or the reverse? In any case, the content of daydreams no less than nocturnal dreams may give the therapist a key in unraveling some psychological difficulties that the individual may be experiencing.

Masturbation is sexually frustrating and not as satisfactory as sex relations with a partner. Refutation: Masturbation is frustrating only when the person feels guilt or shame about it, or when he expects more from it than is reasonable. It is certainly true that heterosexual relations are usually preferable to solitary masturbation. But if coitus is for some reason not possible or advisable, masturbation offers a satisfactory substitute in the release of sexual tension. In the case of women, furthermore, masturbation may be the only means of achieving orgasm (Ellis a; "M"; Sullivan). One additional note: women observed during various sexual acts in a laboratory setting reported that orgasms resulting from such direct but noncoital methods as masturbation were physiologically more satisfying than those produced coitally, although the latter were more satisfying emotionally (Masters and Johnson n).

Certainly it is advisable, if an individual has anxieties concerning masturbation, and if self-stimulation causes him extreme guilt, that he avoid it until the underlying psychological problem is corrected. Similarly, if one has extreme and severe guilt about head-scratching, one should also avoid head-scratching until the underlying psychological difficulty in that instance is rectified.

The technique of masturbation customarily used by men is to grip the penis and move the hand back and forth at the desired pressure and tempo along the length of the penile shaft. The glans is stimulated somewhat as it is by in-and-out body movements during penile penetration of the vagina. The degree of pressure, the speed of stroking, and the use or nonuse of lubrication naturally vary from man to man.

About 67% of women who masturbate prefer to stimulate the clitoris by manual or digital friction of the vulval region (Ford and Beach b), although Masters and Johnson's research indicates that arousal is best accomplished when the stimulation is to the side of the clitoris rather than on the clitoris directly (Masters and Johnson n). About 20% of women prefer vaginal stimulation to other methods, and insert foreign objects into the vagina during masturbation; about 11% prefer stimulation of the urethral meatus; and 2% attain orgasm by pressing their thighs together in a rhythmical manner (Ford and Beach b). Some women achieve self-arousal and orgasm through directing a stream of water onto the genitals while bathing—either from the faucet of a tub or from the peppery spray of a shower (Kronhausen and Kronhausen). The running water provides a continuous pressure, with just enough variation in constancy to satisfy the physiological requirements involved in producing an orgasm. Women describe the sensation received from this method of self-arousal as being somewhat similar to that created by an electric vibrator, although less intense. Perhaps the use of water in self-stimulation has some psychological advantage in that an unconscious need to "cleanse away the guilt" engendered by masturbation is satisfied along with the sexual need. . . .

LEARNING ABOUT ONE'S OWN SENSUALITY

As described vividly in the best seller *The Sensuous Woman* ("J"), women can learn to heighten their sexual responsiveness through certain exercises. The woman who, because of a lifetime of sexual taboos and restrictions, is not freely responsive to sexual stimulation is advised to explore and experiment with her body to uncover its full sensitivity. She can begin by exercising her tactile senses while blind-folded. She can slowly and gently feel objects of different textures, allowing the resulting tactile sensations to become firmly fixed in her memory. She can then lightly stimulate various parts of her nude body with furry or fluffy material.

She is advised to relax by lingering in a hot bath while all stresses of the day float away. After delicately drying her body, she should stretch, roll, curl up, and otherwise ma-neuver herself in her bed, mist-sprayed with cologne, as she listens to music, with a flickering candle as the only source of illumination. She should follow this bit of self-indul-gence by delicately rubbing and massaging her breasts, abdomen, and other curves of her body with her favorite lotion, all the while making herself as acutely aware as possible of the various tactile sensations that she is experi-encing.

Since the mouth and tongue are highly important in lovemaking, the woman who wishes to develop her sensu-ousness should practice various flicking, stretching, clock-wise, and counterclockwise movements of the tongue. These maneuvers can be practiced by running her tongue over her palms, between her fingers, and on her wrists and arms. She can also use an ice-cream cone, directing her tongue in various swirling patterns on the ice cream. This exercise not only enhances the finesse of tongue movement but also allows a woman to fantasy her own body's being thus caressed and stimulated by her lover.

The woman who wants to give and gain the greatest pleasure from lovemaking must practice muscle control. She must learn techniques of strengthening, tightening, and controlling muscles of the vagina, abdomen, back, and gluteal area. She is also advised to learn to coordinate her body movements with those of her lover; one of the best ways that this can be accomplished is through dancing. She should close her eyes and allow her body to melt into his

and be led by him throughout the steps. She should concentrate on the feel of his body next to hers as they become
attuned in rhythm, movement, and style. The feeling of
sensuousness is also heightened if a woman permits herself
the luxury of beautiful, delicate, and high-quality lingerie;
a sensitive and responsive body deserves such pampering
("J").

Learning to masturbate successfully is probably the
most important step for the woman in learning to come to
orgasm easily and quickly: she learns what is required of
herself and of her lover to give her the fullest sexual response. In addition, learning to breathe in a manner to
reduce muscular tension is a valuable lesson in training
oneself to reach orgasm. Tension begins to build with inha-
lation but is released with exhalation. Proper breathing can
remove muscular tension from the groin, the pelvis, and
buttocks, producing a warm and tingling sense of aliveness
in the genital area that can add significantly to sexual pleasure and orgasmic response. Freedom from muscular tension, coupled with free, uninhibited fantasy of an erotic
subject that her sexual imaginativeness can conjure up, are
essential "keys to sexual heaven" (Hamilton).

*BIBLIOGRAPHY

Dearborn, L. W. Masturbation. In M. F. DeMartino (Ed.), *Sexual behavior and personality characteristics.* New York: Grove, 1966.

Duffy, J. (a) Masturbation and clitoridectomy, *Journal of the American Medical Association,* 1963, **19** 246–248. (b) Masturbation and clitoris amputation. *Sexology,* May 1964, 668–671.

Ellis, A. (a) *Sex without guilt.* New York: Lyle Stuart, 1958. (b) *The art and science of love.* New York: Lyle Stuart, 1960. (m) Masturbation. In M. F. DeMartino (Ed.), *Sexual behavior and personality characteristics.* New York: Grove, 1966.

Ford, C. S., & Beach, F. A. (a) *Patterns of sexual behavior.* New York: Harper, 1951. (b) Self-stimulation. In M. F. DeMartino (Ed.), *Sexual behavior and personality characteristics.* New York: Grove, 1966.

Hamilton, E. Emotions and sexuality in the woman. In H. A. Otto (Ed.), *The new sexuality.* Palo Alto: Science and Behavior, 1971.

"J." *The sensuous woman.* New York: Lyle Stuart, 1969.

Kinsey, A. C., Pomeroy, W. B., & Martin, C. E. (a) *Sexual behavior in the human male.* Philadelphia: Saunders, 1948. (c) & Gebhard, P. H. *Sexual behavior in the human female.* Philadelphia: Saunders, 1953.

*These are only a few of the many references listed by J. L. McCary in his book, *Human Sexuality.*

Kronhausen, P., & Kronhausen, E. *The sexually responsive woman.* New York: Ballantine, 1965.

"M." *The sensuous man.* New York: Lyle Stuart, 1971.

Masters, W. H., & Johnson, V. E. (n) *Human sexual response.* Boston: Little, Brown, 1966.

Sullivan, P. R. What is the role of fantasy in sex? *Medical aspects human sexuality,* April 1969, 79–89.

Chapter 17

CHANGES IN MASTURBATORY ATTITUDES AND BEHAVIOR

Morton Hunt

ATTITUDE CHANGES TOWARD MASTURBATION IN THE PAST GENERATION

The tradition concerning masturbation is over two millenia old, while the countertradition barely existed two decades ago and has become a significant force only in the past ten years. That being the case, one could hardly expect the massive bulwark of tradition to have been completely torn down since Kinsey's time, nor has it been. Nonetheless, our data show that it has been badly battered and frequently breached; the classic attitudes toward masturbation, the frequency of masturbation (especially in adults) and the feelings of most masturbators about their own behavior have all undergone changes of striking magnitude and importance.

As one measure of attitude change, we offered questionnaire respondents the simplistic moral platitude "Masturbation is wrong," asking them to signify agreement or disagreement.* It might have been useful to have asked, in separate questions, whether they considered it wrong for children, and wrong for adults. Since, however, this item occurred in the context of a long series of other attitude questions relating to adult sexual practices, it is reasonable to assume that the replies refer essentially to postadolescent masturbation. Unfortunately, there is no comparable body of attitude data from the 1940s against which to contrast our own. Even Kinsey, though he had much to say about attitudes toward masturbation, presented little statistical information about them. But we are justified in assuming that any significant difference in attitudes between the older people in our sample and the younger ones would be at least a partial measure of the change occurring in the past generation: The 35-and-over respondents, even if they have been somewhat influenced by the new voices, will tend to reflect primarily the dominant social attitudes of their own formative period (roughly, 1915 to 1945) while the under-35 respondents will reflect the impact of the liberalizing influences existing during the past 30 years. And whatever change we do find, we can feel fairly sure that it will augur still greater change in the next generation, for as the attitudes of young parents grow more permissive, they will be less likely to impose guilt feelings upon their own children—who, in turn, will be even more receptive to scientific findings and nonmoralistic views concerning masturbation.

*As with other attitude questions, respondents were offered five choices: Agree strongly, Agree somewhat, Disagree somewhat, Disagree strongly, Have no opinion. Since both "strong" and "somewhat" responses to this question proved to be of roughly equal dimensions, we present the results in collapsed (combined) form. Except where otherwise noted, the percentages are based on those who made some reply, the nonanswerers being omitted from our calculations.

What, then, does our survey reveal? Somewhat to our own surprise we find that, even in the older half of our sample, men and women are not generally harsh in their views on masturbation: For each man who agrees that masturbation is wrong, a little over two others disagree; and even among women, who have traditionally been sexually more conservative than men, for each one who agrees that it is wrong, two others disagree. We cannot take these data to mean that a majority of older people think well, or approvingly, of masturbation; in all likelihood they still regard it as immature behavior or as indicative of personal inadequacy, and probably most of those older people who sometimes masturbate still experience guilt feelings or self-contempt. Nevertheless, the majority of the older half of our sample has at least begun to repudiate the categorical moral condemnation of masturbation taught them during their own childhood.

Table 9   Masturbation is Wrong: Total Sample,
Percents Agreeing

	18–24	25–34	35–44	45–54	55 and over
Males	15	16	27	28	29
Females	14	17	27	33	36

In the younger half of the sample, however, the vote is considerably clearer: For every male who says masturbation is wrong, five others say it is not; and the same ratio holds true among females. What is even more remarkable is the evidence of a withering away of the moralistic tradition decade by decade. We can see a continuing long-term shrinkage of disapproval when we look at our entire sample arranged by age (see Table 9). And Table 10 presents the corollary set of data, showing the increasing percentages of people who, decade by decade, have adopted the viewpoint of the countertradition.

Table 10   Masturbation is Wrong: Total Sample,
Percents Disagreeing

	18–24	25–34	35–44	45–54	55 and over
Males	80	81	67	67	63
Females	78	77	68	55	52

We were concerned that there might be a bias in these figures, since a sizable fraction of the younger age groups consisted of single people and it is reasonable to suppose that single people might be more inclined to justify masturbation than those who are not so often in need of it. But when we examined the responses of married people alone, we found that, age group for age group, the percentages of those who regard masturbation as wrong and those who do not were almost identical with those for the total sample. The counter-tradition is affecting not only those who currently benefit the most from it but nearly everyone in the younger segment of American society.

Kinsey and various other observers had noted that the taboos against masturbation were distinctly stronger at lower social levels of the population and among the less-educated than at higher levels and among the college-educated.[1] Our data indicate that this is still so. Both at the blue-collar and the white-collar occupational level, and among noncollege-educated people as well as college-educated, the traditional view is being eroded; the under-35 half of the sample is distinctly more permissive about masturbation than the 35-and-older half in every category. But the gap between the occupational categories and the gap between the educational categories does not narrow, among the young, as we reported it does elsewhere; in some cases it even seems to widen. This does not mean that blue-collar and noncollege-educated people have become more conservative about masturbation; in all likelihood, it simply indicates that among the more articulate parts of the society the permissive trend has developed faster. Perhaps this is truer of masturbation than of most other forms of sexual activity; people now freely discuss all kinds of sexual acts—and so strip away their traditional hostility toward them—but autoeroticism, by virtue of its historic position as the lowliest and most ignoble sexual act, is less freely discussed than other acts. This being so, it would follow that the more articulate part of the public would adopt the new outlook more rapidly than the less articulate part.

Changes in Masturbatory Behavior: Accumulative Incidence and Age at First Experience

It is, however, in measurements of actual behavior that we find more concrete and telling evidence of the extent to which masturbation has been stripped of much of its culturally imposed burden of sin, pathology and shame. One might suppose that the most obvious indication of that change would be in a marked increase in the total percentage of males and females who have ever masturbated. But while this is a revealing parameter for most kinds of formerly disapproved or deviant behavior, it is not so in the case of masturbation, an act so simple, so biologically natural and so likely to be spontaneously discovered on one's own that it has probably always been a part of the total life experience of nearly all men and a majority of women. This was known, at least intuitively, to most sex researchers prior to Kinsey, and confirmed and quantified by his finding that in his very large sample of Americans the accumulative incidence of masturbation, ever, or to orgasm, was 92 percent for males and for females was 62 percent ever, and 58 percent to orgasm.[2] ("Accumulative incidence" was Kinsey's projection of the ultimate lifetime experience of his total sample.) Our own results look virtually identical—94 percent of our males and 63 percent of our females have masturbated at some time—but this is not an accumulative incidence; it represents what has happened up to this time, in the lives of our respondents. Presumably, some of the younger people in the sample and at least a few of the more mature people who have not yet experienced masturbation will still do so during their lifetimes. Accordingly, our incidence data suggest at least a small overall increase since Kinsey's time.*

But where a sexual act had been experienced by nearly all males and by most females even before the advent of sexual liberation, we must look for change by means of more subtle tests, such as how early in life people first do it, how often they do it, when and why they do it and how they feel about it. The first of these tests is based on the common-sense assumption that the total weight of parental, religious and social disapproval, plus the warnings of folklore and the medical profession, will delay the beginning of masturbation until the growing power of the sexual drive and the increasing strength of the teen-age or young-adult ego breaks through the psychosocial barriers. The corollary assumption would be that if those barriers have been weakened, the breakthrough will come sooner after puberty, or even concomitantly with it.

And we do, in fact, find that just such a shift has taken place. In Kinsey's sample, 45 percent of all males had masturbated by the time they were 13;[3] in our own sample, fully 63 percent have done so by that age. Among the females the shift is, as we might have anticipated, still more striking, since they have traditionally been subject to far greater psychosocial inhibiting forces than males. In Kinsey's sample only 15 percent had masturbated to orgasm by the time

*Here, as in almost all of our comparisons with Kinsey's data, we have omitted our black respondents, in order to make the comparison with Kinsey's all-white sample as close as possible.

they were 13,[4] while in our own sample the figure is 33 percent, or more than twice as large. In every age grouping, our males and females seem to have begun somewhat earlier, on the average, than Kinsey's people in comparable age groupings a generation ago. Even within our own sample, our younger people started earlier than our older people. Evidently it has been far easier for people passing through adolescence and the teens in the past decade or so to perceive masturbation as acceptable, at least internally, than it was for people in their parents' generation.

Even those who are restrained by fear, guilt or ignorance tend today to acquire liberating information as they grow older, or, in the case of females, to experience masturbation in petting or marital sexual relations, and to try it themselves thereafter. As a result, more of the young married females in our sample have masturbated, at least at some time, than have our older females. The same change is revealed by a comparison of our figures with Kinsey's: 44 percent of his married females had experienced masturbation at some time or other while married,[5] as against 61 percent of ours.

Thus, even though our overall total incidences of masturbation are only slightly larger than Kinsey's accumulative incidences, there has been a major change in the age at which masturbation is first experienced: Both sexes are beginning it earlier than formerly, although females still begin masturbating, on the average, a good deal later than males, many females doing so for the first time in their dating or early marital years.

The tendency for both boys and girls to masturbate earlier does not, however, mean that it is now largely devoid of struggle and inner conflict. Americans exhibit a very wide range of feelings about their own desires to masturbate, some being thoroughly liberated from the tradition, a majority being partially liberated and ambivalent, and a minority still having the powerful negative feelings about it that their great-grandparents did. Working-class men and women, and men and women without any college education, are still distinctly more apt to be troubled by their own masturbatory desires or acts, or to believe the folklore warnings about it, than are white-collar men and women, and men and women who have had at least some college education. Even more marked is the restraining effect of religion, though only on women. Those who attend services frequently, whether Protestant, Catholic or Jewish, are distinctly less apt ever to have masturbated than those who never attend services, as Table 11 illustrates:

Table 11   Ever Masturbated: All Faiths, by Regularity of Church Attendance, Percents

	Regular churchgoers	Irregular churchgoers	Non-churchgoers
Males	92	92	93
Females	51	69	75

The survey data and the interviews suggest, moreover, that among those who have ever masturbated, strong religious feelings tended to delay the beginning of such activity for both males and females. . . .

CHANGES IN MASTURBATORY BEHAVIOR: FREQUENCY, CONTINUING USE, USE BY THE MARRIED

The earlier beginning of masturbation in the adolescent years thus does reveal, more sharply than the increase in total incidence, the impact of sexual liberation on contemporary behavior. But even more interesting and meaningful revelations emerge from an analysis of the frequency of masturbation, the number of years during which it is actively used and the continued use of masturbation beyond the adolescent years and early teens by adults, and particularly by the married, for whom heterosexual contact is easily and more or less continuously available.

We begin with the hypothesis that the past generation of sexual liberation should have resulted in measurable increases both in the active incidence* and in the frequency of masturbation by late teen-agers and young single adults; but, more than that, we hypothesize that there should also be increases in both the active incidence and frequency of continued masturbation by married adult males and females. These hypotheses may seem strange to some readers. Surely (they may argue) an increase in masturbation by single people in their late teens or early adulthood would be no evidence of liberation, since the genuinely liberated should be enjoying more frequent and satisfying intercourse, and ought not need self-relief; by the same token, and all the more so, an increase in masturbation by the married would not be evidence of salutary sexual liberation but an indication of a spreading inability of contemporary men and women to achieve sexual satisfaction with each other in marriage.

We agree that a high frequency of masturbation in a single person can be symptomatic of gross inadequacy in heterosexual relationships or of neurotic compulsions, and that masturbation by a married person may be the result of marital conflict, impotence or frigidity. But nothing else

*"Active incidence" signifies the percentage of an age group who have performed the activity in question within a specified period of time; e.g., if half of all females aged 18 to 24 masturbated at least once while they were in that age bracket, the active incidence for the 18–to–24 cohort would be 50 percent; or if half of all females masturbated while they were 18, the active incidence for age 18 would be 50 percent.

"Accumulative incidence," as indicated earlier, signifies the total percentage who have ever performed the activity in question, even once, within a lifetime, or up to any specified age.

about our overall sample or any component part of it indicates a rise in the overall incidence of sexual, psychological or marital pathologies, as compared to Kinsey's era, and it therefore seems unlikely that they account for any significant increases we find in masturbation rates.

We also agree that sexual liberation should result in more frequent, varied and satisfying intercourse for both single and married persons, but this need not preclude a simultaneous rise in masturbation; the two things could be compatible and coexisting results of the same cause. Indeed, as we will see in later chapters, our males and females, single and married alike, are generally having more frequent, more varied and more satisfying coital experiences than their counterparts of a generation ago. Any increase in masturbation is therefore not a case of *faute de mieux* but a natural and normal result of the lessening of psychosocial restraints against most forms of sexual expression.

This is not to argue that masturbation is a *should* for every liberated man or woman, or that those adults who never practice it are necessarily unliberated; the use of masturbation ought to be a matter of preference and need. There are many who find it so unrewarding compared to intercourse—for which they have ample opportunity—that they very rarely or never have any desire to masturbate; but there are others who, even though paired or happily married, do have occasion to need one or more of the various benefits offered by masturbation. The easing of inner restraints and of social disapproval does not force anyone to masturbate; it merely makes masturbation acceptable in situations where it can satisfy an unfilled want.

This is a very different thing from those special cases in which a man or woman masturbates compulsively, or relies on masturbation because other and more rewarding kinds of sexual satisfaction lie outside his or her capabilities. Certain militant feminists, denigrating the nature of heterosexual interaction, have urged women to use vibrators or their own fingers for sexual relief, and have waxed rhapsodic over the fact that a woman can give herself numerous orgasms in a single uninterrupted session. But while this kind of performance results in total sexual satiety, it yields none of the complex emotional satisfactions, and none of the replenishment of the ego, produced by loving heterosexual intercourse. Masters and Johnson, while judging the masturbatory orgasm to be physiologically more powerful in women than coital orgasm, noted drily that, nonetheless, it is "not necessarily as satisfying as that resulting from coition."[6] The few compulsive masturbators among our interview subjects all boastfully accounted for their masturbation as necessitated by their unusually powerful sexual desires and capacity—but in truth they seemed more driven than desirous, more sated than satisfied by their masturbating, and without exception they had only shallow and brittle relationships with their sexual partners. This statement by a 35-year-old man is illustrative:

> I can have sex for two hours with a girl, and half an hour later I'll wake up completely turned on, and have to masturbate to get back to sleep. I can come in a woman and stay hard, which is very strange, and not feel I've had enough. My whole life is oriented towards sex—everything I do is aimed at getting it—but I get a *mental* satisfaction out of balling, not a *sexual* satisfaction; I don't know if that makes any sense. Anyway, I masturbate at least once a day, whether or not I've been with a girl that day, because I need it.

But such cases are the exception; from other data yielded by our survey and from the general tenor of the interviews we conducted, it is clear that neither compulsive masturbation nor frenzied hedonism accounts for any overall increase we may find in general masturbatory activity, especially beyond the adolescent years; rather, it is explainable as one result of the unleashing of natural sexual desires, concomitant with the increased use of formerly rare techniques of coital foreplay and of variant coital positions, and the increased frequency, duration and enjoyment of heterosexual intercourse.

These being our hypotheses, what do we find? First, let us look at the experience of young single males. In Kinsey's survey more than four out of five single young men had masturbated at least once within a five-year period. In precise terms, the active incidence for single males between the ages of 16 and 20 was 88 percent, and for single males between 21 and 25, 81 percent.[7] Our most nearly comparable group consists of a cohort ranging from 18 to 24 years in age; data for that group should compare well with Kinsey's two cohorts combined and recalculated. For our cohort the active incidence is 86 percent—exactly the same as for his two cohorts recalculated as one. But this does not mean that there has been no increase in active incidence, for we defined it much more narrowly than Kinsey did: We took it to mean any activity within a one-year period, while he took it to mean any activity within a five-year period. Obviously, if we had used the five-year measurement, our active-incidence figures would have been higher than they are, though by how large a percentage we cannot say. In any event, since our figures are almost identical to Kinsey's, it is clear that there has been an increase of some sort in the active incidence of masturbation by single males between the ages of 18 and 24.

We can make a somewhat more precise statement concerning the frequency with which these active individuals masturbate. In Kinsey's sample the median frequency for those single males in the 16–to–20 cohort who were masturbating was 57 times a year, and in the 21–to–25 cohort, 42 times a year.[8] Taking into account the size of these two samples and their age distribution, the Kinsey rate with which our own median frequency should be compared is 49 times a year; in our own sample the actual median proves to be just under 52 a year. There is thus evidence of at least a small increase in this age group.

A more striking change, however, is the far greater tendency of young single men in recent years to continue masturbating beyond their teens and into early adulthood. In Kinsey's sample, by age 30 over a fifth of his single men had ceased being "active" masturbators,[9] while in our own sample less than a tenth had stopped—this despite the fact that our males have more opportunity for, and experience of, coitus than their predecessors. Even more striking is the contrast in frequencies. By age 30 those of Kinsey's single males who were masturbating at all were doing so about 30 times a year (this, again, is the median, or most typical, rate),[10] while the median for our own comparable sample is a little over 60 times a year—even higher than for the younger cohort in our sample.

With women, some of the changes are far greater, and genuinely remarkable. A generation ago only a little over a quarter of all single girls in their upper teens, and only a little over a third of those in their early twenties, were masturbating;[11] today over 60 percent of girls 18 to 24 are doing so. (Once again, we must point out that even this remarkable increase understates the reality, since our definition of active incidence is so much more restrictive than was Kinsey's.) There is also a sharp increase in typical frequency as shown by medians: Kinsey's active single females in this age span were masturbating about 21 times a year;[12] our own do so about 37 times a year.

Beyond the age of 24 our sample is too small for statistically rigorous comparisons; it is at least suggestive, however, that by their late twenties and early thirties nearly half of Kinsey's single women were masturbating,[13] while over four-fifths of our comparable sample are doing so.

As interesting as the foregoing contrasts may be, what

is far more interesting, and even astonishing, is the evidence of greatly increased use of masturbation by younger married men and women. Prior to Kinsey there had been almost no systematic collection of data in this area; it seems to have been taken for granted that masturbation all but ceased when marriage began. It was, therefore, startling—and at the same time immensely guilt-relieving to many persons—when Kinsey revealed in 1948 and 1953 that far larger numbers of young husbands and wives were masturbating, and far more often, than anyone had supposed. In their late twenties and in their early thirties, for instance, over four out of ten husbands still masturbated from time to time, their median frequency being about half a dozen times per year.[14] Today, half again as many husbands (72 percent) in our most nearly comparable cohort masturbate, and with a median frequency of about 24 times per year, a truly remarkable increase. In Kinsey's sample about a third of all wives in the same age range masturbated, and with a median frequency of some 10 times per year.[15] Today, although the median frequency is the same, over twice as many wives in this age group (68 percent) are actively involved.

In sum, far more women, both single and married, and far more married men masturbate today than formerly, and while typical frequencies have increased only slightly for young single men and not at all for married women, they have risen considerably for single women, single men of 30 and married men. These changes, though confusing at first sight, have a common thread of causality in the central ethos of sexual liberation. Formerly, men felt that masturbation was more or less acceptable for adolescents and even teenagers, but not for young adults and certainly not married adults. They now see no evil in the practice at any time, if it does not preempt or replace heterosexual coitus. Formerly, girls were far more inhibited about masturbating than boys, and even in adulthood wives were, in general, somewhat less likely than husbands ever to permit themselves the solace of masturbation. Today, both young single females and adult married females have moved much closer to the male patterns of behavior as they are today, in consonance with the basic egalitarianism of sexual liberation.

The principal inhibitory demographic factors identified by Kinsey were lower occupational level, lower educational level and religious devoutness. These factors tended to reduce the likelihood that the individual would ever masturbate, or to delay the first such experience or restrict the incidence of active masturbation.[16] Today, the only one of these factors that still has significant influence is religious devoutness. In our sample, the nonreligious are more likely to masturbate, to start doing so early and to continue doing so in adult life and even (though at a reduced rate) in married life than are the devout. But here, as in most other areas, the inhibitory force is operating less effectively among the young than among older people.

Religious preference still has some noteworthy correlations with masturbatory activity, as it did a generation ago. To be sure, in our sample religious preference is somewhat allied with religious devoutness, the Jews being the least religious, the Protestants more so, and the Catholics most of all. But there are two correlations that deserve mention. First, while Catholics and Protestants have similar patterns of activity, Catholics who are active masturbators masturbate more frequently than Protestants. One might speculate that the relieving effect of confession makes it easier for them to perform the act without prolonged guilt feelings. Second, a much higher proportion of Jewish men than of Catholic or Protestant are currently active masturbators. Jewish women, too, are more likely to be active masturbators than non-Jewish women, though by a narrower margin.

At first glance, the large active incidence of masturbation for Jewish men is mystifying in view of the historical origins of the condemnation of masturbation and the severity with which it has been punishable in orthodox Judaism. We can suggest several explanations. One, already mentioned, is that our sample includes a smaller proportion of orthodox Jews than of devout Protestants and devout Catholics (orthodox Jews are ethnically somewhat insular and defensive, and thus hard to reach by sampling techniques). Another is that our Jewish sample is weighted toward higher occupational and educational levels, which introduces a liberal bias. Finally, Judaism, for all its moral strictness about sexual matters, has never been as generally ascetic and antisexual as was Christianity for most of the centuries since its beginnings. Kinsey, though his data on this point were admittedly inadequate, seemed to find Jewish husbands somewhat more active sexually with their wives than non-Jewish husbands.[17] Our data, though rather imperfect, seem to show that Jewish husbands are no less active, within marriage, than non-Jewish husbands. If Jewish men, and especially Jewish husbands, masturbate more than non-Jews, it is not because they are all Portnoys, afflicted and compulsive, but perhaps because they are somewhat less blocked, by culture and upbringing, from perceiving masturbation as a normal and legitimate sexual activity.

NOTES

1. Kinsey (1948), pp. 339–43; (Kinsey 1953), p. 190. Note, however, that for females, the social taboo seemed to make little difference in either accumulative or active incidence: Kinsey (1953), pp. 182–83.

2. Kinsey (1948), pp. 499–500; Kinsey (1953), pp. 142, 177, 180.

3. Kinsey (1948), p. 500. This is a "U.S. Correction," but even if we use the raw data and exclude the 0–8 educational level for closer comparability to our own sample, the accumulative incidence by age 13 would be only about 50 percent, or considerably lower than our figure.

4. Kinsey (1953), p. 141, (Fig. 9).

5. Kinsey (1953), p. 177. Actually, this is the accumulative incidence for the oldest cohort in Kinsey; an overall figure more closely comparable to our own would be on the order of 40 percent or less.

6. Masters and Johnson (1966), p. 118.

7. Kinsey (1948), p. 240.

8. Same as Note 7.

9. Same as Note 7; also Kinsey (1948), p. 270 (Fig. 55).

10. Same as Note 7; also Kinsey (1948), p. 271 (Fig. 58).

11. Kinsey (1953), p. 178.

12. Same as Note 11.

13. Same as Note 11.

14. Kinsey (1948), p. 241.

15. Kinsey (1953), p. 178.

16. Kinsey (1948), pp. 507–9, Kinsey (1953), pp. 148–58 (N.B.: Overall, parental occupational level was only weakly correlated with the inhibition of masturbation, nonetheless, for some cohorts the correlation is considerable enough to merit inclusion on our list).

17. Kinsey (1948), p. 482, comparing medians for inactive Jews and inactive Protestants. No medians of marital coitus for inactive Catholics are included, but in other areas of sexual activity Kinsey's data show inactive Catholic males and inactive Protestant males to have quite similar medians. See Kinsey (1948), pp. 478–81.

Chapter 18

THE ART AND SCIENCE OF
MASTURBATION

Albert Ellis, Ph.D.

Although we have remarkably liberalized our attitudes toward masturbation during the last fifty years, writers on sex rarely take a completely objective, nonmoralistic attitude toward this touchy subject. Complete public endorsement of self-stimulation prevails only among some widely scattered primitive peoples; and when raised in any civilized nation we find it almost shocking to read about the unusual freedom experienced by such peoples.

Thus, Linton tells us that among the Marquesan Islanders, "The child found early in life that it got nowhere by yelling, for if the adults got busy, they just let it cry. However, if the child turned too troublesome, an adult might quiet it by masturbating it. The masturbation of

Abridged from *Sex and the Liberated Man*, by Dr. Albert Ellis. New York: Lyle Stuart, 1976. Copyright © 1976 by The Institute for Rational Living. Published by arrangement with Lyle Stuart. Reprinted by permission of Dr. Albert Ellis and Lyle Stuart.

female children began very early; in fact from the moment of birth there existed systematic manipulation of the labia to elongate them, as elongation was considered a mark of beauty.". . .

Devereux notes that among the young Mohave Indian males "Masturbating and urinating competitions occurred frequently. In masturbating competitions both the short-ness of the time required to cause ejaculation and the distance to which the sperm projected got taken into consideration. Urinating competitions consisted of urinating figures and letters on the ground."

So much for some of the "uncivilized" primitives. In our own "higher" civilization, attitudes toward masturbation appear infinitely primmer. Menninger notes that "even today few authors seem brave enough and honest enough to make the flat statements that masturbation never harms a child and that the child whose sexual life evolves without a period of masturbation exists as an exceptional and, one may say, an abnormal child." He also points out that even psychoanalysts tend to view masturbation as self-destructive because it represents a preoccupation with the self, based on aggressive feelings toward others. He fails to acknowledge this psychoanalytic concept as largely a biased view, not based on any factual evidence, since only a small minority of individuals masturbate because of their hatred of others. . . .

As Morton Hunt points out, ever since the 1960s and the widespread publication of unexpurgated editions of books by Henry Miller, the Marquis de Sade, D. H. Lawrence, and other "sexy" writers, there has occurred "a liberation of sexuality from a two-millennia-long tradition of Judeo-Christian asceticism, a liberation so sweeping that nearly everyone can now think about, talk about and read about sex as freely as they can about food, politics or money and most people have turned grudgingly tolerant, even if not warmly approving, of many forms of sexual behavior they would formerly have regarded with loathing or even righteous indignation."

Yet in his large-scale study of sexual behavior in the 1970s, Hunt makes this almost astounding conclusion: "Most persons who masturbate remain more or less guilt-ridden about it, and nearly all of them appear extremely secretive about their masturbating and would feel horribly embarrassed to have anyone know the truth.". . .

OBJECTIONS TO MASTURBATION

In my books *Sex Without Guilt* and *The Art and Science of Love,* I have examined various objections raised against masturbation and shown their invalidity. Let me again briefly consider these objections, particularly as they apply to the single adult male, to see if they hold any water.

Supposed Immaturity

People claim that although masturbation may remain perfectly normal for adolescents, it denotes immature behavior for older males, who should completely forgo it for other, presumably heterosexual outlets. Nonsense! As every study of masturbatory activity has shown, not only youngsters, but most unmarried individuals, particularly males, practice it as their main—yes, *main*—sex outlet. How senseless to call autoerotic activities names when humans practice them so universally and harmlessly!

This includes married people, too. Beigel noted that "among the married men, between 21 and 25 percent supplemented their marital relations by this means at one time or another." And he found this practice "entirely harmless and perhaps even helpful in some instances."

Studies by Kinsey and his associates and by Yankowski not only showed self-stimulation widespread among males and females, but as Gillette pointed out, "Active incidence of masturbation among men over fifty proves generally higher than among any other post-adolescent group. Among females, masturbation appears as widespread in adulthood as in adolescence."

Morton Hunt, in his large-scale study of American sexual behavior, also found that adolescence hardly constitutes the time when masturbation reaches its highest peaks, since "as young adults, single males and single females masturbate considerably more frequently than formerly." . . .

We'd better acknowledge, of course, that autoeroticism *may* prove childish or compulsive when you have the choice of several other modes of sex activity and find that you can enjoy *only* this one or when you use masturbatory fantasies and activities to reduce your feelings of anxiety. But this pathological use of masturbation seems relatively rare, and the great majority of people who masturbate regularly or irregularly show, by mere virtue of this activity, no pathology whatever. We probably can't say the same for most people who never bring themselves to orgasm!

Supposed Antisocialness

Autoerotism often gets considered an asocial or antisocial habit, because those addicted to it presumably tend to withdraw from social life. No evidence whatever backs this hypothesis; the facts actually show that some of the most extraverted and highly socialized individuals masturbate steadily. Certainly *some* males may masturbate rather than face their anxieties about engaging in heterosexual relations, but this hardly proves *most* or *all* masturbators socially anxious. . . .

Emotional maturity, moreover, largely consists of your striving, as a human, to remain alive and to enjoy yourself during your lifetime, while bringing on yourself a minimum amount of needless pain and misery. It includes your getting along, as well as you can, with yourself and others and avoiding needlessly self-defeating behavior, particularly short-range pleasures, such as smoking and drug addiction, which may well lead to future pain and death. Masturbation, although it certainly proves immediately gratifying, also has many long-range gains—it helps you to discover what *you* really like sexually, to imagine interpersonal relations with others that you and they would want to achieve, to train yourself to enjoy sex in a maximally satisfying way. These comprise distinctly self-interested, but hardly antisocial, goals; and evidence shows that, particularly in the case of females, these goals usually aid heterosexual (and homosexual) arousal and orgasm. How, then, can we look upon this kind of masturbatory experience as *im*mature?

Mary and John Ryan take a dim view of masturbation because "Anyone capable of moral decisions can understand the difference between treating oneself and others as persons or as things. The normal adolescent can certainly see, for example, that reading 'girlie' magazines constitutes a means of stirring up sexual excitement for its own sake as an impersonal source of pleasure; what seems wrong doesn't include the pleasure but the purpose—clearly not a loving one. This way of evaluating the morality of sexual behavior would seem to offer very convincing arguments against masturbation, as a clear instance of seeking self-centered, unloving sexual pleasure.". . .

These critics of autoeroticism do not see that masturbation actually tends to involve people in imagining themselves having sex with *others* and rarely proves as narcissistic as it may at first sound. Moreover, it gives them sex practice, which, again, enables them to get along more successfully later in their interpersonal relations.

Again, as we know from recent research in sex fantasizing, even when you have sex with another, you tend to get highly aroused and come to orgasm, on many occasions, through your focusing and imaging about (1) the bodily parts of these others or (2) the arousing features of third parties whose presence exists only in your head.

In all kinds of sex, therefore, you basically remain self-involved; you focus on what feels exciting to *you* and on your *own* sensations. As Dr. Lonnie Myers has aptly indicated, this holds particularly when you approach orgasm. Before you reach this point, you may get very involved in your sex partner, and even primarily think of her. But as you ascend toward orgasm, your own sensations and feelings tend to take over, true *intimacy* gets temporarily lost, and you probably wouldn't reach climax at all if you didn't focus almost exclusively on yourself for at least a few moments. Interpersonal sex does not differ too significantly from masturbatory sex in this connection; we wrongly *assume* that it does. . . .

Supposed Lack of Emotional Gratification

Masturbation, people say, does not produce full emotional or sexual gratification. Havelock Ellis, for instance, noted that "in the absence of the desired partner, the orgasm, whatever relief it may give, must get followed by a sense of dissatisfaction, perhaps of depression, even of exhaustion, often of shame and remorse." With all due apologies to the great sage of sex, this sounds like claptrap.

Certainly masturbation leads to depression and remorse—*when* you do not wholeheartedly accept it as a good and beneficial act, when you erroneously *view* it as unsatisfying, or when, again, you act so childish that you absolutely refuse to accept a lesser, and available, sex satisfaction instead of an ideal, and presently unavailable, one.

No sex act, in fact, including heterosexual coitus, can give ideal or full emotional or physical gratification at all times to all persons, simply because humans exist as unique individuals and continually differ from *themselves* from day to day (as well as from each other). Objective observation reveals literally millions of people who at least *at times* obtain more emotional and physical gratification from masturbation than from any other kind of sex. Only (as noted above) when these individuals *always* enjoy autoerotism more than intersexual relations do they act oddly. . . .

Supposed Leading to Sexual Inadequacy

Some people allege that masturbation leads to impotence in the male or frigidity in the female. This allegation has no factual evidence to support it. On the contrary, I have found in my clinical practice that impotent males tend to engage in considerably less autoerotism than potent ones. And the Kinsey research group discovered that although approximately 33 percent of females who did not masturbate before marriage felt unresponsive in intercourse during the early years of their marriage, only about 15 percent of females who did masturbate felt equally coitally unresponsive. In treating both males and females for sexual inadequacy, I often find that inducing them to masturbate to orgasm helps them to overcome their sexual inadequacy.

As Professor Douglas Sprenkle points out, control over your sexual response tends to prove greater in masturbation than in coitus—and some therapists therefore prescribe self-stimulation as a part of a treatment program for learning to control fast ejaculation. . . .

Supposed Excessiveness

Many so-called authorities hold masturbation dangerous because it easily leads to sexual excess on the part of the masturbator. This allegation is directly contradicted by the findings of Kirkendall, who studied the masturbatory activities of young males and showed that they usually have considerably more sexual potential than they actually use. Moreover, as I have pointed out in previous writings, you will find it almost impossible to masturbate to excess, unless you turn practically psychotic—because erotic response depends upon a remarkably foolproof mechanism. When you reach the limit of your physiological endurance, you no longer respond sexually. . . .

To illustrate that "excess" rarely stems from autoeroticism, Professor Sprenkle cites the case of a prisoner in a German concentration camp during the Second World War. His captors forced him to masturbate every three hours, twenty-four hours a day, for two years. But upon his release, physicians could not find any evidence of physical damage. When he later married, he had excellent potency and fathered a child.

Similarly, evidence lays to rest the myth that masturbation leads to energy loss and fatigue and that athletes must therefore not engage in it before an important game. Dr. Wardell Pomeroy notes, in this regard, the case of a national track record set within an hour after the athlete masturbated. And Dr. William Masters has pointed out that athletes can perform at peak efficiency if they allow themselves sufficient time to relax after a sexual experience. How much times does this take? One to five minutes!

Supposed Unnaturalness

Few writers on sex these days put down masturbation as an "unnatural" practice because it obviously precludes procreation. . . . Especially in today's world, when overpopulation seems much more of a problem than human extinction, masturbation provides one of the best ways of helping the individual and the race as a whole!

ADVANTAGES OF MASTURBATION

As you can see from the foregoing discussion, the main objections raised against autoeroticism turn out, upon closer examination, specious and nonsensical. At the same time, the indubitable advantages of masturbation frequently get ignored in our literature. What constitute some of these reasons? Let me list a few salient ones.

1. Self-stimulation consists of a harmless, exceptionally repeatable sex act that virtually never interferes with the desires, activities, or rights of others.
2. It keeps you completely free from the dangers of venereal infection, pregnancy, abortion, illegitimacy, and other difficulties that may go with intersexuality.
3. It serves as a fine and effective apprenticeship in erotic fantasy that often proves good for later relationships.
4. It has a most calming effect on your sex urges and emotional excitation if you want quick relief from erotic tension.
5. It involves a minimum of monetary expense.
6. It requires much less expenditure of time and energy than do most forms of sex.
7. You can practice it in many circumstances and under many conditions where you can't very well engage in heterosexual or homosexual activity.
8. It makes no demands whatever on any of your sex partners.
9. It encourages all kinds of sex experimentation that will very likely help you discover what kind of sexuality you have (and have not!), what you really want, and how to satisfy yourself maximally

in masturbatory and other kinds of sex pursuits. . . .

Do these advantages of masturbation seem products of my own prejudices? In some ways, yes, for I have frankly favored masturbation myself, since my teens, and consider myself greatly benefited and little harmed by it. Just to show you, however, that my permissive attitude toward autoeroticism, once somewhat unique among writers in the field, has also received endorsements from some other outstanding authorities, let me quote:

> Boston's Women's Health Book Collective: "Masturbating can exist as a useful part of a person's sexual development. Besides helping you learn to enjoy your body, it can also teach you what techniques prove best for arousing yourself, so that you can show your sexual partner how to arouse you. . . ."

> Sex Information and Education Council of the U.S.: "We find sexual self-pleasuring, or masturbation, a natural part of sexual behavior for individuals of all ages. It can help to develop a sense of the body as belonging to the self, and an affirmative attitude toward the body as a legitimate source of enjoyment. It can also help in the release of tension in a way harmless to the self and to others, and provide an intense experience of the self as preparation for experiencing another. Masturbation, and the fantasies that frequently accompany it, can show themselves as important aids in maintaining or restoring the image of one's self as a fully functioning human. . . ."

> Betty Dodson: "Masturbation holds the key to breaking this socially approved bondage of women simply because it reverses the whole process of repression. With sexual independence, we gain control of our bodies and stand up straight and strong. By making no secret of our masturbation, we challenge those who have a stake in our repression, who perpetuate the conspiracy of grim silence. By openly advocating masturbation and debunking myths about it, we get less intimidated and more confident about ourselves and

our bodies. . . . Masturbation represents our primary sex
life. It constitutes our sexual base."

My conclusion from this material? Not that self-stimulation seems better or more desirable than intersexual
union. For some people some of the time, it does, but for
the most part, it doesn't. As long as heterosexual and homosexual intercourse remain as intrinsically enjoyable as
they seem for most people, they will not get totally or even
mainly replaced by masturbation. Most men and women
would much rather copulate with other people once a week
than masturbate daily, and I fully believe that they will
continue to feel this way for some time to come.

Your choice, however, doesn't rest between whether
you'd better masturbate or have heterosexual relations, but
whether you may, at various times, do both. The answer
seems obvious to any sane and thinking person. When interpersonal sex seems truly unavailable, or when it would
require your going far out of your way to obtain it, can you
find any reason why you should not *then* masturbate? If you
don't do so in such circumstances we may suspect you to
have some disturbance.

As I say in the concluding paragraph of my chapter on
masturbation in *Sex Without Guilt,* "We would find it difficult
to conceive of a more beneficial, harmless, tension-releas-
ing human act than masturbation, spontaneously performed with (puritanically inculcated and groundlessly
held) fears and anxieties. Let us, please, now that Kinsey
and his associates have stoutly reaffirmed this fact, see that
our sex manuals and sex education texts unequivocally say
it in plain English."

TECHNIQUES OF MASTURBATION

Although almost innumerable books exist on coital techniques, exceptionally few consider in detail the attitudinal

and physical methods of achieving autoerotic satisfaction. Betty Dodson's paperback volume *Liberating Masturbation* constitutes one of the rare volumes of its kind, and she had unusual difficulties compiling the material for the book and finally getting it published. It deals, moreover, almost exclusively with female masturbation and with liberating women's attitudes more than with showing them exactly what to do.

The following section will largely include techniques of self-stimulation. . . .

Self-fulfilling Attitudes

In his article "Autoeroticism: A Sociological Approach," Dr. Edward Sagarin highlights some of the negative attitudes toward self-stimulation that have existed for centuries and that still continue. He notes that if you really want to enjoy this kind of activity, you'd better release yourself from most of your inhibiting puritanism. How true! Women, especially, tend to think that they have no right to pure sex pleasure and that they must not take advantage of their own bodies; but so do millions of men!

First and foremost, then: Look forward to masturbation joyously, eagerly. Fully convince yourself that *any* pleasure you can give yourself, as long as it does not lead to subsequent pain or sabotage, has legitimacy. . . .

See masturbation, therefore, as good, great, even marvelous. . . .

So *look for,* actively *seek out* masturbatory satisfactions. As in any other endeavor, try to *maximize* your pleasure in this respect. Don't think you *have* to get the best autoerotic joys in the world; but feel determined that you *want to* reach some summits.

Fantasies

Although authorities often state that many animals masturbate, and therefore we can consider this act "normal," human masturbation seems unique in the animal kingdom, in that it almost invariably includes thinking, imagining, and emotion. Young children may masturbate mechanically, for sheer physical gratification. But older children and adults almost always arouse themselves and bring themselves to orgasm with distinct ideas and fantasies. Otherwise, they rarely get aroused or satisfied; and some of them have orgasmic failure.

To masturbate well, then, think your goddamned head off! Don't *desperately* try to get aroused and satisfied; but determinedly and experimentally discover what seems highly exciting to *you* and use that kind of thinking and imagining. For years, sexologists (including Kinsey) believed that men easily and naturally fantasize about sex, while women much more seldom do. Evidence by Nancy Friday, Barbara Hariton, J. Aphrodite and other investigators tends to show that women, too, can easily have fantasies similar to those of males and that many fantasize to good effect.

What kind of fantasies can you use in this respect? Virtually any kind that work! Lester Dearborn indicated that even bizarre or "sick" fantasies appear legitimate—so long as you do not actually carry them into practice to any considerable or compulsive degree. Thus, you can put yourself, in your head, into various masochistic or sadistic scenes. But don't, in real life, go on to actual bloodshed! Also, if your sex fantasy reinforces some of your self-defeating *general* ideas, watch it and try to change it! . . .

Fantasies also may prove compulsive and therefore limiting. If you can see yourself *only* in one way in your fantasy—for example, having sex with an animal—and refuse to let yourself get aroused when you use other fantasies, you arbitrarily limit yourself. You might, therefore, try to broaden your range of fantasizing, employ more variety, and train yourself to use, at least from time to time, other fantasies as well. With these exceptions, fantasies generally remain harmless and can, even when bizarre, lead to excellent results. Sometimes, just *because* they seem bizarre, they add novelty, strangeness, or interest to your sex life. . . .

Sexual Focusing

A form of sex thinking or attending that somewhat resembles fantasy but also has distinct differences consists of focusing—usually on your own sensations. While you masturbate, you can focus on your own sensual and sexual feelings and actually bring yourself to arousal or orgasm by doing this quite intently. Women especially use focusing to arouse and satisfy themselves, but men do it much more than they think they do, since they usually intersperse it with actual fantasy and may do more of the latter than the former. If you will attend to your own sensations, you can heighten them by this kind of concentration, and that can make all the difference between coming and not coming. . . .

Persistence

For some strange reason, people often believe that sex arousal and satisfaction should come quickly and easily. Drivel! Frequently, you can bring yourself to excitement and orgasm *too* quickly, before you have much of a chance to enjoy yourself very much. But at other times, you may take a fairly long time either to get fully aroused or to reach a climax. Persist! . . . Many tasks that at first appear uncompletable—hitting a tennis ball over the net, for example, or playing the piano well—later turn successful. Masturbatory play may well get included in the same category. If at once you don't succeed, try, try again!

Sounding Off

Sex with another person often gets enhanced by your or his or her accompanying sounds. If you talk in a sexy manner or moan and sigh and groan as your excitement mounts, you frequently turn yourself and your partner on. Fantasies themselves can come into play mutually—you tell your partner yours, and he or she relates to or adds to these or goes off on his or her own kick. Similarly with masturbation —sex talk can add to the proceedings. . . .

Just as you may employ sex literature, so you may use sex sounds. Music, the noises of two or more people making love, other recorded sounds that you find personally arousing—go to it, if you will, in these connections. Try what you will—even if others won't!

Scenic Aids

Some people get distinctly turned on by the sight of their own bodies. In women, this often requires self-training, as Betty Dodson points out, since women frequently put down their own bodies, especially their genitalia, and consider them ugly and disgusting. Such individuals could well use hand mirrors and other devices to see themselves more fully when they masturbate, and train themselves to like their bodies—or to turn what Ms. Dodson calls "cunt positive." Seeing photos of themselves, especially in sexual positions or with their genitalia very visible, also may help.

Erotic art involving others has its great advantages too. For years—probably centuries!—males have had their pin-ups and have often used them largely for masturbatory purposes. But women and couples, too, have done the same thing, as witnessed by the ancient Chinese practice of giving brides and grooms well-illustrated "pillow books" to help them with their sex lives. . . .

Mutual Sex

Technically, masturbation does not include another individual's manipulating your genitalia until you come to orgasm, since that constitutes petting or noncoital sex. But it does include your masturbating in the presence of another, and perhaps when that other stimulates you in some non-genital way. Thus, as a male you can have a partner hold or kiss you, while you take care of your own genitalia. And as a woman, you can do the same—and often to great advantage, since many women get turned off if another person manipulates their genitalia and they have to keep instructing this other to go faster, go slower, make this motion, try it that way, etc. . . .

Physical Movement

Speaking of moving, many individuals find it good to mas-turbate while simulating coital or other sexual positions. Not only do they move their hands aptly and strongly while bringing themselves to climax, but they also move their genitalia or other parts of their bodies. Some of them simu-late actual coitus—for example, males who lie on their bel-lies and "fuck" their hand, a bed, or some other object. Others lie on their backs, sit, or stand, and still actively move their pelvic regions, thighs, or other parts of their bodies while masturbating. What do you prefer? Experi-ment! Find out!

Lubrication

Great numbers of people, especially those who masturbate for long periods at a time, find it best to use lubrication—such as Vaseline, oil, K-Y jelly, soap, saliva, or other lubri-cants. For one thing, such lubrication often makes mastur-bation closely resemble coitus. For another, it avoids excessive and painful friction. Again, it may provide a sen-suous quality that otherwise they find lacking. Whatever the reason, it can distinctly add to sex satisfaction. . . .

Variety

Almost all sexuality feeds on a certain amount of variety, and a position or a technique that really excites you today may turn into a routine, unstimulating performance tomorrow. Masturbation sometimes proves an exception to this rule, since some individuals really seem to enjoy almost exactly the same procedure day after day; and, as a matter of fact, without it, they can hardly climax at all. But most of us don't fit this category. We like the same old jacking-off technique, but we like other methods, too. And the old favorite often gains new gloss when we forgo it for a while and substitute different methods. . . .

Speed and Pressure

What works for you, works! You may like very speedy stimulation of your genitalia or very slow or somewhere in between. You may desire great pressure, medium pressure, or low pressure. Sometimes you will prefer one mode; sometimes, another. Don't go by what others adore—or by what they think you *should.* One of the great advantages of masturbation, as against having your genitalia massaged by a partner, consists of your having the greatest leeway to vary procedures as befits your sexual mood—to start fast, then go slow, then speed up again . . . or whatever! . . .

Sensitive Zones

All penises and all female genitalia hardly have the same sensitized zones. Most males seem to feel most sensitive on the underside of the penis, about one inch behind the head or prepuce. But not all! Most females tend to bring themselves to orgasm by massaging the clitoral area, especially the sides of the clitoris, as Masters and Johnson have shown. The shaft itself, and the head of the clitoris, often remain too stimulatable for these females. But not always! At times, they want direct stimulation of the clitoral shaft or head. At other times, they crave massage of the inner labia or the entrance to the vagina. Occasionally, they want deep penetration—as with a penis or artificial phallus.

What constitute *your* sensitive genital zones? How can you tell, without experimenting? And how will you know unless you try different areas, with various kinds of procedures, at different times? Answer: You most probably won't!

Positions for Masturbation

As in the case of intercourse, positions for masturbating vary—and you have several basic choices and a good many minor variations on each major theme. You might think that people who bring themselves to orgasm, particularly those who have done so for twenty or more years, would have explored all possible positions and finally hit on those which prove most satisfactory. Well, frequently they haven't!

For one thing, partly for reasons connected with privacy, they use convenient places that limit their techniques. Thus, boys frequently masturbate in the bathroom—where they have little chance to lie on their backs or bellies. And women often masturbate at work, by rubbing their thighs together—an effective but still limited position. Relatively few individuals seem to try almost all possible places and positions, even when they live by themselves and have almost unlimited possibilities.

Does place or position really matter? It certainly may! In my own case, I have found that squatting in the bathroom, taking a shower, and jerking off in bed can give quite different sensations and that each of these positions may prove most desirable at certain times. Other positions—

such as lying prone upon a bed and rubbing against the sheets—work, all right, but rarely as well as the three mentioned above. . . .

Timing

Most people seem to take a minimum of time masturbating, and their game seems to include the goal of discovering the great heights of pleasure they can achieve in relatively few minutes. Fine—if that truly consists of the way you want it. Sex hardly amounts to the acme of human existence, and the more efficiently you learn to masturbate, the more time and energy you may save for other worthwhile pursuits.

But some things, including self-stimulation, would better not always get rushed! . . .

Mechanical Devices

Men and women have employed mechanical devices for masturbatory purposes from the beginning of human history to the present. Males have frequently used hollowed-out objects of various sorts, such as melons, bottles, pipes, jars, and rubber or plastic appliances. Women have employed cucumbers, candles, sausages, ears of corn, bananas, bottles, tubes, mercury balls, etc. Both sexes have used smaller objects, such as hairpins, bobby pins, and pencils, for urethral stimulation, and both have used a wide variety of small and large objects, including hairbrush handles and necks of bottles, for anal masturbation.

Nothing unusual here—except that when objects get inserted in the urethra or the anus, they may find themselves sucked into the bladder or the lower intestine; and urologists, proctologists, and other physicians not infrequently get called to remove such objects, which can lead to minor or serious damage. Obviously, therefore, if you decide to resort to mechanical devices for masturbatory purposes, you'd better use your common sense regarding what you do and how you do it. You normally wouldn't eat by putting a sharp knife in your mouth, and you'd better use at least as much caution about what objects you stick in your genitalia! . . .

In regard to masturbation in both men and women, however, mechanical instruments and objects rarely get used only in their own right. They tend to *represent* something else, in most cases—symbolize the genitalia, the body, or even the personality of a partner. If a male, for example, employs a roll of toilet paper for masturbatory purposes, and even oils it so that it resembles a vagina more closely than it normally would, he tends to think of it as part of a female. . . .

The one outstanding sex invention of the last few thousand years consists of the electric vibrator. Many different kinds of instruments powered by electricity may get used for sex purposes—an electric toothbrush, for example. But the vibrator, ostensibly devised to massage the scalp or body, proves most useful and harmless in connection with specific sexual manipulation. When correctly applied to the genital area, it provides both sexes, especially women, with an exceptionally rapid and exciting form of stimulation that virtually no manual technique can provide. And in many instances, particularly when the individual has difficulty coming to orgasm, the vibrator promptly and uniquely brings it about. Once achieved in this manner, as Dr. LeMon Clark showed a good many years ago, orgasm may then get brought on by nonmechanical methods. . . .

As usual, mechanical devices have their limitations—especially when used in disturbed ways. Dr. Warren J. Jones, Jr., who generally endorses the use of vibrators and other mechanical aids to sex, writes, "I have seen two or three guilt-ridden wives on emergency consultations in a state of decompensated depression after their spouses discovered the power of the vibrator and proceeded to use it compulsively without regard to the wife's feelings."

How true! Any kind of sexuality, including normal intercourse, can get performed compulsively. I, too, have seen several women who felt they kept getting driven "up the wall" by their partners' compulsively insisting that they achieve orgasm in various ways, as well as several males who compulsively kept trying to achieve orgasm themselves and felt utterly desperate when they did not succeed. . . .

Too much of a good thing can get obsessive-compulsive! And compulsion constitutes a large part of sex disturbance. So try, if you want, all kinds of sex and all kinds of mechanical devices to aid you in your masturbatory and interpersonal practices. But not compulsively! Not desperately! Learn to want strongly without direly needing. Then your experimentation can remain sexy—and sound!

Some final words on masturbation. Humans remain inevitably *human.* They use all kinds of mechanical devices in sex (and even in love); but they use them *imaginatively,* and they *invent* partners for themselves while so doing. Their "animalism" gets embedded in a uniquely human context.

To make yourself more enjoyably human, teach yourself—with, I would naturally recommend, rational-emotive procedures—to do away with practically all your sexual (and nonsexual) shame, embarrassment, and humiliation. Stop gratuitously upsetting yourself by your own self-downing.

For *you* invariably bring on feelings of shame and self-denigration by convincing yourself of two points, at least one of which turns out wrong: (1) "This act that I have committed appears mistaken, foolish, or immature"; (2) "therefore, I must rate myself as an idiot, a fool, or a rotten person." Although the first of these views may certainly have some sense to it, the second never does. *You,* by performing a mistaken, foolish or immature act, can only remain a *person who acts wrongly.* You can never, except by word-magic, make yourself into a *foolish* or *bad person.* To down, and later try to correct, your acts may prove very wise. To down *yourself* for doing such acts amounts to an overgeneralization that interferes with, rather than aids, your correcting your poor behavior.

Remember this in regard to practically every sex act that you perform—particularly in regard to masturbation! For although your autoeroticism may at times seem wrong-meaning, productive of less enjoyment or more disadvantages than you could obtain by other forms of sex—*you* never amount to a louse for engaging in it. Always remember that! . . .

BIBLIOGRAPHY[1]

Beigel, H. Masturbation in marriage. *Sexology,* 1966, **33** (4), 234–236.

Benjamin, H. Sex happiness in marriage. *Medical Record,* July 5, 1939.

Benjamin, H. Impotence. *Sexology,* November 1959, 240–243.

Benjamin, H. Seven kinds of sex. *Sexology,* 1961, **27**, 436–442.

Boston Women's Health Book Collective. *Our bodies, ourselves.* New York: Simon and Schuster, 1973.

Clark, L. A doctor looks at self-relief. *Sexology,* 1959, **24**, 785–788.

Clark, L. *101 intimate sexual problems.* New York: New American Library, 1967.

Comfort, A. *More joy.* New York: Crown, 1972.

Dodson, B. *Liberating masturbation.* New York: Bodysex Designs, 1974.

Ellis, A. *Sex without guilt.* New York: Lyle Stuart, 1958. (Revised ed.) New York: Lyle Stuart and Grove Press, 1965. Hollywood: Wilshire Books, 1968.

Ellis, A. *The art and science of love.* New York: Lyle Stuart, 1961. (Revised ed.) New York: Lyle Stuart and Bantam Books, 1969.

Ellis, H. *Studies in the psychology of sex.* New York: Random House, 1936, 4 vols.

[1]Included here are only some of the many authors listed in the bibliography of *Sex and the Liberated Man.*

Friday, N. *My secret garden.* New York: Trident, 1973.

Gillette, P. J. *Psychodynamics of unconventional sex behavior and unusual practices.* Los Angeles: Holloway House, 1966.

Gillette, P. J. *The big answer book about sex.* New York: Award Books, 1970.

Gordon, D. C. *Self-love.* New York: Verity House, 1968,

Haft, J. S. Foreign bodies in the female genitourinary tract; some psychosexual aspects. *Medical Aspects of Human Sexuality,* 1974, **8** (10), 54–78.

Hariton, E. B., & Singer, J. L. Women's fantasies during sexual intercourse. *Journal of Consulting and Clinical Psychology,* 1974, **42**, 313–322.

Hunt, M. *Sexual behavior in the 1970's.* Chicago: Playboy Press, 1974.

Jones, W. J. Mechanical sexual devices. *Medical Aspects of Human Sexuality, 1975,* **9** (1), 131.

Kinsey, A. C., Pomeroy, W. B., & Martin, C. E. *Sexual behavior in the human male.* Philadelphia: W. B. Saunders, 1948.

Kinsey, A. C., Pomeroy, W. B., Martin, C. E., & Gebhard, P. H. *Sexual behavior in the human female.* Philadelphia: W. B. Saunders, 1953.

Massey, F. A new look at sex toys. *Sexology,* 1973, **40** (3), 6–10.

Masters, R. E. L. *Sexual self-stimulation.* Los Angeles: Sherbourne, 1967.

Masters, W. H., & Johnson, V. E. *Human sexual response.* Boston: Little, Brown, 1966.

Masters, W. H., & Johnson, V. E. *Human sexual inadequacy.* Boston: Little, Brown, 1970.

Pomeroy, W. *Girls and sex.* New York: Dell, 1973.

Ryan, M. P., & Ryan, J. J. *Love and sexuality.* New York: Holt, Rinehart and Winston, 1967.

Part V

USE OF AUTOEROTICISM IN THE TREATMENT OF SEXUAL DYSFUNCTION

INTRODUCTION

The chapters in this section are perhaps not only the most important ones in this book from a psychotherapeutic viewpoint, but they also represent the most dramatic changes in attitude currently being witnessed in reference to the desirability of the use of autoeroticism. Because here, far from condemning the practice, masturbatory activity is strongly recommended by leading sex therapists in the treatment of sexual dysfunction in women. In addition, impressive evidence is presented clearly showing how effective the use of masturbation can be in helping women overcome their inability to attain orgasms either by themselves or during sexual encounters with others. The studies that appear in Part 5 are presently exerting an enormous influence on the thinking of persons in the field of human sexuality, especially sex therapists; in the years ahead these studies will undoubtedly be viewed as the forerunners of a new era concerning the beneficial and therapeutic uses of auto-erotic activity.

In Chapter 19, which is a landmark in the field of sex therapy, Dr. Joseph LoPiccolo (psychologist) and Dr. W. Charles Lobitz begin by reminding us of the very negative attitudes toward masturbation still held as late as the 1960s, even by many graduating medical students and some faculty members in medical schools. To support their view of masturbation as being "normal" and "healthy," LoPiccolo and Lobitz refer to the research of Ford and Beach, Kinsey et al., W. R. Johnson, and Dearborn. They then go on to emphasize that in the case of women "since masturbation is the most probable method of producing an orgasm and since it produces the most intense orgasm, it logically seems to be the preferred treatment for enhancing orgasmic potential in inorgasmic women." While the use of masturbatory activity to aid orgasm attainment was recommended in the past by some prominent therapists, as LoPiccolo and Lobitz observe, masturbation was never employed as "a systematic part of a therapy program." These clinicians also discuss their methods of counteracting any negative attitudes toward autoeroticism that may be experienced by the participants in their therapy program and describe in detail the role masturbation played in a nine-step therapy program in the treatment of primary orgasmic dysfunction in women at the University of Oregon Psychological Clinic Sexual Research Program. LoPiccolo and Lobitz further point out that their masturbatory program is part of a larger behavioral program that is conducted by a male as well as female therapist and includes both the inorgasmic wife and her husband. Although the general program is patterned after the one originated by Masters and Johnson, as LoPiccolo and Lobitz state, "The masturbation component of our program is unique to our work, however, and has been developed by us." As part of the evidence presented to demonstrate the effectiveness of their therapeutic approach it is reported that all eight women who took part in the treatment process "gained the ability to achieve orgasm" and "six women . . . achieved orgasm through intercourse with their husbands and continue to experience orgasm in this way."

Of the many professional women now engaged in sex therapy, one of the best known, as well as the most outstanding, is the author of Chapter 20—Helen Singer Kaplan, M.D., Ph.D. In addition to being a psychiatrist and leading sex therapist, Dr. Kaplan is also a prolific researcher and well-known writer. She begins Chapter 20 by stating that although many women appear to be inorgastic because of ineffective sexual stimulation, true orgastic dysfunction in a woman occurs only in those instances in which a "woman reveals that she has tried to masturbate to no avail and/or that her husband's attempts to stimulate her have not enabled her to reach orgasm." In treating such women, the "initial objective" is to help them attain their first orgasm, and basic to the treatment process is the removal of both remote as well as immediate orgastic psychological inhibitory forces (or mechanisms). As Kaplan states, "The therapist attacks the defenses the patient has erected against the perception of her sexual sensations on both deep and immediate levels. He draws certain inferences with respect to their underlying sources and he also makes specific behavioral suggestions to counteract their destructive effects." When, however, a woman is not able to achieve an orgasm through "joint treatment tactics" that involve the use of her sex partner, the method of treatment becomes that of autoeroticism (which is viewed as a transitional step). To counteract the anxiety feelings often experienced by a woman in this regard, the therapist discusses the woman's attitudes relating to masturbation and also makes specific suggestions concerning her practice of self-stimulation. And as Kaplan points out, in the beginning the woman is told to masturbate manually but if this approach does not produce an orgasm, a vibrator is recommended even though it may have some disadvantages. To further assist the woman in reaching an orgasm from self-stimulation, she is told how to tense her muscles, to breathe, and to fantasize. At times the therapist also has to engage in a "psychotherapeutic exploration of the patient's unconscious fears of orgasm" in order to help the patient attain an orgasm. After a woman is able to reach several orgasms with the aid of a vibrator and has become sufficiently confident concerning her orgastic ability, she is directed to discontinue the use of a vibrator and employ digital stimulation. Kaplan notes that "erotic fantasy during sex is an excellent distractor and is an invaluable tool for overcoming orgastic inhibition," and discusses the importance of the control of various muscles during orgasmic attainment. In the final step of the therapeutic approach outlined by Kaplan, the woman's husband is brought into the situation and specific instructions are given to the wife as well as the husband concerning their respective modes of behavior during their lovemaking encounters. The therapeutic procedure delineated by Kaplan definitely appears to be a highly effective one since, as she observes in view of her clinical experience, "virtually all the totally inorgastic women are able to achieve orgasm by the tactics described above. Many of these patients become progressively more facile in attaining orgasm and go on to achieve a good sexual relationship with their husbands."

Dr. Lonnie Garfield Barbach, a clinical-social psychologist, first points out, in Chapter 21, that the Playboy Foundation investigation (Hunt, 1973) showed no improvement had occurred in the percentage of married women who had ever attained an orgasm since the Kinsey et al. study of 1953. She then suggests that the lack of effective therapeutic methods in general, and psychoanalysis in particular, are responsible for the continuing problem of "primary orgasmic dysfunction." The mistaken psychoanalytic notion that regards a clitoral orgasm as being immature and inferior to the vaginal orgasm is especially criticized by

Barbach as having interfered with the successful treatment of women with orgasmic dysfunction. In refuting the claims of psychoanalysts concerning the importance of a vaginal orgasm, Masters and Johnson's findings are referred to and the underlying principle of their sexual therapeutic program is stated: sexual dysfunction is a relationship problem and not a "personality problem of one of the individuals in the relationship." Barbach also mentions the masturbatory program developed by Lobitz and LoPiccolo. Following this commentary of previous therapeutic approaches relating to orgasmic dysfunction in women, Barbach notes that a "group treatment program for primary anorgasmic women," created at the University of California in 1972, was later instituted at the University of California Medical Center in San Francisco. The group treatment program described for "preorgasmic" women (a more optimistic term), which includes only women who work as a group, uses masturbation as "the major learning tool." Male partners are excluded because they are felt to reduce a woman's sense of security and serve as a "distracting element in a masturbation program." The specific program reported in detail by Barbach involved 83 women ranging in age from 19 to 48. As a result of this therapeutic program, 91.6% of the women "were orgasmic with masturbation by the end of the 10 sessions" and a number of positive personality and behavioral changes were reported to have been experienced by the women. Male partners (husbands, steady mates) of some of the participants also viewed the undertaking as having been very successful. While several essential factors are believed to have accounted for the success achieved in counteracting orgasmic dysfunction in women, as viewed by Barbach, "The use of self-stimulation as opposed to partner stimulation as the method of becoming familiar with orgasm is central; having the orgasm under the woman's own control allows her to go at her own pace while eliminating outside distractions provided by the presence of another person."

Chapter 19

THE ROLE OF MASTURBATION IN THE TREATMENT OF ORGASMIC DYSFUNCTION

Joseph LoPiccolo, Ph.D. and W. Charles Lobitz, M.A.[1]

It is proposed that a program of directed masturbation can be effective in treating primary orgasmic dysfunction. A brief review is made of the normality of masturbation and its effectiveness in producing orgasm in women. A nine-step program of masturbation, designed to lead to heterosexual coital orgasm, is described. Techniques for dealing with clients' negative emotions towards masturbation are discussed. Case material and treatment outcome statistics are presented to illustrate the effectiveness of this masturbation program.

INTRODUCTION

"No other form of sexual activity has been more frequently discussed, more roundly condemned, and more universally

[1]Department of Psychology, University of Oregon, Eugene, Oregon.

From *Archives of Sexual Behavior,* 1972, *2,* 163–171. Reprinted by permission of the Plenum Publishing Corporation.

practiced than masturbation" (Dearborn, 1967). In contrast to this general condemnation of masturbation, we feel that masturbation is not only a normal, healthy activity but is an extremely effective aid in the treatment of primary orgasmic dysfunction in women. This paper will describe the role directed masturbation plays in therapy at the University of Oregon Psychology Clinic Sexual Research Program.

Greenbank (1961) studied the attitude toward masturbation of graduating medical students and the faculty in five Philadelphia area medical schools. His research indicated that "half of the students have a feeling that mental illness was frequently caused by masturbation. Even one faculty member in five still believes in this old, and now discredited idea." Because of the apparently still widespread misconceptions about masturbation, even among health professionals, a note on its normality is in order.

Among subhuman primates, masturbation occurs in many species even when ample opportunity to copulate with receptive partners exists (Ford and Beach, 1951). Although masturbation is more common in male than in female animals it has been observed in female dogs, chinchillas, rats, porcupines, elephants, and dolphins, among other species (Ford and Beach, 1951; Kinsey et al., 1953). The phylogenetic evidence, then, is that masturbation is a "natural" rather than an "unnatural" act and is seemingly an inherent part of our biological endowment.

Other cultures vary considerably in their attitudes toward masturbation (Ford and Beach, 1951). In some cultures, the Lesu in Melanesia, for example, masturbation is acceptable and is practiced casually in public. In other cultures, it is severely prohibited. Such prohibitions seem to have only the effect of causing people to masturbate in secret rather than actually reducing the occurrence of masturbation. For example, Apinaye boys and girls masturbate frequently, even though such activity is punished if detected, and despite the fact that at a ceremony conducted when they are half-grown, their genitals are examined and they are severely beaten if there is any "evidence" of masturbation (Ford and Beach, 1951).

Masturbation is culturally prohibited in American society despite the total lack of any scientific evidence that it has any psychologically or physiologically harmful effects (Johnson, 1968; Dearborn, 1967). This prohibition seems to have arisen from religious doctrine rather than from any rational scientific basis (Johnson, 1968).

In spite of this cultural prohibition, masturbation is more common in our society than many parents, therapists, and clients realize. The Kinsey data (Kinsey et al., 1948, 1953), now over 20 years old, indicate that 94% of men and 58% of women masturbate to orgasm at some point in their lives. Other more recent studies have obtained higher figures, up to virtually 100% of men and 85% of women (Dearborn, 1967). These incidence figures can be useful in reassuring clients (and therapists) about the "normality" of masturbation.

THEORETICAL BASIS FOR THE USE OF MASTURBATION IN TREATMENT

Although the high incidence of masturbation is useful information for encouraging its acceptance by clients, the ability of masturbation to produce orgasm has more therapeutic importance. Masturbation is especially therapeutic for the primary inorgasmic woman, i.e., one who has never experienced an orgasm from any source of physical stimulation. For this problem, it seems most sensible to begin treatment with the technique most likely to produce an orgasm. Kinsey et al. (1953) reported that the average woman reached orgasm in 95% or more of her masturbatory attempts. This figure considerably exceeds the probability of reaching orgasm through coitus (about 0.73 for average married women).

Not only is masturbation the most probable way of producing an orgasm, it also produces the most intense orgasm. In a now famous study, subjects' subjective reports as well as recordings of their physiological responses (heart rate and vaginal contractions) indicated that masturbation produced a more intense orgasm than either coitus or manipulation of the genitals by a partner (Masters and Johnson, 1966). It has been suggested that an intense orgasm leads to increased vascularity in the vagina, labia, and clitoris (Bardwick, 1971). In turn, there seems to be evidence that this increased vascularity will enhance the potential for future orgasms. "Frequent orgasms will effect an increase in vascularity, which in turn enhance the orgasmic potential. Nothing succeeds like success, and the increased number of orgasms will lead to the psychological anticipation of pleasure in sex" (Bardwick, 1971). This notion that increased vascularity enhances orgasmic potential is supported by the findings of Kegel (1952). He discovered that patients who strengthened the pubococcygens muscle through his prescribed exercises experienced an increase in their frequency of orgasm. Since exercising a muscle leads to increased vascularity, it is possible that the increased vascularity in the pubococcygens was responsible for the increased orgasmic frequency. An increase in pelvic vascularity has also been suggested to explain the effectiveness of androgen therapy in facilitating orgasm (Bardwick, 1971).

To summarize, since masturbation is the most probable method of producing an orgasm and since it produces the most intense orgasm, it logically seems to be the preferred treatment for enhancing orgasmic potential in inorgasmic women.

Although masturbation has been noted in the past to facilitate orgasmic potential, it apparently has not been a systematic part of a therapy program. Hastings (1963) reported that some of his patients increased their sexual responsiveness by increased masturbation. Similarly, sex authorities from Albert Ellis (1960) to "J" (1969) have recommended masturbation with an electric vibrator to facilitate an orgasm. We have developed such a systematic masturbation program for treating primary orgasmic dysfunction.

THE MASTURBATION PROGRAM

The masturbation program does not form the totality of our treatment program for inorgasmic women, but is an adjunct to a behavioral, time-limited (15 sessions) treatment program involving both the husband and wife. The general program involving both husband and wife and a male-female cotherapy team is modeled very directly after the procedure developed by Masters and Johnson (1970) for treating inorgasmic women. The masturbation component of our program is unique to our own work, however, and has been developed by us.

In prescribing a masturbation program, the therapist must obviously deal with both the woman's and her husband's attitudes toward masturbation. It is typical of our clients to have learned very negative attitudes toward masturbation. Several of our clients were directly instructed by their parents that masturbation would have dire consequences ranging from acne to cancer to insanity and were severely punished for masturbating as adolescents. One of our clients was forced, as a child, to bathe wearing her underpants, so that she would never directly see or touch her own genitals. In such cases, it would be extremely naive to expect a simple order to "go home and masturbate" to have any therapeutic effect if these negative attitudes, fears, and simple errors of fact were not dealt with.

There are several techniques which can be used to help overcome the client's negative attitudes toward masturbation. One such technique is to ask the client to estimate what percentage of people masturbate, before and after marriage. Even well-educated clients typically grossly underestimate these figures (i.e., estimates of 20 to 30% premaritally and 5 to 10% postmaritally are common). The client can be given the correct information, with the therapist also correcting other misconceptions about the normality and universality of masturbation at this point.

However, a lecture by the therapist on the true facts about masturbation does not always deal with the client's irrational emotional reaction to masturbation. In cases where resistance to masturbation is not based so much on ignorance and misinformation as on emotional conditioning, therapist self-disclosure is often useful in changing the client's attitude. That is, given that the client has had time to develop some regard and respect for the therapist, the therapist's calmly and unashamedly discussing his or her own masturbation can be extremely effective in changing the client's negative attitude. The therapist, of course, must be truly unconflicted and comfortable about revealing this information for it to be effective.

When prescribing masturbation for an inorgasmic woman, it is crucial to enlist the cooperation and support of her husband. That is, if the woman has to sneak off to masturbate and feels her husband disapproves, there is little chance that masturbation will be effective in producing orgasm. The husband should be made fully aware of what his wife is doing, the reasons for it, and should be instructed by the therapists to fully support his wife's masturbation. In our treatment program, we typically split up initially. The female cotherapist discusses masturbation with the female client, while the male cotherapist does the same with the male client. In these individual sessions, the male therapist explains to the husband the rationale for a masturbation program for the wife and deals with any negative reactions the client has. The therapist then directly trains the husband to support his wife's masturbation. With modeling and role-play techniques, we train the husband to make convincingly supportive statements. Our male clients typically take to this procedure well, since they are highly motivated to help their wives become sexually responsive.

In this individual session, the male therapist also suggests to the husband that he should masturbate or, if the husband does masturbate, that he tell his wife about it. We advocate this for two reasons. First, for the wife to feel truly guilt-free about her masturbation, she needs to know not only that her husband approves but that he masturbates as well. In addition, masturbation by the husband is useful in keeping him cooperative, in that the early phases of the Masters-Johnson (1970) treatment for inorgasmic women involve abstinence from intercourse. While the male co-therapist is following this procedure with the husband, the female therapist is similarly explaining the necessity of masturbation to the wife and dealing with any negative reactions she has.

Following these individual sessions, the therapy team rejoins, and the masturbation program is explained in detail to husband and wife.

This program usually consists of nine steps, with the client typically working on one step per week. These steps will be described, with case history data to exemplify the principles involved.

STEP 1

In step 1, the client is told that she is "out of touch" with her own body, that indeed she has never really known her own body nor learned to appreciate the beauty of her sexual organs. Accordingly, she is given the assignment to increase her self-awareness. She is told to examine her nude body carefully and try to appreciate its beauty. The client is to use a hand mirror to examine her genitals closely, identifying the various areas with the aid of the diagrams in Hasting's book, *Sexual Expression in Marriage* (1966). We recommend this genital exploration be done just after bathing, for reasons of cleanliness and to capitalize on the relaxing qualities of a warm bath. Many of our clients express amazement after following this step. Typical statements are "I never really knew what was down there" and "I was amazed at how little I knew about myself."

At this time, the client is also started on a program of Kegel's (1952) exercises for increasing the tone and vascularity of the pelvic musculature, which presumably will increase her orgasmic potential. We advocate having the client tense and relax her pelvic muscles ten times, repeating this exercise three times daily.

Step 2

Next the client is instructed to explore her genitals tactually as well as visually. She is instructed to explore through touch the various parts of her genitals. To avoid putting her under any performance anxiety to arouse herself sexually, the client is not given any expectation that she should be aroused at this point. In these first two steps, we merely want the client to become desensitized to the sight and feel of her genitals and become used to the idea of masturbation. Interestingly enough, it is in these first two steps that we get most resistance from clients. Not uncommonly, the woman reports that she tried, but could not bring herself to look at or touch herself. Additional support from the therapists and the husband will usually overcome this problem. It is also useful for the therapists to tell the client that we expect her to feel some apprehension or aversion at this point but that these feelings usually disappear once she begins actually following the program.

STEP 3

Next the client is instructed to continue visual and tactual exploration of her genitals, but with an emphasis on locating sensitive areas that produce feelings of pleasure. She is not to focus on any area in particular but to thoroughly explore the clitoral shaft and hood, the major and minor labia, the vaginal opening, and the whole perineum, especially that area immediately adjacent to the clitoris. In line with the findings of Kinsey et al. (1953) and Masters and Johnson (1966) we have yet to have a client locate the vagina as a strong source of sexual pleasure; most of our clients focus on the clitoral area as the most pleasurable.

STEP 4

With the pleasure-producing areas located, the client is now told to concentrate on manual stimulation of these areas. The female cotherapist at this time discusses techniques of masturbation with the client. As most of our clients locate the clitoris as the most pleasurable area, this is usually a discussion of techniques of clitoral manipulation; topics covered include variations of stroking and pressure and the use of a sterile lubricant jelly to enhance pleasure and prevent soreness.

STEP 5

If orgasm does not occur in step 4, the client is told to increase the intensity and duration of her masturbation. She is told to masturbate until "something happens" or until she becomes tired or sore. We think of 30 to 45 min.

as a reasonable upper limit for duration of masturbation and indeed have had clients achieve their first orgasm after as much as 45 min. of continuous, intense masturbation. We also recommend the use of pornographic reading material or pictures to enhance arousal. In addition, we suggest the use of erotic fantasies to further increase arousal. Interestingly, the concept of fantasizing during masturbation does not seem to occur spontaneously to our female clients. This is consistent with the data of Kinsey et al. (1953) that a much smaller proportion of women than men fantasize during masturbation.

STEP 6

If orgasm is not reached in step 5, we instruct the client to purchase a vibrator of the type sold in pharmacies for facial massage. These can be purchased for as little as 5 dollars and, as the classified ads in any underground newspaper will attest, are extremely effective in producing sexual arousal. There are two general types of vibrators available: those that strap on the hand and cause the fingers to vibrate and those that are applied directly to the object to be massaged. Both types are effective, but individual preference varies. We have prepared a fact sheet for our clients which lists the various types of vibrators available in town, the price, and where they may be purchased. The client is instructed to masturbate, using the vibrator, lubricant jelly, and pornographic materials. In our most difficult case to date, 3 weeks of vibrator masturbation, with daily 45 min. vibrator sessions, was required to produce orgasm.

We have found a technique of use in cases where orgasm does not occur after some time in step 6. A woman may simply be embarrassed or afraid to have an orgasm, fearing an undignified loss of control with muscular convulsions, inarticulate screaming, and involuntary defecation or urination. To desensitize them to their fears of loss of control, we have such clients role play the experience of orgasm in their own homes.

STEP 7

Once a woman has achieved orgasm through masturbation, our focus shifts to enabling her to experience orgasm through stimulation by her husband. As the first step in this process, we instruct the woman to masturbate with her husband observing her. This desensitizes her to visibly displaying arousal and orgasm in his presence and also functions as an excellent learning experience for her husband. He learns just what techniques of genital stimulation are effective and pleasurable for his wife, from the only person who is truly expert in this subject. Some clients are initially reluctant to masturbate in front of their husbands, but the same techniques of therapist's verbal self-disclosure and coequal involvement of the husband that are used to overcome initial reluctance have also proven effective here.

STEP 8

Step 8 simply involves having the husband do for his wife what she has been doing for herself. If she has been using a vibrator, he now uses it on her. If she has been manually manipulating her genitals, he now begins to do this for her.

STEP 9

Once orgasm has occurred in step 8, we instruct the couple to engage in intercourse while the husband concurrently stimulates the wife's genitals, either manually or with a vibrator. We recommend the female superior sitting, lateral, or rear entry coital positions for this activity, as all these positions allow the male easy access to the female's genitals during intromission. Once orgasm has occurred at this step, the client should logically be considered "cured," since the clitoris and not the vagina is now known to be the major locus of sexuality and orgasm in the normal woman (Masters and Johnson, 1966; Kinsey et al., 1953; Lydon, 1971; Weisstein, 1971; Ellis, 1962). Some clients, however, especially those who have been exposed to psychoanalytic theory and its specious distinction between "clitoral" and "vaginal" orgasm, express a wish to achieve orgasm without the necessity for concurrent manual stimulation during coitus. For such clients, we emphasize the importance of achieving adequate clitoral stimulation from some source (e.g., the husband's symphysis) during coitus and point out that this stimulation is most effectively achieved through direct manual manipulation.

In assessing the effectiveness of this program, two questions arise: how successful is the program in producing an orgasm for the totally inorgasmic woman, and how regularly does this woman become orgasmic in sexual activity with her husband?

We have completed treatment (15 therapy sessions) with eight women who had never previously experienced orgasm. In all eight cases, these women have gained the ability to achieve orgasm.

In regard to the second effectiveness question, two of these women are now orgasmic with clitoral manipulation by their husbands, but not yet during intercourse. The other six women have achieved orgasm through intercourse with their husbands and continue to experience orgasm in this way. Four of the six no longer require direct manual manipulation of the genitals during intercourse to reach orgasm. The regularity of coital orgasm varies—one client reports orgasm on about 25% of coital opportunities, one on about 50% of coital opportunities, and the other four on nearly every occasion. We are continuing to gather follow-up data on these clients, to assess the stability of change. So far, our follow-up (up to 6 months) indicates no relapses but rather further gains in the enjoyment of sexual relations.

It is also of interest to note that the crucial first orgasm may occur seemingly at almost any step in this program or indeed in response to nonmasturbatory stimulation following exposure to the program. Of our eight clients, one client first experienced orgasm at step 2, one client at step 3, two clients at step 4, and two clients at step 6. The other two clients did not experience first orgasm through masturbating, but in sexual activity with their husbands. One woman experienced first orgasm in clitoral manipulation by the husband, which was temporally concurrent with step 4. The other client achieved first orgasm in intercourse with her husband, which followed several weeks on step 6. While it cannot be proven, it is our feeling that neither of these women would have achieved orgasm without having first experienced our masturbation program.

Although our sample is as yet small, we feel that this masturbation program offers considerable promise in the treatment of primary orgasmic dysfunction.

REFERENCES

Bardwick, J. M. *Psychology of women: A study of biocultural conflicts.* New York: Harper & Row, 1971.

Dearborn, L. W. Autoeroticism. In A. Ellis and A. Abarbanel (Eds.), *The encyclopedia of sexual behavior.* New York: Hawthorn Books, 1967.

Ellis, A. *The art and science of love.* New York: Lyle Stuart, 1960.

Ellis, A. *The American sexual tragedy.* New York: Lyle Stuart, 1962.

Ford, C. S., & Beach, F. A. *Patterns of sexual behavior.* New York: Harper & Bros., 1951.

Greenbank, R. K. Are medical students learning psychiatry? *Medical Journal,* 1961, **64,** 989–992.

Hastings, D. W. *Impotence and frigidity.* Boston: Little, Brown, 1963.

Hastings, D. W. *Sexual expression in marriage.* New York: Bantam, 1966.

"J." *The sensuous woman.* New York: Dell, 1969.

Johnson, W. R. Masturbation, SIECUS Study Guide No. 3, Sex Information and Education Council of the United States, 1968.

Kegel, A. H. Sexual functions of the pubococcygens muscle. *Western Journal of Obstetrics and Gynecology,* 1952, **60,** 521.

Kinsey, A. C., Pomeroy, W. B., & Martin, C. E. *Sexual behavior in the human male.* Philadelphia: W. B. Saunders, 1948.

Kinsey, A. C., Pomeroy, W. B., Martin, C. E., & Gebhard, P. H. *Sexual behavior in the human female.* Philadelphia: W. B. Saunders, 1953.

Lydon, S. The politics of orgasm. In M. Garskof (Ed.), *Roles women play*. Belmont, Calif.: Brooks/Cole, 1971.

Masters, W. H., & Johnson, V. E. *Human sexual response*. Boston: Little, Brown, 1966.

Masters, W. H., & Johnson, V. E. *Human sexual inadequacy*. Boston: Little, Brown, 1970.

Weisstein, N. Psychology constructs the female, or the fantasy life of the male psychologist. In M. Garskof (Ed.), *Roles women play*. Belmont, Calif.: Brooks/Cole, 1971.

Chapter 20

ORGASTIC DYSFUNCTION

Helen Singer Kaplan, M.D., Ph.D.

PRIMARY ABSOLUTE ORGASTIC DYSFUNCTION

When a woman says that she has never experienced an orgasm, the therapist's first task is to obtain detailed information about her sexual experiences. For it is important to establish at the outset whether she is truly suffering from an orgastic inhibition or whether she has never experienced an orgasm simply because she has never received sufficient stimulation to enable orgastic discharge. One continues to be astounded by the fact that a significant number of totally inorgastic women have never experienced orgasm simply because they have never been effectively stimulated.

Abridged from Chapter 19, "Orgastic Dysfunction" in *The New Sex Therapy* by Helen Singer Kaplan. New York: Brunner/Mazel, Inc., 1974. Reprinted by permission of the publisher.

In cases where the woman's problem can be attributed to poor sexual techniques, therapy is simple and the results are excellent. Treatment consists of working with the husband and wife conjointly to relieve guilt, correct misconceptions regarding their sexual roles, and enhance communication between them. We also inform the couple of the importance of clitoral eroticism in the production of female orgasm, as well as suggesting effective techniques to enhance the wife's sexual response. Provided the couple's sexual problems are not rooted in serious psychopathology, they respond quickly and favorably to these counseling techniques.

On the other hand, the woman who remains inorgastic although she receives stimulation which should bring her to orgasm presents a more difficult therapeutic problem. When, in the course of the initial interview, the woman reveals that she has tried to masturbate to no avail and/or that her husband's attempts to stimulate her have not enabled her to reach orgasm, it is apparent that one is dealing with a true orgastic dysfunction.

Our initial objective in the treatment of such patients is to help them to achieve their first orgasm. This is an extremely important first step in the therapeutic process. For the first orgastic experience dispels the woman's fear that she is not capable of an orgastic response. Also, once she has had an orgasm, she has taken a first step toward extinguishing her conditioned inhibition.

Essentially, treatment is based on the premise that the orgastic reflex has merely been inhibited in these patients; it has not been destroyed. It follows, then, that it is always possible to achieve orgasm if the stimulation provided is sufficiently intense to overcome the inhibition. To achieve this goal, every effort must be made to diminish the inhibitory forces, while at the same time maximizing stimulation.

During the therapeutic sessions the remote roots of the patient's inhibition are explored and identified, to the extent that this is possible within the brief treatment format. But the primary goal of treatment is the identification and modification of the immediate psychological mechanisms by which the patient impairs her orgastic response. As a general rule, patients are not aware of these mechanisms; therefore, they may not come to light during the initial evaluation. The devices and defenses she employs to inhibit her orgastic response may become apparent to the patient only as a consequence of the prescribed sexual exercises and after these have been discussed with the therapist. For example, in the course of these experiences the patient may discover, to her surprise, that her mind begins to wander or that she feels sleepy whenever she attains a certain level of erotic arousal by masturbation or by reading erotic literature. Even then the patient may not make the necessary connection between her anxiety-motivated defenses and her orgastic inhibition; frequently, the therapist must actively intervene to foster such insight. The patient's awareness of these self-induced inhibitory factors is an important step in therapy. The therapist exploits the temporary distress created by this awareness by confronting the patient with the reality that she is inhibiting herself for a variety of reasons.

The therapist attacks the defenses the patient has erected against the perception of her sexual sensations on both deep and immediate levels. He draws certain inferences with respect to their underlying sources and he also makes specific behavioral suggestions to counteract their destructive effects. For example, the patient may be instructed to consciously control her "spectatoring" or obsessive thinking, or she may be told to empty her mind of all irrelevant thoughts and focus on her erotic sensations. If these procedures are not sufficiently effective to produce orgasm, the patient may be advised to "distract her distractor" by losing herself in erotic fantasy while she is being stimulated. Some patients are able to achieve their initial orgasm only when they engage in behavior which is highly distracting from their tendency to "hold back," such as actually reading erotic material while they receive stimulation.

Treatment

1. MASTURBATION.   Sex therapy usually requires the presence and cooperation of both partners. However, as noted above, the initial, crucial objective in the treatment of primary absolute orgastic dysfunction is to eliminate as many inhibitory factors as possible in order to enable the woman to have her first orgasm. The presence of an "audience" has a major inhibitory effect on many women. Consequently, in our program, when the totally inorgastic patient has not become orgastic in response to the joint treatment tactics which are designed to enhance her general arousal, the treatment strategy is often shifted to enable her to attain her first orgasm in response to self-stimulation.

Not surprisingly, the instruction that the patient masturbate to reach orgasm often evokes considerable anxiety in patients who have been taught from childhood to regard masturbation as dangerous and shameful. Therefore, these attitudes must be dealt with in the therapeutic sessions. The patient is advised to engage in this activity under the most reassuring conditions. It is suggested, for example, that she masturbate when she is alone and free from the fear of interruption and discovery.

The therapist also attempts to reduce the anxiety which inhibits orgastic discharge by giving her "permission" to release the orgasm and by actively encouraging her efforts to this end. Usually, initially the patient reports that she is able to reach a certain level of erotic excitement, but then begins to feel tense and uncomfortable and stops stimulation at this point. She is then instructed to "stay with" these uncomfortable feelings and, on her next attempt, to continue stimulation at this point. She is also told to contract her abdominal and perineal muscles when she feels high levels of sexual tension. This maneuver often facilitates orgastic discharge, possibly because of its distraction value.

2. THE VIBRATOR.   Initially, the patient is instructed to masturbate manually. If the stimulation produced thereby is not sufficiently intense to evoke orgasm, she is advised to use a vibrator for this purpose. The vibrator provides the strongest, most intense stimulation known. Indeed, it has been said that the electric vibrator represents the only significant advance in sexual technique since the days of Pompeii. Nevertheless, it is not without its disadvantages. The previously inorgastic woman may have to rely on the intense clitoral stimulation provided by a vibrator in order to achieve orgasm during the initial phase of treatment. However, there is some danger that such patients may become unable to achieve orgasms by any other means. They may become "hooked" on their vibrator. To guard against the possibility that the woman will be limited to vibration-induced orgasms, we recommend the use of the vibrator initially only when less intense manual stimulation of the clitoris is not effective; in addition, we discourage sole reliance on the vibrator to produce orgasm and to encourage exploration of alternative means of stimulation.

Although it is a potent source of sexual stimulation, the use of the vibrator does not automatically ensure orgasms. Some women reach orgasm easily the first time they try the vibrator, but others have reported that they were able to achieve their first orgasm only after 45 minutes or so of stimulation. Typically, such women approach orgasm, feel tense and uncomfortable, inhibit themselves, "go down," and then resume stimulation with the vibrator until they approach orgasm again, only to experience a repetition of the same sequence of responses. When the patient experiences a great deal of difficulty in achieving her first orgasm, she requires the therapist's active support and encouragement. In addition, she needs instruction in how to "let go" when she feels that she is on the verge of orgasm; she must learn how to tense her muscles, how to breathe and, if necessary, how to reach for an appropriate fantasy to distract herself from her defensive inhibitory tendency.

It has been our experience that the therapeutic strategy of exposing the woman to intense clitoral stimulation and, at the same time, teaching her to distract herself from her habitual tendency to "hold back" enables most inorgastic women to attain orgasm surprisingly quickly.

3.   RESOLUTION OF UNCONSCIOUS FEARS OF ORGASM. In some cases, the orgastic inhibition remains intractable; in addition to these experiental procedures, such patients need to gain some insight into the unconscious roots of their inhibition. Thus, the specific instructions outlined above are usually supplemented by psychotherapeutic exploration of the patient's unconscious fears of orgasm.

A variety of fears, both conscious and unconscious, underlie orgastic inhibition. Some women are afraid that they will die if they have an orgasm; some equate orgasm with a loss of control; other women fear that once they have had their first orgasm they will become preoccupied with sex, to the extent that they will become promiscuous; almost all patients believe on some level that their lives will change drastically once they experience climax.

Although they effectively prevent orgasm, most patients are not in touch with these fears. It is important to foster conscious awareness of such fears. The therapist must also confront the patient with the fact that her fears are irrational and help her to understand their genesis. She must gain insight into the fact that the disasters she anticipates, both consciously and unconsciously, will not really occur if she has an orgasm. Interestingly, the therapist's efforts to this end will sometimes entail exploration of these patients' anxieties about success, which may be activated by the prospect of sexual fulfillment. Paradoxically, it is the patient's realization that her life will not improve dramatically once she becomes orgastic which has proven most effective in breaking the orgasm barrier in such cases. Briefly, we emphasize the fact that the orgasm is merely a reflex and has none of the symbolic qualities so often attributed to it by inhibited women; at the same time, we work with the psychodynamic forces which underlie this symbolism.

Usually, after she has achieved her first climax, the patient requires progressively shorter periods of stimulation to produce subsequent orgasms. After she has been able to achieve several orgasms and no longer doubts her capacity to do so, the patient is "weaned" from the vibrator and proceeds to digital stimulation. In some instances, this is done abruptly—the patient is told to put the vibrator away and to begin all over again with digital stimulation. In other cases, the woman is initially instructed to use the vibrator to reach a high level of arousal and then "finish off" with her finger, so that she can gradually become accustomed to reaching climax in response to less intense stimulation if she so chooses.

4. DISTRACTION.   The use of distraction during stimulation, which plays an exceedingly important role in the treatment of orgastic dysfunction, has universal application to the release of any inhibited reflex. For example, neurologists know that when a patient inhibits his patellar reflex, it may be elicited readily by distracting him by having him focus his attention on clasping his hands together

tightly while he receives the stimulus. Again, constipation is often relieved when the patient reads while he is on the toilet, so that his attention is diverted from the act of defecation. When it is free from the inhibitory control of self-observation, the defecatory reflex is automatically triggered by distention of the rectum.

Similarly, if the inhibited patient consciously focuses her attention on her sexual experience, if she is an "orgasm watcher," if she stands apart and judges herself, it is often impossible for her to experience orgasm, even in the face of intense stimulation. Therefore, during coitus or clitoral stimulation, it is very useful to have her focus her attention on an erotic fantasy instead, or on the contractions of her vaginal muscles, or on coital thrusting, or on breathing, or on her partner. The trainees in our program refer to this therapeutic maneuver as "distracting the distractor."

Erotic fantasy during sex is an excellent distractor and is an invaluable tool for overcoming orgastic inhibition. However, patients often feel guilty about their sexual fantasies and may require the therapist's encouragement and reassurance to free them to employ their most arousing fantasies during stimulation. As is true of the vibrator, there is a danger that the patient may become habituated to its use and so be deprived of really experiencing the sexual act. Thus, while erotic fantasy is the ideal distraction in that it is simultaneously a distraction and a source of stimulation, in the normal course of treatment the patient's use of fantasy diminishes progressively along with her sexual anxiety. On the other hand, it should be noted that fantasy and the vibrator are not just therapeutic crutches, but may be used to extend the limits of the patient's sexual experiences and enhance her sexual pleasure.

5.   MUSCULAR FACTORS.   As mentioned earlier, the orgastic discharge involves clonic contractions of the pubo-

coccygeal and circumvaginal muscles. The orgastic reflex can be inhibited by over-relaxation or, in rare instances, by spastically contracting the pelvic muscles. Again, the orgastic reflex is analogous to the patellar reflex. A patient can frustrate the examining neurologist by relaxing the muscles of the thigh which are involved in expression of this reflex. Similarly, many inorgastic patients report on questioning that their vaginal muscles, which contract during orgasm, are very lax during erotic stimulation. In such cases, discharge of the orgastic reflex can be facilitated if the woman thrusts actively and contracts her vaginal and abdominal muscles when she feels the sensations of impending orgasm. Or the advice to bear down, as in childbirth, at the height of excitement may help to trigger the orgasm. During coitus, the active rhythmic contraction and relaxation of the perineal muscles is important in facilitating coital orgasm. Many women do not do this automatically and need specific instruction on this point.

6.   TRANSFERRING THE ORGASM TO THE HETEROSEX-UAL SITUATION.   Our practice of initiating the treatment of primary absolute orgastic dysfunction with masturbatory orgasm is based on two considerations. First, as mentioned earlier, the presence of an "audience" has an inhibitory effect on many women; treating the patient alone eliminates a major source of stress. Secondly, the lengthy period of stimulation which is often necessary initially before the woman is able to overcome her severe orgastic inhibition may be destructive to the couple's sexual relationship. It is tedious for the man to engage in what may initially amount to hours of stimulation, and the sensitive patient who cannot fail to perceive this is likely to be further inhibited as a result. However, teaching a patient to masturbate in solitude is much better than the patient's not

being able to have an orgasm at all, but this hardly is a satisfactory treatment outcome. We regard it as an important, transitional step in the therapeutic process.

Once the time required to reach orgasm on automanipulation is reduced to a reasonable period, which will not be destructive to the couple's lovemaking rhythm, the husband is involved in the next step in treatment to help the patient to experience orgasm when she is with her partner. The specific method used to accomplish this varies, depending on the couple's dynamics and on their particular needs. Typically, we instruct them to make love in the usual way, and the wife is told not to make any special attempt to achieve orgasm during coitus. After the husband has ejaculated and there is no pressure on the patient to "perform" quickly, he might use the vibrator, guided by her hand, to bring her to orgasm. She is again cautioned to refrain from "spectatoring"—*"I wonder if I'll climax?," "This is taking too long; he'll get sick of it,"* etc. She is told to be utterly "selfish," and to focus on her own sensations. If despite her efforts she finds that she is "turning off," she is encouraged to employ her favorite erotic fantasy to "distract her distractor," in order to counteract her involuntary conditioned tendency to inhibit herself.

Reference was made earlier to our experience that virtually all the totally inorgastic women are able to achieve orgasm by the tactics described above. Many of these patients become progressively more facile in attaining orgasm and go on to achieve a good sexual relationship with their husbands. However, some find it more difficult to progress from masturbatory orgasm to orgasm in the presence of a partner, and require additional therapy before they can function under such conditions.

Chapter 21

GROUP TREATMENT OF PREORGASMIC WOMEN

Lonnie Garfield Barbach, Ph.D.

Abstract

The preorgasmic women's group treatment program for the treatment of primary anorgasmic dysfunction relates to a combination of physiological and psychological components of orgasm. At home, the women explore their physical responses through masturbation. In the group they share their experiences with the homeplay assignments, the difficulties and fears that accompany them, and other issues of personal importance affecting their ability to experience orgasm. At the end of the five-week treatment program, 91.6 percent of 83 women were experiencing orgasm consistently through masturbation. Transfer of orgasmic capability to the partner relationship usually occurs in women who are in satisfactory emotional relationships, within eight months after the group treatment has ended.

From the *Journal of Sex and Marital Therapy,* 1974, **1,** 139–145. Reprinted by permission of the *Human Sciences Press* and *Dr. L. Barbach.*
Dr. Barbach is Clinical-Social Psychologist, Sex Advisory and Counseling Unit, University of California Medical Center, San Francisco, California 94143. Reprint queries should be directed to the author at the University of California Medical Center.

Kinsey, Pomeroy, Martin, and Gebhard,[1] in *Sexual Behavior in the Human Female,* reported that 10 to 15 percent of married American women have never experienced an orgasm. The same figure was obtained 20 years later in a survey sponsored by the Playboy Foundation.[2] Masters and Johnson[3] have labeled this problem "primary orgasmic dysfunction." The apparent lack of reduction in the frequency figures between 1953 and 1970 is perhaps due to the absence of an effective treatment technique. Traditionally, psychoanalysts have considered orgasmic difficulties to be symptoms of more severe underlying psychological problems and, consequently, have proposed years of psychoanalysis as a solution.[4] Psychoanalysis has proved to be extremely costly both in terms of time and money,[5] while therapeutic results have not kept pace with theoretic formulations—less than 25 percent of the females were cured and 36 percent improved.[6]

The relative ineffectiveness of analytic treatment may have been due in part to the erroneous belief held by Freudians[7] concerning a distinction between a clitoral and a vaginal orgasm. Psychoanalysts have led their female patients to strive for and believe in the superiority of the so-called mature vaginal orgasm, while they discounted clitoral sensations as immature and interfering with the "mature vaginal response."

Laboratory studies by Masters and Johnson of human subjects participating in various forms of sexual activity have exposed the vaginal orgasm to be a myth. They found that "from an anatomic point of view, there is absolutely no difference in the responses of the pelvic viscera to effective stimulation, regardless of whether the stimulation occurs as a result of clitoral body or mons area manipulation, natural or artificial coition, or, for that matter, specific stimulation of any other erogenous area of the female body."[8]

Masters and Johnson[3] developed a treatment program for sexually dysfunctional couples based upon the results of their research. They defined sexual dysfunction as a relationship problem and not as a personality problem of one of the individuals in the relationship. Consequently, their program has male-female teams of therapists treating couples as units rather than as individuals. Masters and Johnson report that for a sample of 193 primary nonorgasmic women, 83.9 percent became orgasmic after having been treated in a two-week program.

Drs. Lobitz and LoPiccolo[9] developed a nine-step masturbation desensitization program for primary anorgasmic women. They worked with the women individually in conjunction with the Masters and Johnson style couple program and reported 100 percent success in a sample of only three women, the slowest of whom required three months to achieve orgasm via masturbation.

It appeared that a new approach to the treatment of primary anorgasmia was required for a number of reasons. First of all, Masters and Johnson style treatment was only available to women who were currently involved in a relationship of some solidarity and in which the functional partner was willing to participate in treatment. In addition, this treatment has proved to be too expensive for most women seeking assistance, since it required the time and cost of two co-therapists for each dysfunctional woman treated.

In 1972, a group treatment program for primary anorgasmic women was developed at the University of California at Berkeley. Subsequently, the research has been carried out at the University of California Medical Center in San Francisco. The groups have been called "preorgasmic" women's groups to counteract the negativity of the words "anorgasmic" or "non-orgasmic," and to express the optimism regarding the expected outcome.

Masturbation is the major learning tool. Kinsey et al.[1] reported that of the 62 percent of women in his sample who masturbated, 58 percent achieved orgasm. Since only 4 percent failed to attain orgasm this way, we felt that masturbation would be the easiest and most reliable process by which to teach a woman to experience her first orgasm.

We have excluded the male partners from direct treatment in the therapy program. We felt that women who are afraid of losing consciousness with orgasm would have a greater sense of security if they were regulating the intensity of the stimulation themselves rather than fighting against a loss of control initiated by their partner. Also, partners can be a distracting element in a masturbation program, and we wanted to eliminate as much external interference as possible. We have the women work as a group in order to capitalize on the supportive features provided by women's consciousness-raising groups. The group format also provides a low-cost treatment option for women with low to moderate incomes, permitting us to treat a number of dysfunctional women simultaneously regardless of the status of their relationship.

METHOD

Subjects

Information on the first eighty-three women who participated in the group treatment program has been compiled. They ranged in age from 19 to 48 and included women of all races, religions, economic brackets, educational and work backgrounds, and even some foreign visitors in this country. The majority of participants responded to announcements regarding the availability of help on a radio sex talk show. The remainder were referred by private physicians, therapists, and by word of mouth.

Procedure

The treatment program consists of six women meeting together as a group with two female co-therapists. The groups meet for 1½ hours twice a week for five weeks for a total of 10 sessions.

During the group meetings, the women delve directly into the shameful feelings about sex and masturbation as well as early sexual traumas. We reexplore the impact of subtle messages given to the women by their family and society—messages such as those delineated by Dreifus.[10] We actively assist women in realizing that they have a right to sexual pleasure and that their body and sexuality is a positive thing.

Exercises to be practiced at home, called "homeplay," are assigned at each session. The homeplay follows a modified version of Lobitz and LoPiccolo's[9] nine-step masturbation program. The women are required to practice the assignment for an hour each day at home. During the following group sessions, each woman explicitly relates her experience with her assigned homeplay. The homeplay assignments progress as the woman's sexual responsivity progresses. For the first few sessions, all the women receive identical assignments. Then, later, homeplay is assigned according to the specific needs of the individual woman.

Step one consists of having the women examine their nude body in a full-length mirror in minute detail in order to help them become more comfortable and more accepting of their bodies. The Kegel[11] exercises are assigned as well as readings in *Our Bodies Ourselves.*[12]

In the second session, we explain the anatomy of the female genitals and the sexual response cycle. For homeplay, the women examine their genitals carefully with the aid of a hand mirror.

In the third session, we show the women a female masturbation movie produced by the Multi-Media Resource Center of the National Sex Forum which helps to demystify the process of orgasm. The women are assigned to go home and masturbate, but not to the point of orgasm.

After the fourth session, the masturbation homeplay is tailored to the individual's pace and specific difficulties.

No restriction is ever placed on sexual intercourse. After a woman has become proficient in experiencing orgasm with masturbation, we assign homeplay that includes her partner, if she has one. The exercises stress the necessity of specific and direct sexual communication if the woman is to become orgasmic in the relationship.

The first step of including the partner consists of having the woman masturbate to orgasm while her partner is observing her. After that, both nongenital and genital exploration is encouraged by teaching the woman to guide her partner's hands over her body in the manner she prefers. In our last step, the woman masturbates herself while her partner's penis is inside her if she desires orgasm with intercourse.

Women who have not previously masturbated usually have intense prohibitions against it that are difficult to overcome. These prohibitions deter them from being able to perform the masturbation assignments. Prolonged procrastination is minimized by limiting the number of group sessions to 10 and by directly confronting the resistance through traditional therapeutic approaches, paradoxical injunctions, diversion techniques, and through peer group support.

For many people, sex is equivalent to intercourse. However, the indirect clitoral stimulation afforded through intercourse alone is often insufficient to enable many women to reach orgasm. Rather than stressing orgasm through intercourse as a goal for the women, we try to expand their repertoire of sexual activities by encouraging them to seek sexual satisfaction in whatever manner is mutually acceptable. Therefore, rather than attempting to fit a woman into a mold that may not fit her specific physiological requirements for orgasm, we attempt to broaden the acceptable sexual practices to meet her unique needs or capabilities.

RESULTS

Of the first 83 women who participated in the groups, 91.6 percent were orgasmic with masturbation by the end of the 10 sessions. Of these, three predesignated research groups have been studied exhaustively and have been followed for a period of eight months after the termination of treatment. A detailed analysis of these 17 women is presented by Wallace and Barbach.[13]

After the groups were over, women indicated that they had undergone a number of positive changes as the result of the group. Enhanced self-esteem, increased assertiveness and expression of feelings, body and sexual acceptance, and increased satisfaction with intimate relationships were all mentioned.

Seventeen women were questioned on their orgasmic status eight months after their last session. Each of the women was still orgasmic via masturbation at this time. In addition, seven women were orgasmic with their partners during 90 to 100 percent of their sexual encounters; four achieved a 50 percent orgasmic rate; three were orgasmic less than 50 percent; two had still not achieved orgasm with their partners. In addition, there was one woman whose success could not be determined due to the absence of any partner. At this time, additional questionnaire information was obtained from the women that indicated that compared to pretreatment, they were experiencing improvement in their lives in general, their level of happiness, level of relaxation, and communication with their partner, as well as in their sexual activities.

This continued progress past the termination of the treatment is noteworthy. In one case, a woman called 12 months post-treatment to inform us that she had experienced her first orgasm during coitus. This suggests that the treatment program supplies the necessary techniques that the women can continue to utilize beyond the termination of therapy.

The male partners (N = 13) of the women who were either married or who had *steady* partners were interviewed at the end of the group. These men were very enthusiastic about the changes that occurred in their female partners as the result of the group treatment. Although many felt threatened while the group was in progress, they seemed to overcome those feelings as the sexual relationship became more positive. They were generally supportive of their partner's struggle and wanted to be as helpful as possible. Most men were thankful that their partner could finally give them some specific information that they could apply during lovemaking, hence reducing their responsibility for their partner's orgasm. Most couples felt the sexual relationship was well on the way toward mutual satisfaction and were determined to continue working on that aspect of the relationship by themselves or to get assistance if they could not change things on their own. This is a significant change considering that many of these men were unfavorably disposed to sex therapy when their partners first entered the group.

DISCUSSION

There seem to be five essential factors that account for the reversal of the orgasmic dysfunction: (a) the supportive nature of the group; (b) its permission-giving aspects; (c) the therapists' ability to confront and cut through the clients' resistance while (d) insuring that the client and not the therapist assumes responsibility for the orgasm; and (e) the use of masturbation as the main learning technique.

The use of self-stimulation as opposed to partner stimulation as the method of becoming familiar with orgasm is central; having the orgasm under the woman's own control allows her to go at her own pace while eliminating outside distractions provided by the presence of another person. In this manner, the woman can take gradual steps and learn to become familiar with the feelings that accompany sexual excitation rather than having to guard against them for fear they will overwhelm her. She can stop the stimulation if she feels afraid, or continue on as she grows more secure. As the result of growing familiarity and confidence, the woman becomes capable of experiencing an orgasm on her own. Then, after a period of time of dependably repeating this experience, she becomes secure enough in the response to become capable of experiencing the orgasm while sexually interacting with her partner.

The group leaders are highly important. Their ability to keep the group focused on sex and yet leave room for the expression of feelings and problem solving in related areas is essential. Also essential is their ability to provide warmth and support to the group members while still confronting the group members' resistance.

The group leaders are authority figures in the sense that they focus group interaction and assign homeplay and elicit feedback on its performance. However, they perform their role while placing the responsibility for the achievement of orgasm on its rightful owner, the client. The leaders must also be familiar with the concepts of the group process as described by Yalom.[14] They must be capable of discerning inconspicuous group norms that may be interfering with the attainment of orgasm by the group members. It was observed that more experienced therapists appeared to achieve greater success rates in their groups than less experienced leaders.

The supportive group provides an important medium within which the women can work to redefine their sexuality and sometimes their lives. The women who were interviewed after their groups were over agreed unanimously that the effect of sharing their problems with other women who were like themselves and who could understand them and with whom they could personally identify was of crucial importance.

The permission-giving aspect of the group is important because women have grown up being told over and over again *not* to be sexual. After receiving this message so many times, women become conditioned to ward off sexual feelings rather than expand and enjoy them. When any of the women report positive experiences with their masturbation or other sexual stimulation, the therapists and group members respond with genuine acceptance and praise. This positive response from both peers and authority figures helps to recondition the women to be more accepting of their natural sexual urges.

Sexual permission giving from other women may help to recorrect early learning. Like Fisher,[15] we find that many of the women who have never experienced orgasm came from families where the father was absent, physically or emotionally. Our clinical research is supportive of a speculation Fisher has made indicating that the factor most responsible for the woman's lack of orgasmic response is not the absent father as much as it results from the mother's attitude toward the absent father and men in general. Fisher states: "Illustratively, if the mother relates to the father in a way that suggests that the mother thinks the father to be a dependable person and that his love can be counted upon, this might convey to her daughter the message that not only her father, but also men in general can be taken as dependable love objects."

This would account for the success of a group where women are giving other women permission to be sexual, with the outcome that the women learn to respond sexually alone and with their partners. This goal is achieved without ever including any direct work with their partners and, hence, not directly influencing the level of trust of the partner or his credibility as a dependable love object.

Encouraged by the results of the preorgasmic women's groups, we modified the technique and developed a program for women who have orgasm only with masturbation, and not with partners. We called this a sexual enrichment group because the success of this mode of group treatment of the secondary orgasmic dysfunction was unknown. Results appear promising and research is currently being conducted to evaluate the success of the sexual enrichment groups.

REFERENCES

1. Kinsey, A., Pomeroy, W., Martin, C. et al. *Sexual behavior in the human female.* Philadelphia: W. B. Saunders, 1953.

2. Hunt, M. Sexual behavior in the 1970's. *Playboy,* 1973, **20** (10), 84–88, 194–207.

3. Masters, W., & Johnson, V. *Human sexual inadequacy.* Boston: Little, Brown, 1970.

4. Lorand, S. Contribution to the problem of vaginal orgasm. *Int. Journal Psychoanalysis,* 1939, **20,** 432–438.

5. Bergler, E. Frigidity in the female: Misconceptions and facts. *Marital Hygiene,* 1947, **1,** 16–21.

6. O'Connor, J., & Stern, L. Results of treatment in functional sexual disorders. *New York State Journal of Medicine,* 1972, **72,** 1927–1934.

7. Freud, S. *New introductory lectures on psychoanalysis.* J. Strachey (Ed.) New York: W. W. Norton, 1965.

8. Masters, W., & Johnson, V. *Human sexual response.* Boston: Little, Brown, 1966.

9. Lobitz, W., & LoPiccolo, J. Methods in the behavioral treatment of sexual dysfunction. *Journal of Behavior Therapy & Experimental Psychiatry,* 1972, **3,** 265–271.

10. Dreifus, C. *Woman's fate: Raps from a feminist consciousness raising group.* New York: Bantam, 1973.

11. Kegel, A. Sexual functions of the pubococcygens muscle. *Western Journal of Obstetrics and Gynecology,* 1952, **60,** 521.

12. Boston Women's Health Collective. *Our bodies ourselves.* New York: Simon and Schuster, 1971.

13. Wallace, D. H., & Barbach, L. G. Preorgasmic group treatment. *Journal of Sex and Marital Therapy,* 1974, **1,** 146–154.

14. Yalom, J. *The theory and practice of group psychotherapy.* New York: Basic Books, 1970.

15. Fisher, S. *The female orgasm: Psychology, physiology, fantasy.* New York: Basic Books, 1973.

Part VI

RESEARCH ON AUTOEROTICISM: AN OVERALL VIEW

Manfred F. DeMartino, M.A.

Introduction

PREVALENCE

The extent to which autoeroticism is *actually* practiced by females and males in our society at present is not really known. Different researchers and authorities, as was observed in the previous sections and will be seen here, have reported various percentages both with respect to females as well as males. In the case of males, however, there is much greater unanimity concerning the overall percentage of those who masturbate at some point in their lives than there is in regard to females. Several factors appear to contribute to the lack of agreement among researchers relating to the incidence of autoeroticism by females, including the definition of what constitutes autoeroticism in females, and whether the act results in orgasm. Also, some females who actually engage in autoerotic activity are unaware of the nature of their sexual behavior. Furthermore, especially during the last decade, marked changes have occurred both in the attitudes and practices by females with respect to sexual expression in general. Moreover, many sex therapists and other professionals for the past several years have been recommending the use of masturbation for therapeutic purposes.

Although the incidence of masturbatory behavior among women and men is still open to question, as Kinsey et al. have stated, for females it is the activity "in which the second largest number . . . engage both before and after marriage" (1953, p. 132). For males autoeroticism is the second most important sexual outlet of gratification (1948).

Before presenting some of the important statistical and qualitative findings relative to masturbatory activity, which thus far have not been included in this book or were just briefly mentioned by the contributors, or warrant repeating, it should be emphasized that in evaluating research data pertaining to masturbation a number of factors need to be taken into account, including the following: (1) age range of subjects, (2) religious affiliation and degree of devoutness, (3) social class and level of education or intelligence of subjects, (4) whether the study is based on *current* masturbatory activity (active incidence) or whether the study reports findings related to an autoerotic experience at some time or another (accumulative incidence), (5) personality characteristics of subjects, (6) strength of the subjects' sexual drives, and (7) whether the subjects were virgins or nonvirgins.

DURING INFANCY AND EARLY CHILDHOOD

As one would imagine, it was Freud who was one of the first scientists to write about the occurrence of masturbation during infancy. In his discourse on "Infantile Sexuality," he commented: "We can scarcely ignore the fact that the infantile masturbation from which hardly anyone escapes, forms the foundation for the future primacy of this erogenous zone for sexual activity" (1938, p. 590). Nevertheless, while he and a number of other writers (e.g., Townsend, 1896; Bühler, 1931; Lees, 1944; Spock, 1946; Dearborn, 1947; Spitz & Wolf 1949) made it known over the years that infants of both sexes masturbate, it was Kinsey and his associates, more so than any other researchers, who first enlightened the *general public* to this fact.

With respect to very young females, Kinsey and his co-workers disclosed the following: "masturbation had occurred among females of every group from infancy to old age. . . . We have records of 67 infants and small girls three years of age or younger who were observed in masturbation, or who as adults recalled that they had masturbated at that age. We have one record of a seven-month-old infant and records of 5 infants under one year of age who were observed in masturbation. . . . We have records of 23 girls three years old or younger who reached orgasm in self-masturbation. There are more records of small girls than there are of small boys masturbating to orgasm at such an early age. It requires some experience and some development of muscular coordinations to effect the rhythmic manual movements on which masturbation depends, and the small boy does not so often manage to achieve that end" (1953, pp. 141–142). By the age of 3 years, as noted by their sample of women, 1% had experienced masturbation and 0.3% had achieved orgasms from the practice. By the age of 7, 4% of those who had masturbated had reached an orgasm. At 10 years of age, 13% of the women acknowledged having masturbated and 8% recalled having attained an orgasm from doing so. Prior to the attainment of "adolescence," 19% of the women in the Kinsey group had experienced autoerotic behavior.

In the study by Miller and Lief, 19% of the females stated that they had experienced autoerotic activity before the age of 10 (1976). (This is a higher percentage than was true in the case of boys.)

As for very young males, Kinsey et al. reported: "Erection may occur immediately after birth and, as many observant mothers (and few scientists) know, it is practically a daily matter for all small boys, from earliest infancy and up in age" (1948, p. 164). In reference to autoeroticism, these pioneer sexologists observed: "there are cases of infants under a year of age who have learned the advantage of specific manipulation, sometimes as a result of being so manipulated by older persons; and there are some boys who masturbate quite specifically and with some frequency from the age of two or three" (1948, p. 501). While deliberate self-stimulation is definitely known to occur among male as well as female babies, according to the Kinsey group, "a relatively small number of the younger preadolescents . . . in any strict sense, masturbate" (1948, p. 501). In the Kinsey et al. sample not more than 16% of the young boys began to masturbate before the age of 10. And the majority did not engage in the practice until they were about 12 years old. Those who masturbated during the preadolescent years almost always continued the practice into adolescence. The importance of masturbation as a form of sexual expression in the lives of young males was made apparent by the Kinsey et al. finding that 68.4% of them experienced their first ejaculation from this practice. This occurrence was not significantly affected by social class affiliation. Interesting, too, were the following observations by Kinsey and his associates: "Some adolescent boys and many adults recall specific orgasm with all of its adult characteristics occurring before they had acquired the ability to ejaculate; and there are definite records on several hundred boys who have been observed in preadolescent orgasm which was achieved through self-stimulation or through socio-sexual contacts" (1953, p. 503).

Only 14% of the males in the Miller and Lief investigation signified having masturbated before the age of 10 (1976).

Dr. René Spitz has pointed out not only that genital play and masturbation during infancy and puberty are normal forms of behavior but they are also desirable in terms of personality formation. Moreover, as he discovered, a positive correlation exists between the practice of genital play during infancy and the quality of the relationship that prevails between mother and child (1962). A positive association between genital play and emotional response has also been described by Dr. Georgene Seward. In regard to boy babies "within the first two years" she has reported: "On the one hand, genital tension indicated by tumescence has been found to occur under frustrating feeding conditions, such as difficult nipple, delay in feeding, or with holding the breast. . . . On the other hand, the comforting finger sucking is sometimes accompanied by a rubbing contact with the genitals. . . ."[1] (1946, p. 146).

And Kaplan has remarked: "Boy infants have erections from birth on. They show interest in manipulating their genitals as soon as hand coordination permits. Infantile masturbation is a normal phase of development" (1974, p. 106). She has further stated: "Infants seems to crave erotic pleasure. Babies of both genders tend to touch their genitals and express joy when their genitals are stimulated in the course of diapering and bathing, and both little boys and girls stimulate their penis or clitoris as soon as they acquire the necessary motor coordination" (1974, p. 147).

During Adolescence

In the Kinsey et al. study of females, by age 12 some 12% of the subjects had masturbated to the point of orgasm and

[1]From *Sex and the Social Order* by Georgene H. Seward. Copyright, 1946 by The McGraw-Hill Book Co. Inc. Used with permission of McGraw-Hill Book Company.

by 15, 20% had done so. Furthermore, by the age of 20, 33% of the participants had experienced orgasms from their autoerotic behavior (1953). Unlike males, however, no significant correlation was found to exist between the age of attainment of sexual maturation and the practice of masturbation. Differences in autoerotic activity that were revealed in regard to educational levels were as follows: "In the late teens, the active incidences among single females were 27 percent in the grade school group and 34 percent in the graduate school group. . . . Among married females between twenty-one and twenty-five years of age, the active incidences ranged from 11 percent for the grade school group to 31 percent for the graduate school group . . ." (1953, p. 148).

In my investigation of women with very high I.Q.s some 51% of those subjects from 16 to 19 signified having engaged in autoerotic behavior (1974). (This finding is significantly higher than the one reported by Sorensen [39%] —see below.)

Miller and Lief's study revealed that by the age of 13, 34% of their sample of females had engaged in autoerotic activity and before the age of 16, 45% had experienced such behavior (1976).

In the case of males, by the age of 12, 21% of those in the Kinsey et al. study had masturbated to the point of orgasm and by 15, 82% had done so. By late adolescence, age 20, 92% of the males had engaged in autoeroticism resulting in orgasms (1948). And, as revealed by the Kinsey group, the practice of autoeroticism in males was related to early and late maturation. Not only did many more early-maturing boys experience their first ejaculation from masturbation (72%) than late-maturing boys (52%), but as the Kinsey researchers noted: "Males with the highest frequencies of masturbation are most often those who become adolescent first. These are the males who have the maximum total outlet throughout their lives. . . . The highest incidence (99%) of masturbation in any segment of the population is among these younger-adolescent boys. It is only 93 percent of the late-adolescent boys who ever masturbate" (1948, p. 507). The incidence of autoerotic activity among males was also significantly related to educational and social levels. In this regard Kinsey and his associates commented: "At all ages, in all religious groups and in nearly all other subdivisions of the population, the highest incidences and frequencies of masturbation are to be found among boys of the college level, and the lowest incidences and frequencies among boys of lower educational levels. . . . At the college level, masturbation involves most of the males (96%) and continues to be the chief source (about 60%) of the outlet up until the time of marriage" (1948, pp. 507–508). Moreover, during the period of late adolescence as Kinsey et al. reported: "males of the college level masturbate more than twice as frequently as the males of the grade school level" (1948, p. 508). In reference to the population as a whole, however, according to Kinsey and his co-workers: "The highest incidence for masturbation among single males . . . lies between 16 and 20 years of age, when 88 percent is involved" (1948, p. 238).

In the study by Miller and Lief 48% of the males had masturbated by the time they were 13 and about 83% had done so before the age of 16 (1976).

Sorensen, as a result of his extensive study of several hundred male and female adolescents ranging in age from 13 to 19, disclosed that: "49% of all adolescents say they have masturbated; 58% of all boys and 39% of all girls have masturbated at least once. . . . More girls masturbate at an earlier age than do boys. Most girls who masturbate have masturbated before the age of thirteen; the majority of boys who masturbate have had their first masturbation experience before the age of fourteen" (1973, p. 129). (From the above findings it appears that while a somewhat higher percentage of the girls in the Sorensen study indicated having masturbated than was true in the Kinsey et al. investigation, a much lower percentage of the adolescent males in the Sorensen sample reported having masturbated than was the case in the undertaking by the Kinsey group.) Not unexpected, the use of marijuana by adolescents was observed to be related in some ways to autoerotic behavior. As Sorensen noted: "Marijuana users enjoy masturbation in substantially greater proportions than nonusers. . . . More marijuana users fantasize during masturbation than nonusers" (1973, p. 145). "Pot" users also experienced less guilt and anxiety feelings concerning autoeroticism than did nonusers. (Sorensen's reference to the average age when females compared with males begin masturbating, it should be pointed out, is at odds with Hunt's comment recorded below.)

In 1974 Hunt revealed that by the age of 13, 33% of the sample of females and 63% of the males in the Playboy study had masturbated. His findings thus are significantly higher than those recorded by Kinsey et al. mentioned above. In view of these results Hunt stated: "there has been a major change in the age at which masturbation is first experienced. Both sexes are beginning it earlier than formerly, although females still begin masturbating on the average a good deal later than males, many females doing so for the first time in their dating or early marital years" (1974, p. 77).

DURING ADULTHOOD

It is interesting from an historical standpoint that the eminent English sexologist of the early 1900s, Havelock Ellis, mistakenly believed masturbation was more prevalent among women than men. As he commented: "After adolescence I think there can be no doubt that masturbation is more common in women than in men. Men have, by this time, mostly adopted some method of sexual gratification with the opposite sex; women are to a much larger extent shut out from such gratification. . . ." (1936, p. 245). In the early study by Peck and Wells of about 250 college males, 86% of the respondents were found to have masturbated, a finding that is fairly consistent with those of present-day research (1923). And in regard to his study of men and women of a "relatively high level of culture" Hamilton observed: "97 of the 100 men and 74 of the 100 women had masturbated at some time or other in their lives after they were old enough to remember it. . . ." (1929, p. 539). In the major study of 2200 women undertaken by Davis, 64.8% and 40.1%, respectively, of the unmarried and married subjects indicated having masturbated at some point in their lives. The average age of the unmarried sample was 36.8 years, while 38.3 years was the average age of the married women (1929).

Kinsey et al. in 1948 and 1953, respectively, startled many Americans by discovering that 92% of their male subjects (96% at the college level, 95% at high school level and 89% at the grade school level), and 62% of the females they questioned had engaged in autoerotic activity at one time or another. As in the case of males, the factor of education was also positively related to the experiencing of masturbation by females. Relative to the frequently quoted 1948 finding of "92 percent," the following comments by Dr. Wardell Pomeroy in reference to a letter sent by Kinsey, are somewhat surprising: "Thus, when a . . . medical student . . . wrote to ask whether it was true that 2 percent of males did not masturbate or whether all of them did at one time in their lives, Kinsey was happy to give him an answer which knocked down one more myth: Our survey indicates that ninety-six percent of the males masturbate at some time in their lives. . . ." (1972, p. 313).

In a study of 102 women social nudists (ranging in age

from 17 to 62, with an average age of 34.7 years) and 73 "potential" nudists (with an age range from 17 to 52, and an average age of 26.9 years), undertaken by this writer, 84 and 80%, respectively, of the nudists and "potential" nudists signified having masturbated at one time or another (1969). Both groups of women were rather well-educated.

McCary in surveying the literature on masturbatory behavior has remarked: "From 50% to 80% of all women masturbate at one time or another in their lives, whether or not they are aware of it (the variance in figures resulting from differences among the results of several investigations into the subject)" (1973, p. 298).

And in an international study of 327 women with very high I.Q.s (age range 16 to 61, average age 32), conducted by this writer, 81% of the participants reported having engaged in autoeroticism (1974).

In the study commissioned by the Playboy Foundation, which included 982 males and 1044 females ranging in age from 18 to 77 (most of whom were between 25 and 77) as noted by Hunt, 94% of the males and 63% of the females had masturbated (1974). While these percentages very closely resemble those recorded by the Kinsey group in 1948 and 1953, in reference to his findings, Hunt remarked: "but this is not an accumulative incidence; it represents what has happened up to this time, in the lives of our respondents. Presumably, some of the younger people in the sample and at least a few of the more mature people who have not yet experienced masturbation will still do so during their lifetimes. Accordingly, our incidence data suggest at least a small overall increase since Kinsey's time" (p. 76). Additional evidence for this writer's previous claim (1974) that women of high intelligence are somewhat more sexually responsive than those of average intelligence may be seen by comparing the percentage of women with high I.Q.s who masturbated (81%) with the percentage of those who did so in the Playboy study (63%). Especially significant, Hunt's data were collected in 1972 and were based on subjects up to the age of 77, while all of this writer's data were obtained by 1969, and were based on women up to the age of 61.

Kaplan, in viewing the incidence of autoeroticism on the part of males and females, has commented: "While virtually all normal boys masturbate, approximately 30% to 40% of women report that they either do not masturbate at all or they did not start to masturbate until after they had had a sexual experience which had led to orgasm or to intense arousal" (1974, p. 110).

Shere Hite, in her well-known study of 3000 women ranging in age from 14 to 78, which was undertaken with the cooperation of the National Organization for Women, revealed that masturbation had occurred in the lives of 82% of the subjects (1977).

Finally, in the investigation by Miller and Lief involving 556 women and men (high school, college, graduate and medical students) with an age range of 18 to 35 plus, about 78% of the women and 97% of the men indicated having masturbated (1977).

DURING MIDDLE AGE AND OLDER

Like so many other aspects of human behavior related to the aged, up until rather recently little research had been done in the area of human sexuality even though it is possible for men and women to remain sexually active up until the age of 100 (Lobsenz 1974).

In regard to women, unlike men the practice of masturbation is more prevalent among older persons than younger ones. Kinsey et al. for instance stated: "The active incidences of masturbation were lowest in the younger groups, and highest in the older groups of females" (1953, p. 143). Reasons offered by the Kinsey group in an attempt to explain this finding were (1) an increase in sexual responsiveness may have occurred during the older ages, (2) more women of the older ages turned to masturbation because of a reduction in their available sexual outlets, (3) a lessening of sexual inhibitions was experienced with advanced age, and (4) because of their greater overall sexual experience with other persons, they discovered that pleasure could also be obtained through autoerotic activity.

And Masters and Johnson have commented as follows: "Mention should be made of the increased masturbatory rate of women in the 50–70-year age groups. The pattern of masturbatory release of sexual tensions reportedly increases in frequency after the menopause, at least into the 60-year age range, for many reasons. Unmarried women committed to regularity of manipulative relief as younger women continue their pattern into the older age group. In addition, there are women who are married to men failing in health, and who are widowed, divorced, or socially isolated for any reason in the declining years. They frequently find need for some regularity of the sexual tension release denied them by loss or unavailability of sexual partners. Since these forms of social isolation are particularly prevalent among women in the 50–70 year age group, a relative increase in frequency of masturbatory rate is understandable. Psychosocial freedom to enjoy masturbatory relief of unresolved sexual tensions has more and more become an acceptable behavioral pattern for those women so handicapped by limited partner availability in this age group" (1970, p. 342).

Consistent with the results uncovered by Kinsey et al., and Masters and Johnson, this writer found that a higher percentage of highly intelligent women 30 years and older as compared to those of 29 years of age and younger had engaged in masturbatory behavior (1974).

Kaplan, in comparing aged females with aged males has observed: "In sharp contrast to men, elderly women remain capable of enjoying multiple orgasms. In fact, studies indicate that 25% of 70-year-old women still masturbate" (1974, p. 112).

Apropos of males, Kinsey and his associates found that at age 50, 53.8% of their sample of single males were still masturbating and this activity accounted for a little more than a third (37.9%) of their total sexual outlet (1948). By age 50, the maximum average frequency of masturbation for the males in the study was reported to be 6 per week and "once in two weeks at sixty years of age" (1948, p. 506). While a little more than a tenth of the married men were still masturbating in their middle fifties, only a few of the men 75 years of age were still doing so.

Dr. Isadore Rubin, in reference to the largest sexual study ever conducted of highly professional males over 65 years of age (more than 800) revealed the following: "66 out of 279 married men who reported regular satisfying coitus reported that they engaged in masturbation either currently or in the period over the age of 60 (24 percent). Nine out of 49 men who reported unsatisfactory coitus (18 percent) reported masturbation over the age of 60. Twenty-five out of 105 impotent males (24 percent) reported masturbation over the age of 60. These findings in a group of males over 65, each of whom had attained considerable distinction in his profession, should certainly raise questions in the minds of those persons who characterize masturbation as a 'childish' and 'immature' activity" (1963, pp. 141–142).

How Masturbation Was Learned

The findings reported in the overall scientific literature leave no doubt that the primary way in which females learn to masturbate is through self-discovery (by accident).

Self-discovery or self-exploration, for example, was

the predominant way the females in the Kinsey et al. investigation learned to masturbate (1953). More of the females of the upper educational levels had discovered the practice by themselves than did those of the lower educational levels. Quite remarkably, many of the women who first started masturbating at ages 40 and 50 also learned of the act through self-discovery. About 43% of the women had learned to masturbate from verbal and/or printed sources (this was the most important source for women who started to masturbate after 20, and the second major source for those who had done so before the age of 20), 12% as a result of premarital heterosexual activity, 11% from watching others (including the observation of males), and approximately 3% from homosexual contacts.

In both of the studies undertaken by this writer, self-discovery (exploration, accidentally, experimentation) was also the primary way in which the women had learned to masturbate (1969, 1974). Most of the women in the Hite report similarly discovered masturbation by themselves (1977).

Contrary to females, the great majority of males, according to the Kinsey researchers, masturbate after first having *heard* about the practice. In the Kinsey sample, 75% of the males learned about masturbation from verbal and/or printed sources (mainly verbal), 40% from observing others, 28% through self-discovery, and 9% as a result of having been masturbated by another male. In general, the males began masturbating very soon after having heard about the activity.

REASONS FOR MASTURBATING

Like almost all other forms of human behavior, the motives governing autoeroticism by females and males are many and varied. Kinsey et al. in their study of female masturbation stated: "In the human animal, motivations for the activity lie in the conscious realization that erotic satisfactions and some release from erotic tensions may thus be obtained" (1953, p. 133).

In this writer's research, while the motives given by the various women subjects for engaging in autoeroticism *after* marriage were diversified, the two main ones were husband not present and desire for gratification following unsatisfactory coital relations with husband (1969, 1974). Other reasons reported included feelings of boredom, loneliness, anxiety, depression, insufficient coital activity, release of tension, husband fatigued, ill or impotent, erotic arousal from thinking or reading, frustration, poor marital relationship, not being able to fall asleep, for the pleasure derived from act, response to an erotic dream, as part of heterosexual relations, and pregnancy.

Among the reasons recorded by the women in the Hite study (1977) concerning the *importance* of masturbation were the following: (1) It provides a means of sexual gratification when a partner is either absent or not available. (2) It serves as a sexual self-learning experience. (3) It helps improve sexual relations with others. (4) It is viewed "as a means of independence and self-reliance" (p. 75). (5) It serves to produce feelings of pleasure.

No motives were given by the Kinsey group in reference to masturbation by males. They simply remarked: "The inspiration for the first experimentation in masturbation is a matter which will need more extensive consideration in a later study on sex education" (1948, p. 501). Hunt, however, like other researchers also discovered that the reasons for masturbation by males and females are complex—and many of them are unrelated to sexual interests or biological urges. In addition to the the need for "relief of sexual tension"—the major motive—masturbation was observed to be motivated by "sexual hunger," feelings of insecurity, boredom, apprehension, loneliness, feelings of frustration (especially by a desired sex partner), feelings of "general tension" that interfere with falling asleep, and erotic arousal from seeing erotic movies, pictures, or from reading (the latter is particularly true in the case of women). Then, too, as Hunt noted, autoeroticism "enables people to do, in fantasy, sexual things they do not ordinarily have the chance to do, or with partners they have no access to" (1974, p. 90). The absence or nonavailability of one's sexual mate was also found to lead to the practice of masturbation.

METHODS USED IN MASTURBATING

Although autoeroticism is more prevalent among males than females and is generally engaged in more frequently by males than females, females nevertheless employ a much greater variety of autoerotic techniques than do males. In reference to the main methods used by females, Kinsey and his associates stated: "Masturbation among the females . . . had most frequently involved some manipulation of the clitoris and/or the labia minora" (1953, p. 158). Breast and nipple stimulation had been part of autoerotic activity for only about 11% of their sample of women, and for approximately 10% masturbation on occasion had occurred by the subjects "crossing their legs and appressing them to exert steady or more rhythmic pressure on the whole genital area" (1953, p. 159). Vaginal insertions were employed occasionally during masturbation by about 20% of the subjects. Other methods utilized during autoeroticism by some of the females in the Kinsey et al. study were rubbing genitalia against objects such as pillows, beds, chairs, clothing, and the like, and using a vibrator, running water, douches, enemas, urethral and anal insertions, and "sado-masochistic activity."

And as Masters and Johnson have observed, women

differ in the ways in which they masturbate and rarely "employ direct manipulation of the clitoral glans" (1966, p. 63). Instead, they generally "stimulate the entire mons area."

With respect to the more unusual autoerotic methods that have been used by women, as Havelock Ellis has reported these include *rin-no-tama* (two small lightweight balls that are hollow); artificial penises made of wax, paper, clay, rosin, ivory, gold, leather; a "glass object filled with warm water"; a rubber penis substitute capable of injecting a warm fluid; cucumbers; bananas; turnips; carrots; beetroots; hair pins; bone hairpins; knitting needles; corks; hen's eggs; sitting on the naked heel of one's foot and rubbing the genital area against it; riding on a hobbyhorse; horseback riding; bicycle riding; rubbing against a bureau drawer with a key protruding; operating a foot-peddled sewing machine; and tight lacing of corsets (1936). One woman in the study by Kronhausen and Kronhausen was only able to attain an orgasm "by rubbing her genitals against her husband's knee" (1965). Edward Lea noted the use by some women of "sweet potatoes as dildos" as well as a masturbation machine found in the Dresden Museum that was controlled by a foot pedal and on which different size penises could be attached (1967). During the past few years, mention has also been made of women masturbating by leaning against an on-going washing machine. And recently, Albert Ellis has referred to an advertisement describing a "remote-control vibrator (so that a woman can masturbate while typing or doing other work!)" (1976, p. 64).

The predominant autoerotic technique reported by the women nudists and "potential" nudists investigated by this writer, was one that "involved in some way use of either the finger (or fingers) or hand (manual) and clitoral stimulation (manipulation)" (1969, p. 36). Only a very few women acknowledged having engaged in the manipulation of breasts and/or nipples.

Consistent with the findings revealed by the Kinsey group and those described in the study just mentioned, the main masturbatory technique practiced by this writer's sample of highly intelligent women was "manual clitoral stimulation" (1974). This was followed by "manual manipulation of the external genitalia." And again, breast or nipple autostimulation was experienced by a small number of the women of high intelligence. This latter finding, however, was not surprising in view of Masters and Johnson's disclosure that just three of their women subjects were able to attain an orgasm from breast stimulation alone (1966).

Masturbatory techniques described by women in an unpublished study by this writer included the following: fingers on clitoris and anus; use of drinking glass, baseball bat, door; swinging on bars (ages 10 to 13); use of handle of a knife; reading or driving a car while wearing very tight levis; use of garden hose; medicine dropper rubbed against vagina and inserted in vagina—also warm running water of tub on clitoris till orgasm; clothespins; using rubber hot dog; finger rubber glove—"at times I am able to reach orgasm just by imagining myself in a sexual situation with a man I have an attraction to" (age 33, married).

Some of the autoerotic practices recorded by the women in the Hite investigation included the following: (1) clitoral area stimulation by hand or vibrator (used by the majority of subjects), (2) clitoral and vulva stimulation—use of index finger, middle finger, whole hand, right hand, left hand, (3) breast and nipple massage—rubbing, pinching, pulling, and squeezing nipple—also sucking on nipple and licking breasts, lubricant on breasts, long ruler to stimulate both breasts at the same time, (4) vaginal insertions—fingers, candle, dildo, vibrator, (5) anal penetration, (6) crossing of legs and exerting thigh pressure—method used in classrooms and other public places—legs apart, together, (7) rubbing against objects—pillows, chairs, blankets, bathroom sink, laundry bag, (8) use of running water on genital area, and (9) use of a mirror, of lubricant on the clitoris—vaseline, oil, cream, use of a warm wet towel, feather, pencil eraser, ice cubes, lipsticks (1977).

In a study by Hill, among the various methods of masturbating openly discussed by a group of women were the following: use of water from kitchen sinks, doorknobs, end of broom handles, scissors handles, cucumbers and ben-wa balls (1976).

In view of the ever increasing use of vibrators and massagers for autoerotic purposes, especially by women, a further word of caution seems necessary. Some years ago Dr. Edwin Hirsh in commenting on the "use of the vaginal vibrator or high-frequency electrode" pointed out that: "Not a few accidents have occurred from the indiscrete use of these contrivances. Explosions have taken place within the vagina. Electrocution has also resulted when the electric instrument was employed while the woman was taking a bath" (1938, pp. 140–141).

Since the use of lubricants are sometimes helpful during female autoeroticism, as Heiman, LoPiccolo, and LoPiccolo suggest, while saliva, body oil and "K-Y" jelly may be used inside the vagina, substances that should *not* be inserted are lotions that contain alcohol, perfume, or other strong ingredients (1976).

Contrary to the widely diversified autoerotic methods used by women, as Kinsey et al. have stated: "In the human male, masturbatory techniques are largely manual. . . . There are some boys who attempt to masturbate by moving the penis against a bed or against some other object; but for most males this technique is rare. . . . Self-fellation is an anatomic impossibility for most human males, . . . but a considerable portion of the population does record attempts at self-fellation, at least in early adolescence. Only two or three males in a thousand are able to achieve the objective. . . . Urethral insertions and other masochistic techniques, and anal stimulation and anal insertions occur very occasionally. Sometimes devices which simulate the female genitalia may be used for masturbation, but they are rarely employed" (1948, pp. 509–510).

Kinsey and his co-workers also noted that: "many a boy exhibits his masturbatory techniques to lone companions or to whole groups of boys. . . . There are teenage boys who continue this exhibitionistic activity throughout their high school years, some of them even entering into compacts with their closest friends to refrain from self-masturbation except when in the presence of each other" (1948, p. 169). In their discussion of sexual contacts with animals these researchers have further observed: "In some cases the boy masturbates by friction against the body of the animal. . . . If a boy is alone, he may masturbate himself while he masturbates the animal, and there may be considerable erotic stimulation to the boy involved in such a performance" (1948, p. 675).

As reported by Masters and Johnson, while males show variations in the tightness with which they grip their penis and their speed of movement during masturbation, most males "manipulate the shaft of the penis with stroking techniques that encompass the entire organ" (1966, p. 198). And according to Lea: "Farm youths have frequently reported incidents of 'copulating' with mud along river banks, or with watermelons warmed by the sun into which they cut holes" (1967, p. 328). Moreover, modeling clay formed in the shape of vaginas and the inside cardboard of toilet tissues are also used for masturbatory purposes.

Albert Ellis has mentioned the following artificial devices that may be used by males during masturbation: bottles, jars, pipes, the "Auto-suck," large plastic or rubber dolls, various kinds of artificial vaginas including an electric vagina and anal stimulators (1976).

USE OF FANTASY DURING MASTURBATION

Incidence

Especially in years past, females, unlike males, were not generally thought to engage in fantasy very much while experiencing autoeroticism or other forms of sexual expression. Consequently, the following results uncovered by Kinsey et al. concerning the use of fantasy by women during masturbation came somewhat as a surprise to many persons: "For more than a third (36 percent) of the masturbating females in the sample, nothing more than physical stimulation seemed to have been involved. For the remaining two-thirds (64 percent), psychologic stimulation through fantasy concerning specifically sexual situations had sometimes accompanied the physical stimulation. For just about half (50 percent) of the females, fantasies had occurred in connection with most of their masturbation, at least during certain periods of their lives . . . fantasies were more common among the older females, and less common among the younger females" (1953, p. 164). The experiencing of masturbatory fantasies by women, however, was not found to be related to the factor of education.

The percentages of women in this writer's sample of social nudists and "potential" nudists who revealed having fantasied while masturbating were 53 and 72 percent respectively (1969). In reference to the nudists, fantasy use during autoeroticism was correlated with feelings of high self-esteem ($r = .32$, $p < .05$). Maslow, it will be recalled, in regard to high dominance women stated: "masturbation is often (not always) found to be a highly sensual affair, protracted and making use of all sorts of titillating and stimulating thoughts, objects and acts" (1972, p. 286). In this writer's investigation of women with high I.Q.s, 70% reported the use of fantasy during autoerotic activity (1974).

Adult males and older adolescent males have long been known to fantasize in one way or another during their masturbatory activity. This fact, however, became even more widely publicized when the Kinsey group reported the following: "Nearly, but not quite, all males experience sexual fantasies during masturbation" (1948, p. 510). As to the onset of such fantasy, these researchers found that: "fantasies often do not begin to accompany masturbation until a year or more after such self-stimulation has begun" (1948, p. 523). With respect to males, unlike females, the greatest amount of fantasy was experienced by those of the "better educated groups."

Although Hunt did not specifically indicate how many of the men and women in the Playboy study ever fantasied during autoerotic activity, the percentage who did appeared to be very high (1974).

Nature of Fantasies

In the case of females, Kinsey et al. took the position that the fantasies that occurred during masturbation "were usually in accord with the overt experience of the individual" (1953, p. 164). Masturbatory fantasies related to unconscious desires, impulses or wishes, they believed, unlike those of males, are not often experienced by women. The nature of the fantasies revealed by their sample of women included: heterosexual (by about 60%), homosexual (by 10%), sexual contacts with animals (by about 1%), sadomasochistic (over 4%). Also, "different sorts of fantasies had occurred during different periods of their lives" (1953, p. 164).

The primary masturbatory fantasy disclosed by the women nudists as well as the "potential" nudists studied by this writer, related to the subjects having sexual relations with a desired male (1969). Other fantasies described pertained to the following: being raped, engaging in sex with a black man, sexual contacts with animals, thoughts of how others masturbate or experience coitus, group sex, viewing other women and men engaged in sex, thoughts of penis substitutes, thoughts of experiencing cunnilingus and fellatio at the same time, being a prostitute, of men with large penises, and so on. The main fantasy indulged in during autoerotic activity by this writer's sample of highly intelligent women also involved "sexual thoughts of desirable men" (1974).

While Kinsey and his associates indicated that the nature of the masturbatory fantasies experienced by males tend to reflect their overt experiences as well as conscious and unconscious attitudes toward sexual matters, they, however, also recognized that "there may be some striking disparities between the nature of the fantasies accompanying masturbation and the overt experience of the male, . . ." (1948, p. 511). The autoerotic fantasies indulged in by the males questioned by Kinsey et al. included the following kinds: heterosexual, homosexual, sexual contacts with animals, sadistic, and masochistic.

In the Playboy study, while a variety of masturbatory fantasies were reported by the participants, similar to the findings uncovered by this writer (1969, 1974), the kind described most involved "thoughts of intercourse with a loved person" (1974). This type of fantasy was experienced by four-fifths of the women and three-quarters of the men in the study. And the percentages of single and married subjects who recorded such fantasies were almost the same. Other masturbatory fantasies described included the following: (1) coitus with strangers (by 21% of females and 47% of males), (2) heterosexual group encounters (by 18% of females and 33% of males), (3) engaging in forms of sex that the subject would never actually practice (by 28% of females and 19% of males), (4) someone forcing the subject to engage in sex (by 19% of females and 10% of males), (5) subject forcing someone else to experience sex (by 3% of females and 13% of males), and (6) homosexual encounters (by 11% of females and 7% of males). The younger respondents in the Playboy investigation experienced a wider range of fantasies than older ones.

How strongly related the fantasies one experiences during autoeroticism are to actual life experiences or to one's true conscious or unconscious desires is a question that still needs to be answered, even though the Kinsey group seemed to feel that such fantasies generally reflect the primary interests and overt experiences of the person involved.

Masturbation and Orgasm Attainment

In just about every major scientific study reported, the percentage of women who are able sooner or later to attain an orgasm from autoerotic acitivity is very high. More so than any other researchers it was Kinsey et al. who first highlighted the ease with which women are able to achieve an orgasm from masturbation. As they stated: "Among all types of sexual activity, masturbation is . . . the one in which the female most frequently reaches orgasm" (1953, p. 132). Concerning the very small percent of their subjects who did not attain an orgasm from self-stimulation they pointed out: "The 4 to 6 percent which had masturbated without reaching orgasm was chiefly a group of females who had made only single or desultory and infrequent trials of their capacities, for nearly all of those who had seriously experimented soon learned to reach orgasm" (1953, p. 142).

This writer found that 90 and 84%, respectively, of those women nudists and "potential" nudists who had ever masturbated achieved an orgasm from the activity (1969). And in a group of highly intelligent women studied by this writer, 82% of those women who had engaged in autoeroticism acknowledged having experienced an orgasm from the behavior at one time or another (1974). In the Hite study, 95% of the women who masturbated "could orgasm easily and regularly, whenever they wanted" (1977, p. 59).

With respect to the intensity of orgasm obtained by women from autoeroticism versus heterosexual intercourse, according to Masters and Johnson: "subjects report that usually the experience with orgasm induced by masturbation is more intense than, although not as satisfying as, that resulting from coition" (1966, p. 118).

As for the length of time the average female needs to masturbate in order to reach an orgasm, Kinsey and his co-workers have reported that it is "a few seconds under four minutes" (1953, p. 163). Some of their subjects (45%), however, were able to do so in "three minutes or less." (See also Hite, 1977.) The time required by the average male in the Kinsey et al. study to attain an orgasm from masturbatory activity was only slightly less—"something between two and three minutes" (1953, p. 164).

MASTURBATION SINCE (DURING) MARRIAGE

When in 1953 Kinsey and his associates revealed that a significant percentage of women (44%) had masturbated even though married, many persons in our society were amazed. This was so because of the hitherto generally held belief that autoeroticism was an activity experienced almost solely by unmarried people. Although the general public is now somewhat more knowledgeable concerning the widespread use of masturbatory behavior by married women and men, a goodly number of persons still associate the practice only with unmarried individuals.

In the Kinsey et al. study, while some of the women stopped masturbating after they were married, others first began the activity *after* having engaged in marital petting.

To some extent, the factor of educational level was

noted to be related to the active incidence of masturbation among the married women. For instance, between the ages of 21 and 25 the active incidences of masturbation for those women of the graduate group was 31% while for those of the grade school group it was 11%. Most interesting was the disclosure by the Kinsey group that during marriage while more men than women engaged in autoerotic activity, those women who did so, masturbated *more often*.

In the study of women nudists and "potential" nudists conducted by this writer, of those subjects who were married or had been and reported having masturbated, 93 and 87% of these women, respectively, signified having experienced such activity while married (1969). And in this writer's study of highly intelligent women, of those women who were married or were at one time and had engaged in self-stimulation, 80% indicated having done so while married (1974).

Levin and Levin in regard to the *Redbook Magazine* study of 100,000 women, the great majority of whom were married, reported the following: "Regardless of age and religious belief . . . almost three fourths of all the married women who answered *Redbook's* questionnaire say that they have masturbated since marriage. Seven out of 10 engage in it occasionally, and 2 out of 10 do so often. For wives in poor marriages, the figures are significantly higher. Better than 8 out of 10 say they masturbate, and a little more than 3 out of 10 do it often" (1975, September, p. 56). Consistent with other research findings the *Redbook* study also revealed a relationship in women between a tendency toward sexual experimentation and the use of autoeroticism. Levin noted that: "Cohabiting women [those living with a man] seem generally more inclined to experiment with sexual practices and techniques than newlywed wives. They are more likely to masturbate and do so frequently; to engage, at least occasionally in anal sex; to use vibrators and other stimulating devices. . . ." (1975, October, p. 38).

Masturbation by married males is also a common practice and is one which according to Kinsey et al. was indulged in by many more males of the college level (69%) than those of the grade school (29%) or high school (42%) levels (1948). In general, as the Kinsey group pointed out: "Among married males, the highest incidence (42.1%) [of masturbation] occurs between 21 and 25 years of age . . ." (1948, p. 238). Although the married males engaged in autoerotic behavior mainly when they were away from their wives, some did so for pleasure and "as a source of sexual variety" even when marital coitus was available.

The findings presented by Hunt (1974), not surprisingly, show a significant increase in the use of autoeroticism has occurred since the Kinsey et al. findings were published, both on the part of married men and married women, especially younger ones.

Effect of Premarital Masturbation on Sexuality After Marriage

A question of much importance that now seems to have been answered with some degree of certainty is this: What effect does the experiencing of premarital autoerotic activity have on a person's marital sexual life? Although the Kinsey researchers did not comment on this matter in the case of males, they did so in reference to females. They reported that "Pre-marital experience in masturbation may actually contribute to the female's capacity to respond to her coital relations in marriage" (1953, p. 172). And in this writer's study published in 1969 as well as the one included in this book (1974), while the majority of the married women subjects felt that the use of masturbation had *no* effect on later marital sexuality, the overall results suggested that its use had a *positive* rather than a negative effect on later marital sexuality.

MASTURBATION AND VIRGINITY-NONVIRGINITY

Contrary to the belief held by Freud and other psychoanalysts, the evidence is conclusive in showing that the use of masturbation does *not* prevent a person from engaging in heterosexual intercourse. Maslow was the first sexologist to discover that in the case of females, "masturbation and nonvirginity go together more than do masturbation and virginity" (1942, p. 273).

Kinsey and his co-workers, relative to females observed: "It has been claimed that pre-marital masturbatory experience may so condition an individual that she may want to continue solitary activities in preference to having coital relations after marriage; but we have seen very few histories of this sort" (1953, p. 71).

Additional support of Maslow's finding was uncovered by this writer's study of women nudists and "potential" nudists (1969). In the case of both the nudists ($r = .22$ $p<.05$) and "potential" nudists ($r = .26$ $p<.05$) autoerotic activity was noted to be related more to nonvirginity than to virginity. Furthermore, Abramson concluded, as a result of his extensive study, "that those female subjects who have masturbated tend to be older and have had intercourse. This finding is in accordance with the hypothesis that the disposition to use masturbation . . . signifies a positive interest and attitude toward a wide range of expressions of sexuality" (1973, p. 140). And, in this writer's investigation of women with very high I.Q.s again the practice of masturbation and nonvirginity was found to go together more than did masturbation and virginity ($r = .11$ $p<.05$) (1974).

Concerning the relationship between masturbation and premarital sexual intercourse in the case of males, Kinsey et al. pointed out: "In general, the boys who were first mature are the ones who most often turn to masturbation, and, interestingly enough, to pre-marital socio-sexual contacts as well. They engage in both heterosexual and homosexual relations more frequently than the boys who are last in maturing" (1948, p. 325). Sorensen, based on his study of males and females of ages 13-19, reported: "masturbation is less common among virgins (34%) than among nonvirgins (62%)" (1973, p. 130). He also noted the following: "we see a substantial rise in the incidence of masturbation among those who have had sexual intercourse. . . . Masturbation jumps nearly 50% from male virgins to male nonvirgins . . . and, again, virtually 50% from female virgins to female nonvirgins. . . ." (1973, p. 131).

Then too, in the study by Miller and Lief the use of masturbation was found to be much more prevalent among nonvirginal than virginal females and males, and nonvirgins engaged in the practice more frequently than did virgins. Moreover, in general, nonvirgins began the practice at an earlier age than virgins and were more liberal regarding the activity than were virgins (1976).

ACCEPTANCE OF AUTOEROTICISM

Since in the 1940s (and even later) some physicians and authorities (including the *Boy Scout Manual*) were still publicly proclaiming masturbation to be an undesirable form of sexual expression, it is no wonder, as Gagnon has recently observed: "In the United States, where it is increasingly possible to talk freely about various forms of sexuality that have been forbidden, masturbation still retains many of its taboo aspects" (1977, p. 141).[2]

The Kinsey researchers in their study of females remarked: "Among the females in the sample who had ever masturbated, approximately half had experienced some psychologic disturbance over their experience. . . . There is no other type of sexual activity which has worried so many women" (1953, p. 170). Not surprisingly, acceptance of

[2]Gagnon, J. H. *Human Sexualities.* Illinois: Scott, Foresman and Co., 1977.

autoerotic behavior was related to some degree to level of education.

About 76% of both samples of women nudists and "potential" nudists studied by this writer indicated the practice of masturbation was acceptable to them (1969). And, in the case of the nudists, a significant correlation was noted between feelings of high self-esteem and a positive attitude toward autoeroticism ($r = .41$ $p<.05$). The security-insecurity feelings of the women, however, were not found to be significantly correlated with an accepting attitude toward masturbation.

In this writer's study of highly intelligent women only 68% of the respondents viewed the practice of masturbation as being acceptable (1974). Very noteworthy, significant positive correlations were observed between feelings of high self-esteem ($r = .15$ $p<.05$) as well as security ($r = .17$ $p<.05$) and an accepting attitude toward the use of autoeroticism.

The findings of the Hite study (1977) also show that many women in America continue to view masturbation in a negative manner and as a result, the practice, though physically pleasurable, generally results in feelings of guilt, shame, loneliness, and the like.

As a result of their investigation of the autoerotic behavior of males the Kinsey group reported: "while college men more often admit their experience, there are males in some other groups who would admit almost any other kind of sexual activity before they would give a record of masturbatory experience" (1948, p. 499). And as these researchers discovered, there was a much greater acceptance of masturbation by those of the upper social levels and those who attended college than by males of the lower social levels and those who did not go beyond grade school or high school.

In the Sorensen study (1973) of male and female adolescents, the one sex practice about which the subjects felt most embarrassed and defensive was masturbation.

Concerning the widespread lack of acceptance of masturbatory activity on the part of people in our society, a few years ago Hunt stated, "Yet, aside from pubescent boys (who are often proud of their new accomplishment), most persons who masturbate remain more or less guilt-ridden about it, and nearly all of them are extremely secretive about their masturbating and would be horribly embarrassed to have anyone know the truth" (1974, p. 66). Hunt, however, did find in the Playboy study that there was a much greater acceptance of autoeroticism by subjects who were under 35 years of age than there was by those 35 and older. Moreover, similar to Kinsey et al.'s observations, college-educated participants and those of the higher social classes were more accepting of masturbation than were noncollege persons and those of the lower social levels.

Among the findings uncovered by Miller and Lief (1976) in their study of the masturbatory attitudes, knowledge, and experience of females and males were the following: (1) In the case of high school and college students, males expressed more liberal masturbatory attitudes than did females. With respect to graduate students, however, females exhibited more liberal attitudes toward autoeroticism than did males. (2) Level of education was positively correlated with liberal masturbatory attitudes, masturbatory knowledge, and the practice of masturbation. (3) Significant positive correlations were found between the factors of attitudes, knowledge, and experience, with the strongest correlation being "between attitudes and knowledge." (4) Attitudes toward masturbation were significantly related to the age at which the behavior first began. (5) The subjects who masturbated were much more liberal in their attitudes toward the activity than those who did not. And in college, liberal attitudes were related to the frequency with which masturbation was practiced. (6) Degree of knowledge concerning autoeroticism was related to liberal attitudes toward the practice. (7) Rather startling, more "residents" believed that masturbation causes psychopathology than did medical students. Approximately 16% of the medical students believed this.

PERSONALITY CORRELATES

Maslow first observed a relationship between feelings of high self-esteem or dominance-feeling in women and the practice of masturbation in his classic study of 1942. (Significant too, as will be seen from the findings presented below, was his finding concerning a positive correlation between masturbation and sex drive.) With respect to higher-dominance people he indicated that there is: "widespread incidence of masturbation . . . both before and after marriage" (1942, p. 289).

Kinsey and his associates, moreover, have remarked: "since the frequencies of masturbation depend primarily on the physiologic state and the volition of the female, they may provide a significant measure of the level of her interest in sexual activity" (1953, p. 146). (See also Davis, 1929, pp. 211–212.)

Based on the study of women social nudists and "potential" nudists, this writer noted that in the case of the nudists, the use of autoeroticism was significantly related to high self-esteem ($r = .44$ $p < .05$) (1969).

Abramson in his investigation of undergraduate men and women concluded the following: "there is no significant difference in neuroticism between females who are high and females who are low in their frequency of masturbation per month . . . females who are high masturbators are significantly higher than females who are low masturbators on the sex drive and interest scale. . . . For females, the results indicate that the only variables significantly related to the frequency of masturbation are sex drive and interests" (1973, p. 139). In reference to males, he stated: "males who masturbate more frequently than others are significantly higher (p less than .01) on their neuroticism score on the Eysenck Personality Inventory . . . males who masturbate more frequently were significantly higher (p less than .01) in their sex drive and interests" (1973, pp. 137–138).

Although not related to personality characteristics, nevertheless the following findings thus far reported by Dr. Nathan Wagner relating to the practice of masturbation by cardiac patients are certainly worth noting: "In a study presently being carried out at the University of Washington School of Medicine, we are measuring the cardiac cost of masturbation. . . . In our preliminary data on young males, it is clear that at the time of orgasm by masturbation the heart rate does not go above 130 and it rises to the 110 to 130 level for the briefest moments. These preliminary data are on 10 males, three trials each. This is in contrast to a cardiac cost of up to 180 for coital activity of individuals in this same health and age classification. Physicians should consider discussing the therapeutic use of masturbation as a method of re-entrance into sexual activity for cardiac patients" (1975, p. 177).

RELIGION AND AUTOEROTICISM

As in the past, religion still serves to inhibit the practice of autoeroticism. With regard to females the Kinsey researchers stated: "In the high school, college, and post-graduate groups . . . masturbation had ultimately occurred in an appreciably smaller number of those females who were religiously devout" (1953, p. 154). And in connection with males they commented: "The least frequent experience in masturbation is found among the more devout members of each and every one of the religious groups . . . the males who most often masturbate are the religiously inactive . . ." (1948, p. 473).

Consistent with the Kinsey et al. findings, Hunt has observed: "Religious preference still has some noteworthy correlations with masturbatory activity, as it did a generation ago" (1974, p. 87). Significant too, Hunt reported in the Playboy study: "a much higher proportion of Jewish men than of Catholic or Protestant are currently active masturbators. Jewish women, too, are more likely to be active masturbators than non-Jewish women, though by a narrower margin" (1974, p. 87). The greater prevalence of autoeroticism by Jewish men and Jewish husbands than by non-Jews was explained by Hunt on the basis of their being less inhibited by cultural factors and thus more accepting of the practice.

The Kinsey group, however, both in the case of males as well as females, found "relatively few distinctions between the accumulative incidences of masturbation" among the Jewish, Catholic or Protestant groups "of the same level of devotion" (1948, 1953). (See also Fisher, 1973.)

GENERAL CONCLUSIONS

In view of the overall scientific research on autoeroticism currently in existence the following general conclusions seem warranted:

1. Masturbation essentially is not only a "normal" and healthy form of sexual behavior, but it is also useful as a means of learning about one's own sexual responses.

2. While the great majority of both sexes masturbate at one time or another, more males do so than females (although increasingly more females are doing so) and they generally masturbate more often.

3. Babies and very young children of both sexes experience genital manipulation as well as deliberate self-stimulation, which at times results in orgasms (orgasms,

however, are attained by more young females than males).
Moreover, autogenital stimulation during infancy is a positive behavior and appears to be related to a sense of well-
being and desirable personality development.

4.   Although a number of children masturbate to the
point of orgasm, *most* youngsters do not engage in deliberate autoerotic behavior until about the time of adolescence.

5.   Both females and males are beginning to masturbate at younger ages than in the past, but which of the sexes
is starting to do so earlier still remains an unsettled question.

6.   While at present about 95 or 96% of the men in
our society experience masturbatory activity at one time or
another, the percentage of women who do so is probably
around 80. And an increasing number of women are indulging in the practice.

7.   Autoerotic activity is engaged in by a considerable
number of women and men of advanced age and among the
aged the behavior is more prevalent on the part of women
than men.

8.   The main way in which females acquire a knowledge about autoeroticism is through self-discovery while
males seem to learn about the practice primarily from *hearing* about it.

9.   There are various reasons why people masturbate
and these include specifically sexual ones as well as more
complex psychological motives.

10.   The masturbatory techniques utilized by females
are much more varied than are the ones employed by males
and among other things include the use of the hand or
fingers, vibrators, all sorts of elongated objects, penis substitutes, running water, and fruits and vegetables.

11.   The use of fantasy during masturbation while
more prevalent among males than females, is experienced
by a substantial percentage of females. And more and more

females appear to be employing fantasy during self-stimulation.

12.   Sooner or later almost all women learn to achieve an orgasm from masturbatory activity and the average time needed for women to attain an orgasm from masturbation is approximately "a little less than four minutes." The average time required by males to reach an orgasm from masturbation seems to be "between two and three minutes" (Kinsey et al., 1948).

13.   Many married women and men masturbate and this is a behavior that is increasing. In the case of women, the use of autoeroticism has a positive rather than a negative effect on their marital sex lives. (The same is probably also true with respect to men.)

14.   The practice of autoeroticism definitely does *not* inhibit one from engaging in sexual activity with other persons, and with respect to females, the experiencing of sexual intercourse tends to result in an increased use of masturbation.

15.   While fewer people presently experience feelings of guilt, shame, fear, and embarrassment in reference to the practice of masturbation than was true in years past, nevertheless, a surprising number still do, including college students. Acceptance of autoerotic behavior is greater among college educated persons and those of the upper social levels than among non-college-educated individuals and those of lower social levels. Also, males are generally more accepting of the practice than are females.

16.   Some medical students, residents, and doctors still believe that masturbation causes emotional disorders.

17.   Personality characteristics such as feelings of self-esteem (especially) and security seem to be related to an acceptance of autoeroticism.

18.   Masturbation to the point of orgasm appears to put *less* strain on one's heart as measured by an increase in heart rate than does coital activity that results in orgasm.

19.   The element of religion, as always, continues to exert a negative influence on the practice of masturbation. Autoeroticism is more prevalent among nonreligious groups of people than among those who are devout.

20.   The use of autoerotic activity is being employed more and more in the treatment programs of women and men who have sexual problems and thus far the therapeutic results achieved have been very encouraging.

21.   Self-disclosure by sex therapists and the like concerning their own masturbatory experiences appears to be a new development that is becoming more widespread.

22.   Diametrically opposed to the attitudes toward masturbation held by authorities of the past, reputable psychotherapists and sexologists are now stating that a *lack* of masturbatory experience may be related to psychopathology, rather than the practice of autoeroticism.

23.   In the years ahead, it appears certain that "masturbation" will become a household word and its use by babies, children, adolescents, and adults will be viewed in a far more positive light than ever before.

Previous Books by Manfred F. DeMartino

Understanding Human Motivation (Coeditor)
Sexual Behavior and Personality Characteristics (Editor and
   Contributor)
The New Female Sexuality
Sex and the Intelligent Woman

BIBLIOGRAPHY

Abramson, P. R. The relationship of the frequency of masturbation to several aspects of personality and behavior. *Journal of Sex Research,* 1973, **9,** 132–142.

Annon, J. S. Therapeutic use of masturbation in the treatment of sexual disorders. In R. D. Rubin, J. P. Brady, J. D. Henderson (Eds.), *Advances in behavior therapy.* New York: Academic Press, 1973.

Barbach, L. G. Group treatment of preorgasmic women. *Journal of Sex and Marital Therapy,* 1974, **1**(2), 139–145.

Barbach, L. G. *For yourself: The fulfillment of female sexuality.* New York: Doubleday, 1975.

Beigel, H. G. Masturbation in marriage. *Sexology,* 1966, **33**(4), 234–236.

Bennet, C. J. Female masturbation. *Medical Aspects of Human Sexuality,* 1972, VI, 10.

Buhler, C. *Zum problem der sexuellen entwicklung. Ztscher. f. Kinderheilkunde,* 1931, **51,** 612–641.

Calderone, M. *Release from sexual tension.* New York: Random House, 1960.

Clark, L. A doctor looks at self-relief. *Sexology,* 1959, **24,** 785–788.

Cohen, R. C. Masturbation. *Psychoanalytic Review,* 1952, **36,** 34–41.

Colton, H. S. The real truth about masturbation. *Coronet,* October 1975, 39–44.

Comfort, A. *The anxiety makers.* New York: Delta Publishing Co., 1967.

Comfort, A. *Sex in society.* New York: Citadel Press, 1975.

Davis, K. B. *Factors in the sex life of twenty-two hundred women.* New York: Harper and Brothers, 1929.

Dearborn, L. W. Masturbation. In M. Fishbein & E. W. Burgess (Eds.) *Successful marriage.* New York: Doubleday & Co., 1947.

DeMartino, M. F. (Ed.). *Sexual behavior and personality characteristics.* New York: Grove Press, 1966.

DeMartino, M. F. *The new female sexuality.* New York: Julian Press, 1969.

DeMartino, M. F. Mistakes men make in lovemaking. *Sexual Behavior,* 1972, **2**(4), 18–22.

DeMartino, M. F. *Sex and the intelligent woman.* New York: Springer Publishing Co., 1974.

Dickinson, R. L., & Beam, L. *A thousand marriages.* Baltimore: Williams & Wilkins, 1931.

Dickinson, R. L., & Beam, L. *The single woman.* Baltimore: Williams & Wilkins, 1934.

Dodson, B. *Liberating masturbation.* New York: Published by Betty Dodson (Box 1933, N.Y.C. 10001), 1974.

Dodson, V. *Auto-erotic acts and devices.* Los Angeles: Medico, 1967.

Early, J. T. How masturbation can improve lovemaking. *Sexology,* 1975, **41**(7) 44–46.

Ellis, A. *The art and science of love.* New York: Lyle Stuart, 1960.

Ellis, A. *Sex and the liberated man.* Secaucus, N.J.: Lyle Stuart, 1976.

Ellis, H. *Studies in the psychology of sex.* New York: Random House, 1936.

Evans, D. R. Masturbatory fantasy and sexual deviation. *Behav. Res. Therapy,* 1968, **6**, 17–19.

Fink, P. J. Quality of response in masturbation vs. coitus. *Medical Aspects of Human Sexuality,* 1974, **8**(1), 88–89.

Fisher, S. *The female orgasm: Psychology, physiology, fantasy.* New York: Basic Books, 1973.

Freud, S. *The basic writings of Sigmund Freud.* Translated and edited by Dr. A. A. Brill. New York: Copyright, 1938 by Random House, Inc. Copyright © renewed 1965 by Gioia Bernheim and Edmund Brill.

Gordon, S. *Let's make sex a household word.* New York: John Day, 1975.

Graeber, G. K., & Graeber, B. *Woman's orgasm: A guide to sexual satisfaction.* New York: Bobbs-Merrill, 1975.

Greenberg, J. S., & Archambault, F. X. Masturbation, self-esteem and other variables. *Journal of Sex Research,* 1973, **9**(1), 41–51.

Greenwald, H. Are fantasies during sexual relations a sign of difficulty? *Sexual Behavior,* May 1971, 38–40, 49–54.

Greer, J. H., & Quartaro, J. D. Vaginal blood volume responses during masturbation. *Archives of Sexual Behavior,* 1976 **5**(5), 403–413.

Hamilton, G. V. *A research in marriage.* New York: Medical Research Press, 1929.

Hare, E. H. Masturbatory insanity: The history of an idea. *Journal of Mental Science,* 1962, **108**(452), 2–25.

Hastings, D. W. *Impotence and frigidity.* Boston: Little, Brown, 1963.

Heiman, J., LoPiccolo, L., & LoPiccolo, J. *Becoming orgasmic.* Englewood Cliffs, N.J.: Prentice-Hall, 1976.

Hesselund, H. Masturbation and sexual fantasies in married couples. *Archives of Sexual Behavior,* 1976, **5**, 133–147.

Hill, J. *Women talking.* Secaucus, N.J.: Lyle Stuart, 1976.

Hirsch, E. W. *The power to love.* New York: Garden City Publishing Co., 1938.

Hite, S. *The Hite report.* New York: Dell, 1977.

Hunt, M. *Sexual behavior in the 1970s.* Chicago: Playboy Press, 1974.

"J." (pseud., for Joan T. Garrity). *The sensuous woman.* New York: Dell, 1971.

Kaplan, H. S. *The new sex therapy.* New York: Brunner-Mazel, 1974.

Kaplan, H. S. The classification of the female sexual dysfunctions. *Journal of Sex and Marital Therapy,* 1974, **1**(2), 124–138.

Kaplan, H. S., Kohl, R. N., Pomeroy, W. B., Offet, A. K., & Hogan, B. Group treatment of premature ejaculation. *Archives of Sexual Behavior,* 1974, **3**, 443–452.

Katchadourian, H. A., & Lunde, D. T. *Fundamentals of human sexuality.* (2nd ed.) New York: Holt, Rinehart and Winston, 1975.

Kelly, L. G. et al. *Female masturbation.* Inglewood, Calif.: Banner, 1966.

Kinsey, A. C., Pomeroy, W. B., & Martin, C. E. *Sexual behavior in the human male.* Philadelphia: Saunders, 1948.

Kinsey, A. C., Pomeroy, W. B., Martin, C. E., & Gebhard, P. H. *Sexual behavior in the human female.* Philadelphia: W. B. Saunders, 1953.

Kirkendall, L. Towards a clarification of the concept of male sex drive. *Journal of Marriage and Family Living,* 1958, **20**, 367–372.

Kohlenberg, R. J. Directed masturbation and the treatment of primary orgasmic dysfunction. *Archives of Sexual Behavior,* 1974, **3**(4), 349–356.

Kronhausen, P., & Kronhausen, E. *The sexually responsive woman.* New York: Ballantine Books, 1965.

Lampl-DeGroat, J. On masturbation and its influence on general development. *Psychoanalytic Study of the Child,* 1950, **5**, 153–174.

Landis, C., & Bolles, M. M. *Personality and sexuality of the physically handicapped woman.* New York: Hoeber, 1942.

Lea, E. Instruments for autoerotic stimulation. In R. E. L. Masters (Ed.), *Sexual self-stimulation.* Los Angeles: Sherbourne Press, 1967.

Lees, H. "The word you can't say." *Hygeia,* May 1944.

Levin, R. J. The Redbook report on premarital and extramarital sex: The end of the double standard? *Redbook Magazine,* October 1975, 38–192.

Levin, R. J., & Levin, A. Sexual pleasure: The surprising preferences of 100,000 women. *Redbook Magazine,* September 1975, 51–58.

Levine, M. I. Pediatric observations on masturbation in children. *Psychoanalytic Study of the Child,* 1951, **6,** 117–124.

Lobitz, W. C., & LoPiccolo, J. New methods in the behavioral treatment of sexual dysfunction. *Journal of Behavioral Therapy and Experimental Psychiatry,* 1972, **3,** 265–271.

Lobsenz, N. M. Sex and the senior citizen. *New York Times Magazine,* January 20, 1974.

LoPiccolo, J., & Lobitz, W. C. The role of masturbation in the treatment of orgasmic dysfunction. *Archives of Sexual Behavior,* 1972, **2,** 163–171.

Madison, J., & Meadow, R. A one-day intensive sexuality workshop for women. *Journal of Sex Education and Therapy,* 1977, **3**(1), 38–41.

Marcus, I. M., and Francis, J. J. (Eds.) *Masturbation: From infancy to senescence.* New York: International Universities Press, 1975.

Marquis, J. N. Orgasmic reconditioning: Changing sexual object choice through controlling masturbation fantasies. *Journal of Behavioral Therapy and Experimental Psychiatry,* 1970, **1,** 263–271.

Maslow, A. H. Self-esteem (dominance-feeling) and sexuality in women. *Journal of Social Psychology,* 1942, **16,** 259–294.

Masters, R. E. L. *Cradle of erotica.* New York: Julian Press, 1963.

Masters, R. E. L. (Ed.) *Sexual self-stimulation.* Los Angeles: Sherbourne, 1967.

Masters, W. H., & Johnson, V. E. *Human sexual response.* Boston: Little, Brown, 1966.

Masters, W. H., & Johnson, V. E. *Human sexual inadequacy.* Boston: Little, Brown, 1970.

McCary, J. L. *Human sexuality.* (2nd ed.) New York: Van Nostrand, 1973.

Miller, W. R., & Lief, H. I. Masturbatory attitudes, knowledge, and experience: Data from the sex knowledge and attitude test (SKAT). *Archives of Sexual Behavior,* 1976, **5**(5), 447–467.

Morrison, E. S., & Borosage, V. (Eds.) *Human sexuality.* (2nd ed.) Palo Alto: Mayfield Publishing Co., 1977.

Newman, R. P. Masturbation, madness, and the modern concepts and adolescence. *Journal of Social History,* 1975, **8,** 1–27.

Peck, M. W., & Wells, F. W. On the psycho-sexuality of college graduate men. *Mental Hygiene,* 1923, **7,** 697–714.

Pomeroy, W. B. *Boys and sex.* New York: Dell, 1971.

Pomeroy, W. B. *Dr. Kinsey and the institute for sex research.* New York: Harper & Row, 1972.

Pomeroy, W. B. *Girls and sex.* New York: Dell, 1973.

Reevy, W. R. Adolescent sexuality. In A. Ellis & A. Abarbanel (Eds.) *Encyclopedia of sexual behavior.* New York: Hawthorne Books, 1961.

Reich, A. The discussion of 1912 on masturbation and our present-day views. *Psychoanalytic Study of the Child,* 1951, **6,** 80–94.

Rubin, I. Sex over 65. In H. G. Beigel (Ed.) *Advances in sex research.* New York: Hoeber Medical Division, 1963.

Sagarin, E. Autoeroticism: A sociological approach. In R. E. L. Masters (Ed.), *Sexual self-stimulation.* Los Angeles: Sherbourne, 1967, 161–171.

Schimel, J. L. Commonly asked questions about masturbation. *Sexual Behavior,* 1972, **2,** 4–7.

Schneidman, B., & McGuire, L. Group therapy for nonorgasmic women: two age levels. *Archives of Sexual Behavior,* 1976, **5**(3), 239–247.

Schumacher, W. F. A priest discusses masturbation. *Sexology,* March 1969, 516–519.

Schwartz, G. S. Devices to prevent masturbation. *Medical Aspects of Human Sexuality,* 1973, 141–153.

Segraves, R. T. Conditioning of masturbatory fantasies in sex therapy. *Journal of Sex Education and Therapy,* 1977, **2**(2), 53–54.

Seward, G. H. Sex and the social order. New York: McGraw-Hill, 1946.

Sherfey, M. J. *The nature and evolution of female sexuality.* New York: Vantage Books, 1973.

Snyder, A., LoPiccolo, L., & LoPiccolo, J. Secondary orgasmic dysfunction: Case study. *Archives of Sexual Behavior,* 1975, **4,** 277–283.

Sorensen, R. C. *Adolescent sexuality in contemporary America.* New York: World, 1973.

Spitz, R. A., & Wolf, K. M. Autoeroticism. *Psychoanalytic Study of the Child,* 1949, 3–4, 85–120.

Spitz, R. A. Autoeroticism re-examined. *Psychoanalytic Study of the Child,* 1962, **17,** 283–315.

Spock, B. *Baby and child care.* New York: Pocket Books, 1946.

Sprenkle, D. H. Breaking through those masturbation myths. *Sexology,* 1974, **40**(12), 14–17.

Stacey, C. L., & DeMartino, M. F. *Understanding human motivation.* Cleveland: World, 1963.

Stekel, W. *Autoeroticism.* New York: Liveright, 1950.

Sullivan, P. R. Masturbation fantasies as indicators of deepest sexual longings. *Medical Aspects of Human Sexuality,* 1976, **10,** 154–163.

Townsend, C. W. Thigh friction in children under one year of age. *Trans. American Pediatric Society,* 1896, **8,** 186–189.

Wagner, N. Sexual activity and the cardiac patient. In R. Green (Ed.) *Human sexuality.* Baltimore: Williams & Wilkins, 1975.

Wallace, D. H., & Barbach, L. G. Preorgasmic group treatment. *Journal of Sex and Marital Therapy,* 1974, **1**(2), 146–154.

Wolfe, L. Take two aspirins and masturbate. *Playboy,* 1974, **21**(6). 114–116, 164–171.

NAME INDEX

Abarbanel, A., 293, 365
Abramson, P. R., 145, 165, 352, 361
Adams, C. R., 54
Annon, J. S., 361
Aphrodite, J., 261
Arafat, I., 92, 104
Archambault, F. X., 362
Aronson, L. R., 210, 212

Barbach, L. G., 21, 24, 121, 278, 279, 305, 311, 317, 361, 366
Bardwick, J. M., 283, 293
Baruch, D. W., 54
Beach, F. A., 24, 107, 115, 124, 128, 179, 180, 198, 226, 229, 276, 281, 282, 293
Beam, L., 43, 53, 212, 214, 218, 362
Bee, J., 190
Beigel, H., 271, 361

Bennet, C. J., 361
Benjamin, H., 271
Bergler, E., 107, 115, 316
Bernard, J., 107, 115
Bingham, H. C., 212
Bolles, M. M., 213, 363
Bonaparte, M., 126, 128
Borosage, V., 364
Brady, E. T., 37, 39, 52, 221
Brashear, D. B., 24, 34, 35, 83
Brecher, E., 107, 115
Brill, A. A., 164(n)
Buhler, C., 323, 361
Burgess, E. W., 36(n)

Calderone, M., 361
Carpenter, C. R., 77, 206, 212
Caudill, W., 64, 70
Clark, L., 268, 271, 361
Cohen, R. C., 361
Colton, H. S., 361

SUBJECT INDEX